Did I find the people in the North more friendly, kinder, simpler, straighter, stronger and truer?
I am glad to say I did not.
Some were disposed to be amicable, some disposed to favour me with looks of such deep loathing that the glass in my spectacles came close to melting.
Most northerners struck me as people just like any other.
Others just struck me.
Stephen Fry

CONTRIBUTORS

We would like to thank all the people who have spoken with us:

Ricky Alfred
Katie Arnold
Sharon Balding
Joan Banks
Julie Barnett
Maggie Bellwood
Neil Bishop
Billie-Jean Birch
Roy Blackman
John Bracewell
John Brierley
John Burroughs
Julie Hanson-Brown
John Buttrick
Maggie Cain
Kelly Campbell
Geoff Carline
Andy Clarke
Kevin Cooke
Dave Cooper
Jason Cooper
Barbara Croxton
Bradley Caulsan
Liza Coulman
Vanda Dunackie
Anne Dawson
Lisa Fearn
Vicky Findley
Christine France
Colin Gibson
Isabel Glazzard
Zach Glasby
Harry Gresser
Dee Heim
Frank Houghton
Christine Hyde
Stephen Hyde
Bob Jones
Jack Joyce
Gillian Kapka
Gill Lawrence
Alex Leccardi
Andrew Leeming
Ruth Lewis
Hanif Malik
Harry Malkin
Alex Maynard
Tim Mickleburgh
Helen Miller
Helen Murphy
Caroline Newbold
John Norton
Carys Osborne
Tim O'Connell
Allen Parks
Karlie Peters
Chris Prescott
Parveen Qureshi
Valerie Richards
Zenab Rasool
Vicky Risenham
Charles Robinson
Ashley Rose
Mark Rutherford
Stephen Ryder
Ted Sandland
Matthew Shimells
Bill Savent
Rosie Scurfield
Chelsie Spratling
Alison Spence
Lydia Spence
Barry Spence
Nigel Stakes
Graham Stokes
Enid Thornton
Julie Tunningley
Dave Wilders
Richard Whincup
Tristran Whittingham
Mandi Winterburn
Ben Wood
Kath Wilkie
Catherine Wright
Josh Yorgenson
Yixium Zhang

We would particularly like to thank Alison Robertshaw, Adam Butler and Michael J Adam for their support.

IT'S LIFE JIM BUT NOT AS WE KNOW IT

The Fourth and Fifth
Single Regeneration Budget Schemes
1998 – 2007

BRIAN LEWIS WITH DON STEWART

2006

Publisher **Yorkshire Forward**
Victoria House
2 Victoria Place
Leeds
LS1 5AE

Concept Pontefract Press
17 Linden Terrace
Pontefract
WF8 4AE
01977 793121
pontefractpress1@btinternet.com

Writers Brian Lewis, Ray Hearne, Karen Maitland, Alison Seabrooke, Dee Grijak, Adèle Jagger, Vic Allen and Reini Schühle

Photographer Porl Medlock

Design Jacob Schühle-Lewis and Reini Schühle

Research Adam Butler

Printers Aeroprinting, Jarrow

ISBN 0 9545565 6 9

It is not the strongest of the species that survive, nor the most intelligent, but the ones most responsive to change.
The Origin of Species, Charles Darwin

CONTENTS

FOREWORD

Growing old is mandatory, growing up is optional. When we started out on the road of this off the wall history of the Single Regeneration Budget in Yorkshire and the Humber, we were all a bit younger. As I hope the title of this third book shows, we are still young at heart !

This one is bigger and better still. I have topped and tailed it with what might best be described as policy reflections. Brian and his indefatigable team have filled in the middle with their usual aplomb. The collection of stories, comments, successes and lessons are as readable and informative as ever and do credit to the large number of people who actually delivered the fourth and fifth round of the Single Regeneration Budget.

There will be a fourth book. What the late Douglas Adams might have called the fourth book in the trilogy ! It will be about the Coalfield SRB programme. With luck we will get it written and published before the mines are all re-opened to cope with the energy crisis !

There is a great wisdom that says no matter how hard you try you cannot baptise a cat. The stories that people have to tell in this book show a depth of community regeneration wisdom that bodes well for the future of our communities.

My thanks as ever to Brian and his team for meeting their brief. I hope you find this volume as useful as you tell us you have found the previous two.

Don Stewart

STEWART'S LAW OF REGENERATION

Don Stewart

It's not the way it's got to be, People before Property,
We want a Meeting Place and not a Traffic Jam.
Radical Song of the 1970s

Theories at the Bottom of our Jargon, *Cranes On The Horizon* and *It's Life Jim But Not As We Know It* have traced a popular history of the Single Regeneration Budget in Yorkshire and the Humber. That history is not complete, because no history ever is. History by its very nature influences the present and the future and what was done with SRB will, in some sense at least, live on. When Yorkshire Forward took the decision that Round Six would be the last round in Yorkshire and the Humber, it was doing exactly what it had been set up to do. Regional Development Agencies were invented not to just carry on with existing interventions, but to do things differently. Our first Chair, Sir Graham Hall, was fond of saying, 'If you always do what you've always done, then you will always get what you've always got.'

So our job was to do it differently. The trick though was to learn the lessons from the past for whatever it was we were now going to do. What the three books show is those lessons. There are no bad lessons. One of the maxims I live by is that in my family we win and we learn. We never lose. The books show plenty of 'wins', and some 'learns' as well.

The books never set out to be an academic empirical evaluation of SRB. They simply sought to paint a picture of SRB in this region that might inform us and others and help us all going forward. So what does make the difference? As someone who has been around this agenda for some time now, and latterly has been lucky to have been a Director in Yorkshire Forward, I have a view. I do not for one second suggest that it is the only view or even the right view. It is mine.

The wins and learns together caused me to start thinking about what made regeneration schemes work.

To me the single most important factor in all the successful regeneration schemes comes down to people. Wherever you look and whatever type of project you look at, somewhere in there will be a few sometimes only one or two key individuals who have taken the thing by the scruff of the neck and made it work. This is as true of the big physical projects as it is of the small local community projects. Individuals will stand out as the guiding and often driving force. Dean Clough in Halifax for example would not

have happened but for Sir Ernest Hall. Salt's Mill in Bradford would not have been revived but for Jonathon Silver. Doorstep in Grimsby would not exist today, had Monica Chatterton not given it life, and Manor and Castle in Sheffield would not be the same, had it not been for Dave Clarson.

They of course will all argue that they could not have done it alone. That will be true. But it would not have happened at all without them, and they are not alone. There are good people at the heart of every project. Some of them are never heard of except very locally but when you dig, there they are, driving, prodding, arguing, motivating, nudging things along; leadership skills displayed without fuss, without formal recognition in many cases, and more often than not with no idea that they are leaders at all.

In the institutional world we call them project managers, with skills that are often in short supply, or so we claim. And yet most of them have never actually been trained in regeneration projects at all, falling into the role because nobody else seemed to want to do it, or taking it on after another career has come to an end, or doing a favour for someone else. Take one single example, Laura Moynahan, Chief Executive of Netherthorpe and Upperthorpe Community Alliance. Laura started her working life in marketing and translation for a pharmaceutical company in Brussels; not a straight line career path to NUCA. Latterly of course attempts are being made to capture some of this acquired expertise. It is possible now to learn regeneration skills through formal qualifications in universities, or through the growing regeneration schools or most recently, the development of the Centre for Sustainable Community Skills and through the Leadership Academy. It will be interesting to see if regeneration entrepreneurs can really be made and grown, or whether they just emerge. Proponents of nature or nurture, those old antagonists, now have a new canvas to wrestle on.

People must not do things for fun. We are not here for fun. There is no reference to fun in any Act of Parliament.
A P Herbert, humorist and politician

But can it really be as simple as people? Are there other common elements as well, I asked myself. I think so. And I am not thinking here of stale arguments as to whether area based or thematic initiatives are better. I am looking at common elements that appear in all successful projects. It led me to develop a simple rule of thumb; something I have come to call Stewart's Law of Regeneration. I started with a very basic concept, the

Basic Law. This states that for any given project, objectives divided by resources and multiplied by time will equal result.

STEWART'S LAW OF REGENERATION

BASIC LAW

$$\frac{\text{OBJECTIVES}}{\text{RESOURCES}} \times \text{TIME} = \text{RESULT}$$

The problem with this is, of course, that whilst there would undoubtedly be a result, it might not turn out to be the expected or indeed desired result. It might be more of a learn than a win. So that set me thinking about success factors. And here I need again to give credit to Sir Graham Hall who, amongst many things, taught me to have clear, simple objectives. Graham would, out of habit, telephone me on his way to a meeting for which I had briefed him. He would have read the brief, he always did, but he would want to be sure that he had the key points in his head. He knew that often at meetings your opportunity to make points is limited, what the media trainers call soundbites. So Graham would always demand, 'Don, what are the three key points you want me to make?' and woe betide me if I didn't have them on the tip of my tongue!

I applied that to my basic law. The key thing about objectives is that they need to be clear. Put it in a military context for example, and history shows that campaigns with confused objectives were often costly failures. Hitler might have won the war if he had decided what his key objective was in 1940: did he want to smash the British army or get to Paris? He hesitated. The British were evacuated at Dunkirk and returned to fight another day. He had not prioritised or made clear his objectives, and for a few critical days his generals did nothing. In regeneration projects the clearer the objectives the easier it is to see if they have been achieved. Often, because the visions and the aims have been developed by consultant facilitated focus groups, the objectives are made too woolly through compromise or there are too many of them in order to keep everyone happy. Or, in the worst cases, both too many and too woolly!

Sharp, clear objectives - and few of them - will help a lot in terms of focus. Here on some occasions we can learn from the private sector. It may be apocryphal but legend has it that when Canon set about developing their photocopier business they thought long and hard about their business objective. In the end they decided it was simple: 'Kill Kodak.' So keep your objectives few and clear. Oh and by the way don't let any of these fancy consultants and bureaucrats start talking you into SMART objectives. All that means is 'Spend Money And Rewrite Them'! If you can explain them to a five year old you are on the right track and five year olds are cheaper to consult!

This clarity of objective has a knock-on effect on resources. Resource is always limited. This is particularly true when it comes to public money; which by the way is our money: yours and mine. It's our taxes being recycled. Waste it by spreading it too thin and none of the objectives will be achieved fully. Oddly, too much money can be as bad, although it doesn't occur often. When it does it leads to a desire to take on too much, muddy the objectives again and confuse the picture. And why are we always so cavalier with our money when it comes to us in this public money disguise? Why aren't we as mean with it as we would be if we were actually signing the cheques ourselves? It still makes me angry when people come back to me because the project has overspent. Why, who allowed it to? Down boy, stop ranting.

The same goes for people. Even if you are lucky to have really good people, you will not have enough to do everything. So focusing what is sometimes called your 'human resource' - I think they mean 'people' - will help them to achieve. Again, you can have too many people. As Princess Diana said, 'Three people in a marriage can be a bit crowded.' Too many people and they trip over each other or get bogged down in detail and lose the plot but the bottom line is that you do need adequate resource. A shortage of money or a lack of people with the right skills will compromise delivery every time.

To the person who does not know where he wants to go, there is no favourable wind.
Seneca, Roman playwright and poet

And then there is the question of time itself. Regeneration takes time. It does not happen overnight, except in science fiction! Since this book has a *Star Trek* link, just think of when Captain Kirk's son is involved with the

'Genesis Project'. Here, in a matter of hours as a result of a magical explosion of some fusion device, a barren planet becomes transformed into an Eden-like paradise. Reality is different.

In 1997 a man from the Ministry of Defence came to see me when I was still Director of Regeneration at the Government Office. He had some assets to sell, including a recently decommissioned airfield with a rather long runway at an out of the way place near Doncaster, called Finningley. He was just letting me know that it was going to go on the market and that he was required to get the best price he could for it. Could we, I asked, see if we could get best value, rather than best price? He wasn't sure if the Treasury would allow that. We agreed we could ask; we did and they said yes. OK then, I said, let's market it now as a regeneration opportunity. So instead of the runway becoming aggregate for the next six lanes of the circular car park around London, otherwise known as the M25, a company called Peel Holdings bought it with the idea of turning it into an airport. Nine years later, commercial flights started from Robin Hood Sheffield Doncaster International. (They could afford a long name because of the length of the runway.) And nine years in regeneration terms is not a long time. Oh and by the way, it's not finished of course. Only in this country could we build and open in the twenty-first century the first full service airport for almost fifty years and not put in either modern road or rail access! Can you imagine that happening anywhere else?

Back to time. Typically, there is the time needed for the delivery team to assemble. Often the team that put together the bid for funding is not the same as the delivery team. It takes time for them to assemble, become a team, get up to speed. Consulting with the community and partners about what needs to be done and when, takes time. Planning the work itself takes time, and often getting planning permission takes a long time. Finningley, for example, needed a public inquiry. Assembling the funding, or the personnel, or the land, takes time. Getting the buy-in from the locals takes time. And it takes time for people to learn, develop, realise their abilities and their ambitions and achieve them.

And if you doubt the need for local buy-in, let me tell a little story from Leeds. Way back in the early eighties, a one time boss of mine, the

regrettably late John Lister, headed off up the Chapeltown Road to lead a task force. The premises they parachuted into were above some shops with a separate entrance at the side to the first floor office space. Coming down from a morning's work soon after starting, John found that the door had been bricked up from the outside! Welcome to Chapeltown! More recently, despite a public inquiry the plans for a marina to regenerate Bridlington have been put on hold because of the objections of a small group of individuals using their particular position to frustrate the wish of even the democratically elected local authority. So in the regeneration world there can be many delays along the way.

We also have a habit of trying too soon to evaluate whether projects have been a success. An example I often quote is Leeds Development Corporation. Much pilloried in its time, it was judged to have been less than successful when it closed, particularly in the area of private sector investment. Look now at the area it worked in and you do not need a calculator to assess the private sector investment. You can see the glass and the steel and the concrete from miles away as it rises now 30 storeys into the sky. It just took time.

So Stewart's Expanded Law of Regeneration states that clarity of objectives, divided by adequate resources and multiplied by sufficient time, will lead to the right result.

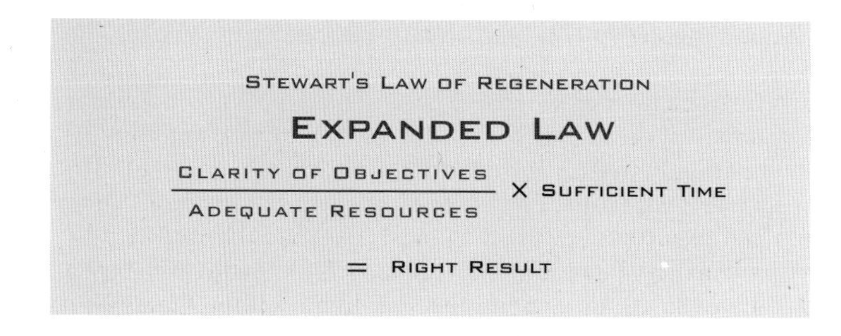

Vision is not enough; it must be combined with venture. It is not enough to stare up the steps. We must step up the stairs.
Vaclav Havel, playwright and President of the Czech Republic

I still thought though, that there was more refining to do. After all, as those of us who work in this arena know, for every complex and complicated issue there is always a single simple solution. And it is wrong! So I developed the refined law. This builds on the points above. Clear objectives are essential, but they also need to be owned.

There needs to be sufficient acceptance that they are the right objectives, otherwise the opposition will be too great. There will always be opposition, that is inevitable. Someone somewhere will not agree with what is being done. When decimal currency replaced pounds, shillings and pence there was a view put about that it should wait until all the old people had died out! It will be the wrong thing to do, take too long, it will be rushed, be the wrong design, be too ambitious or not ambitious enough, in the wrong place, involving the wrong people and so on. Take Bradford at the time of writing. Yorkshire Forward has secured a number of sites in the city centre to avoid speculators buying up prime sites that will be needed to deliver the masterplan for the city's renaissance. One of these is the old Odeon cinema. Immediately there is a ginger group calling for its preservation as an architectural icon. So at a stroke, a purchase with the best of intent has become a headache. In a sense of course it is all healthy. Opposition within our democratic process is a good thing. It should keep us sharp and at its best can turn into a process of scrutiny that helps to enhance and add value to the outcome. So the objectives need to be clear and owned.

As I have suggested, the financial resource needs to be adequate and the people need to be skilled. So adequate resource refined becomes adequate money and human capacity. Sufficient time remains a constant.

But then it struck me that the political environment is an interesting factor that has an effect on the equation. By political in this sense I mean both local and national politics and politicians as well as the small 'p' politics of the surrounding institutional infrastructure. For example, many SRB projects had to survive a change of master as the Government gave their control to Regional Development Agencies. The 'politics' changed. Area Based Initiatives came under question from within the regeneration world in favour of thematic approaches. The 'politics' changed.

Regeneration projects depend on political stability; some might say, a political champion, though in my experience that is probably not true.

Often what they need is a lack of political opposition. Support might be thought to be desirable, but in reality it can lead to polarised opposition which owes little to the project itself but often owes a lot to dogma, personality and ego. And let us face it, when politicians are involved there will be egos as well. A local or even a national politician coming out strongly in favour of a project or scheme can often draw unwanted attention from others who had no reason to oppose it previously. So benign neutrality is ideal. An interesting example of this stability is the contrast between the fortunes of Leeds and Bradford in the last twenty to thirty years of the last century. Where in Leeds political stability saw substantial private sector investment, with a resulting rise in land values leading to a booming economy, Bradford, with relative instability, saw stagnant land values, little investment, piecemeal development and a decline in image which is only now beginning to turn around. Where Leeds was attractive to investors and speculators, Bradford was not. Happily, as I write this, that trend in Bradford is changing for the better, and public developments such as the master planning of the city centre are being mirrored by private sector investment in buildings such as Listers Mill in Manningham and Douglas Mill on the Manchester Road. The small 'p' political message is now clear. Development can happen here, it is welcome and achievable.

So as well as adequate money and human capacity we now add in political stability. The outcome should then be a sustainable result. Sustainable in this case being more than environmentally sound which we take as a given, but having a life beyond the grant dependent regime from which typically regeneration projects will start. That requires the objectives to include what used to be called an exit strategy, and is more commonly now called a sustainability plan. Typically this might mean converting a grant dependent balance sheet into one which sees the entity become a trading or 'social' enterprise, running like any other enterprise on a business footing, delivering services against contract but with a social end in mind. Royds Community Association in Bradford is one example. Or it might mean the departure of the public funding agency from the scene and the hand-over of assets to the community. Or it might simply mean that the 'failed' market has been revived to a point at which the private sector finds it attractive to return, which has for example

A built environment that does not look permanent is unlikely to foster a community that regards itself as sustainable.
Vic Allen, Yorkshire writer

happened in Sheffield on the Manor Estate, where after thirty years negative land values have again become positive.

So the refined Law looks something like this:

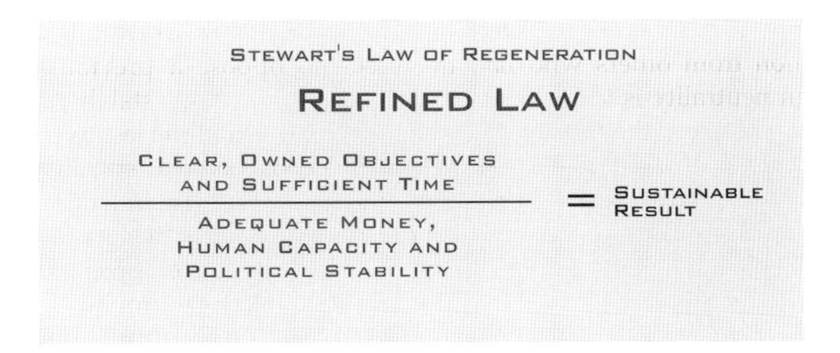

Now I am sure that the world of academia will point out flaws both in my arguments and in the way I have constructed the Law. So be it, if I have done enough to spark that kind of discussion then at least one objective has been achieved.

What of the future? Well, Yorkshire Forward has learnt from the SRB experience. In the final chapter, *Boldly Going Where No One Has Been Before,* I will set out where we now stand with the inclusion agenda.

ROTHERHAM

Ray Hearne

Thomas Paine (1737-1809) sought to write simply candidly and clearly;
to be bold and forthright and to shock readers into attention,
to appeal not only to reason but to the heart.
Encyclopaedia Britannica

THERE ARE FACES I REMEMBER ALL MY LIFE THOUGH SOME HAVE CHANGED

Rotherham - New York Riverside. *This six year scheme will play an important part in Rotherham's regeneration focusing on the New York Riverside area with an ambitious area-based regeneration initiative aimed at linking new development and job creation with the needs of three heavily deprived local communities.*

The Scheme also plays a significant role in helping to deliver the wider regeneration of the Rotherham Partnerships strategy to develop the Rother - Don valley and a vital role in changing the image and perception of Rotherham town centre as a place in which to live, work and invest. The Scheme complements and helps lever in additional resources from the EU Objective One Programme and has strong synergy with Rotherham's Urban Centre and SEZ strategies.

It features a significant market-led element focusing on business and housing development, and public sector funding will be used to attract and consolidate private investment. The Scheme complements existing SRB programmes, the Capital Challenge project, the Templeborough Regeneration Initiative, the Magna development and the local EU Action Plan.

SRB Total: £5.7m, Scheme Total: £36.2m

Nellie Dean's, a less than successful Irish theme pub, used to be the Bridge Inn. Famous and irrepressible, ten yards only from Rotherham's fifteenth century Chantry Chapel, it gave sanctuary for many decades to an assortment of trade union branches, labour movement organisations, single issue groups, CND and the Anti-Apartheid Movement. Most vividly of all, from 1984 to 1985 it welcomed Rotherham Miners' Support Group. Today, garlanded with ringlets of barbed wire, the gates to the Tesco loading bay are directly across the road from Nellie's. In those days before the supermarket, the main entrance to Rotherham Forge and Rolling Mill stood on this spot. The River Don swirled below and the canal came in at right angles; hence the heritage-laden name for the site, 'Forge Island'.

20 SRB 4 & 5

Wherever you might have been in the town centre, at any hour you could hear the repeated rhythmical thump of the great forge hammer beating away within the mill. Watching *Tarzan* in the Odeon just across the river, ululating through the tall jungle trees, or James Bond getting down to serious spy stuff, everything progressed to that same beat, that singular, reassuring, soul-shaking thump. It was the essential heartbeat of the town.

It would have been December 1982 when the hammer was finally stilled and the mill locked up for the last time. Someone painted in big angry letters across the gates: 'Happy Christmas Maggie - Another One Bites The Dust.'

Just along the Riverside towards Bow Bridge was the Don Forge, closed round about the same time. On closure Henry Hudd, a forgeman whose skill with the hammer was legendary, and his mate Peter Hayden, an engineer who could turn the highest precision jobs to a thousandth of an inch less than a 'thou', were dumped out of work. Both in their early fifties these men feared, correctly, that they were doomed never to work again. Their remarkable skills were redundant with not much to show for their know-how and dedication. The firm was a private concern, so beyond the wages they were owed they got next to nothing. Neither of them lived to see the 1990s.

Henry and Peter, representing so many others, lend their faces in my mind to an older Rotherham whose death was so protracted, so painful. Along with others, living and dead, I have spent a good deal of my life thinking and acting to bring about some renaissance of our town. Taken together, those lives, those deaths, those histories, are the kinds of contexts within which I find myself balancing each and every regeneration scheme that comes along, and asking myself, 'What would Henry and Peter make of it?' It is my Hudd and Hayden test.

Pete Bowler, environmentalist, ex-liberal councillor for Central Ward and scourge of river-polluting companies on behalf of 'Waterwatch' - described himself as shit-stirrer 'You show me a pile of crap, and I'll show you who did it.'

When I was nineteen - before all that came about - I went for a job at Guest and Chrimes. In those days it was the biggest foundry in Rotherham and had been so for more than a century. It stood on Don Street just beyond the centre of town, across from the fairground where the 'Stattis', the statutes fair, came twice yearly. I had worked already on gas pipelines with my dad and his navvy mates, I had sweated in steelworks with concrete-gangs and furnace wreckers, I had barrowed bricks on building sites; I was fit, strong, ten ton, ready for anything. The interview was straightforward; could I start the following Monday? A foreman led me out of the office to show me my new place of work. It was the smell, even in the yard, that struck me first; that tincture of something burnt, scalded, roasted and scorched, all at the same time, with an occasional dark chocolate acidity that tickled the back of the throat.

He took me through the doors and into the foundry itself. I was unprepared for the experience, horrendous intense heat, small furnaces seemingly at every corner. I recall no windows, no air to breathe. The shop-floor was littered with piles of what looked like dark sand. Most heaps were smouldering. Muscular men in tattered vests dripping with sweat, hands engulfed in big thick gauntlets, heaved huge metallic moulds around the place. My bottle went. I could not get out fast enough. I remember saying to myself, 'Dante's Inferno.'

I hadn't read the poem but I'd seen an extract from the film. How could anyone spend a life of such toil in such conditions? From that moment Guest and Chrimes came to represent to me Rotherham's hellish underworld, forever present, seething away at its core in perpetual civic heartburn. The price paid by some for economic survival. I had thought myself tough, but I was not made for that. Needless to say, I declined the offer of a start and I never went back for thirty years, not until it came to the moment to write this piece.

You can walk to it from Tesco in three minutes. It stands just to the west of Forge Island, on the patch of ground by the old Central Station where the 'Stattis' had met in its various incarnations since the year 1207. There are now two large red-brick buildings in the way. In the early eighties when the social and economic fabric of the locality was unravelling, these two were the only large scale building projects in the town, and they were highly symbolic indeed. One is the police station; the other, Rotherham Magistrates' Court. The little slip road into the car park is named The Statutes, in tribute perhaps to the playfulness of the fair.

Across the road again to Don Street, and you're back on the Riverside. The fire in the belly of Guest and Chrimes was doused a good while ago. The site is quiet, with little superficial sign of its infernal past, save for the mildly poignant inscription on the metal plaque by the boarded-up entrance, 'World leaders in valve technology'. Nothing here alludes to the fact that the history of civilisation itself was nudged along in no small way by one revolutionary discovery made on these premises in 1845 by the Chrimes brothers: the screw down high pressure tap. Sithee.

These days the building is beautiful in its sad decline. There is a façade of Romanesque window arches, crowned by a magnificent pseudo-Greek pediment. In Bradford it would have been refurbished already with an urban splash and transformed into some kind of gallery. In Rotherham though, in its own determined way, nature is well on the way to reclaiming the whole site. A stout elderberry bush grows somehow out of the very wall of the factory. It rocks in the breeze, festooned with dozens of black caviar-like berry clusters. Daisies, cow parsley, ivy, and the sweetest-scented pink and red roses of early autumn threaten to obliterate entirely the 'Danger Keep Out' sign hanging precariously on a pair of sagging gates.

The riverbank opposite is luxuriant with harebells, thistles and nettles. Masses of blackberries wither on the bramble. Sloes shrivel on undisturbed branches. Bewilderingly enough, a single enigmatic fig tree from who knows where makes its far from modest presence felt, thrusting out at occasional passers-by an exorbitant canopy of rubbery leaves. No clue though as to how it came to be there.

Quiet flows the Don, inexorable as ever. A river that was dead for decades is back with the living. No longer an ever-festering chemical bath, the water once more supports a fish population. Roach, perch, dace, trout; even salmon have been spotted. A fisherman on the bank tells of a pair of herons nesting just upstream, kingfishers are back too; right on cue a couple of swans cruise into sight, though the plumage around their proud necks still looks distinctly mucky.

In the early 80s local poets and members of the Chilean refugee community exiled in Rotherham used to get together in the White Swan for 'worker writer' evenings. I remember organising a Pablo Neruda evening in the belief that poetry could still help to change the world.
Ray Hearne, WEA

The wall at the other side of the water separates Westgate from the river. Several layers of clearly different coloured brickwork are in evidence, bedded one upon another onto much older stone foundations. The New

York Riverside part-funded SRB 4 scheme has allowed the Council to buy up some of the buildings in that row of once thriving shops and pubs, as part of its continuing forward strategy. When the Rotherham Renaissance Project finally takes off, those properties will be available for integration within the extended grand plan for the town centre. For the moment the once haughty White Swan houses the Rotherham Homeless Project.

I'm ready to leave the bloke to his fishing when I notice a shoal of bubbles glooping up through the water. Steadily, incessantly, they break the surface and send little ripples coursing across the current. It might be rotting vegetation, he tells me, or trout feeding possibly. The bubbles keep coming. I have a fanciful Hudd and Hayden moment. Within the great flowing narrative of orthodox history the little bubbles are the voices of those who refuse to shut up, who will not be silenced. Whose questionings and interrogations, frequently awkward and occasionally causing inconvenience, are nevertheless necessary to hold the rest of us to account. I am grateful for the prompt.

If there is not yet a law that states 'the brighter a light shines at its centre the deeper the shadows cast around its edges,' then perhaps it might here be posited, if only for the length of this brief celebration of the SRB 4 scheme.

SHINING LIGHT OR DAMP SQUIB?

The scheme's area of benefit stretches from the town centre along both sides of the Don, out along Sheffield Road, down Westgate and through the Ickles as far south as Templeborough. To the south-east sits Canklow, to the south-west, Masborough and Ferham; three of the town's most seriously deprived communities.

Given the Borough's parlous state towards the end of the 1990s, reeling still at every level from the crushing effects of steel and pit closures, any initiative able to achieve anything at all merits congratulation. In that context, even allowing for a two-year extension on the five-year programme, the New York Riverside's achievement of 1883 jobs created - a huge 89% of its highly ambitious original target of 2120 - seems positively remarkable.

Add in the 'unlocking' of new and improved sites right along the Don and Rother corridor, filled to the brim with businesses, and it is clear that significant inward investment is taking place. On top of that, successes were claimed for 'reducing exclusion' in each of the target communities. There clearly seems cause for celebration. People on the ground confirmed that impression. We spoke to a number of volunteers and paid workers with an involvement in the scheme. The overwhelming sense was that the benefits, as far as they went, outweighed substantially the handful of negative perceptions. From a range of perspectives, including the *Final Scheme Evaluation*, these broad judgements have been generally accepted, and few but the most cynical and begrudging would wish to argue. One commentator went so far as to describe the scheme as 'thunderously successful'. A shining light indeed.

Yet the SRB 4 achievements have not been widely applauded and recognised within the town, or even in the area of supposed benefit itself. How is it that many men in Ferham and Masborough, most particularly men in the Asian communities if one genuine supporter of the scheme is correct, seem not even to know that the SRB programme ever happened, let alone the regeneration which followed?

At its crudest it is probably because local men got few if any of the jobs. The vast majority of the new jobs were high-skilled and located on the newly prepared sites along Sheffield Road, less than a mile geographically but a world away culturally from the heart of the target communities. Moreover, early expectations that homes in the area might be refurbished as they had been under the SRB 2 scheme in Eastwood (described at length in our Yorkshire Forward book *Cranes On The Horizon)* were squashed in their infancy. Hopes of property grants were dashed immediately.

If you've been abroad on holiday, it's like coming home to a backwater. We're getting left behind. There's bits of Rotherham like a third world country, that's why we've got to think positively about this idea o' t' global village, we've got to make it work for us or we'll end up like a shanty town in't Badlands at t'wrong end o' t'village.

Jimmy Lallocks

Doing up houses was not what the New York Riverside money was earmarked for. Its central aim was strategic in reality. It was aimed at business and investment. The main thrust focused on laying down a basis for long-term, borough-wide forward planning and development. It worked. That is the level at which the scheme's undeniable successes took place. A crucial platform for the town's re-making as a viable centre for growth within this South Yorkshire fragment of the global economy was established and consolidated at the point when the comparatively small SRB 4 grant of £5.7 million was introduced. Eventually schemes to the tune of £36.2 million came and locked a whole gamut of public and private funding and investment into the area.

Advocates of the schemes for 'linking local skills to new quality investment, thereby creating benefits for the local communities,' seemed to have a workable strategy. The potential for long-term development, with potential 'trickle down' and 'across' economic benefits, made it likely that the SRB 4 areas would benefit. Within the short life of the scheme itself however, and despite its declared key theme of working to 'ensure that the local communities are best placed to take advantage of the new jobs created adjoining the Riverside', such successes passed way over the heads of the majority of people in those very communities.

This is less the direct fault of the scheme itself or of its hard-working deliverers but rather of the widow's mite culture which spawns such schemes in the first place. What are we to make of a political and social mind-set which seems to hold that for less than the price of a bog standard premier league footballer, whole communities, never much better than 'run-down' for a good half century, can be resurrected, galvanised and rejuvenated within the brief life of even the best laid scheme?

A conscientious Rotherham community activist or a bystander like me can of course afford the luxury of rhetorical questioning. Those involved directly in strategic regeneration and redevelopment of communities cannot. Bids are invited; schemes devised and submitted within punishingly tight deadlines. Ambitious SRB thinkers walk the fine line always between aspiration and fantasy. What might have been feasible, granted the right level of resources, is rendered impossible when the funding eventually allocated falls below the amounts originally costed. Rotherham asked for twice as much as it got. When that happens aims and outputs must be scaled down, ambition's quart funnelled uneconomically into best value's bizarrely-shaped pint-bottle. Trouble at mill, gaffer!

In the New York Riverside case, somewhat strained commitments to so-called 'capacity building' continued to be maintained as objectives. Themes like 'improving the quality of life for residents', working with the targeted areas 'to develop their ability to contribute' and 'to develop enterprise and wealth creation within these communities' are scattered across the documents.

When I read these shibboleths I think of the tombs of one of those great post-Conquest barons; a De Lacy, a De Warenne or a De Busli, who lie in their glory in South Yorkshire churches. Each effigy, a knight in heavy armour, proclaims their power and their magnificence. They once dominated society and the economy for miles around. Lower down, on the side of the great box tomb, are their sons and daughters in reverence and prayer, hands clasped together and kneeling. Carved by apprentices they are there because they have to be. They are sculptural footnotes to the main theme; power and political clout. The first son is hardly distinguishable from the second. The daughters follow and after them come the still-born offspring in winding-sheets. Like the heirs to a fortune, the capacity building references are there because they are expected and because they make the tomb decorous.

We've also got to imagine, even though it almost defies imagination, a new kind of global politics rooted in new ideas of sustainable living in that big single village; Yorkshire and Humberside versions of Indian writer and activist Arundhati Roy's vision: 'Not the politics of governance, but the politics of resistance. The politics of opposition. The politics of forcing accountability. The politics of slowing things down. The politics of joining hands across the world and preventing certain destruction.' At the minute partnerships are just about all we've got.
Ray Hearne

As any observer with an eye on the raft of ever-pertinent issues such as class, economic status, culture, education, history, race, language, might have predicted, the 'capacity building' aspects of the scheme failed lamentably. As the Final Evaluation puts it, 'work on improving the labour market position of residents has been very disappointing…the situation in Central Ward which contains Ferham, has if anything, worsened relative to Rotherham as a whole. The delivery of new business start-ups is no less disappointing'. The evidence seems to suggest that in the specific target communities there were none at all during the period. But observers on the ground know that is far from the whole story.

Admirable success or damp squib? Perhaps both judgements of SRB and the related regeneration schemes are simplistic. Clearly there were complexities to be wrestled with in the framing and delivery of the schemes. The recognition that a new national framework within a new world order had changed wholesale the terrain and the agenda has to be acknowledged. The attempt needed to balance investment needs with the unique requirements of three distinctive and different Rotherham communities. Ultimately it was not easy to focus the capacities and capabilities of those involved coherently and effectively across such a wide, yet supposedly consistent, range of aims.

Cynics of course damn the whole thing as rigged from the start in favour of the purely 'economistic' jobs-at-all-cost impulses of planners and developers. They see the bit of 'community development' as bolted on simply to win the bid. Optimistic futurists do the opposite and remain buoyant. Theirs is a vision of still unfolding successes, of expanding investment programmes, of the New York Riverside scheme as a source of vital and continuing synergy. They see this partly because of its strategic proximity to developments in the south of Rotherham and its location close to the highly successful MAGNA science and adventure park, where there are similar knock-on benefits. It is pivotal. Adjacent to the north on the other hand, the embryonic Renaissance scheme promises over a twenty-five year period little less than the birth of a new town centre.

THE PEACE TALKS OF DIALECTICAL MATERIALISTS

To this unreconstructed bubble-reader, the experience of attempting to place the scheme as a graspable whole somewhere along my own evaluative measuring-stick has been challenging and provocative. I have been forced to confront a range of my own declared prejudices and to interrogate the validity of a number of my own knee-jerk responses, most particularly in regard to the languages and cultures of economic planning, inward investment, and business development. For too long those very same ideas have been regarded by many people in our communities as the mumbo jumbo of those inimical towards us. Such were the idioms presented in the language of the 'plans for your future' employed by the dismantlers of coal and steel. The destroyers of our communities and our ways of life, those to whom we became 'the enemy within', used language in this way. Those who did for Hudd and Hayden wrote their strategies in similar characters.

After such excesses, such intensities, it is difficult not to remain locked emotionally and intellectually in remembrances of communities that have, in reality, disappeared. Looking perennially inward and backwards can become a habit. Over a period, seeking consolation in versions of history which appease and reassure can begin to limit - rather than liberate - imagination. This is particularly debilitating for those like me, who would once have regarded themselves as active agents of change. Times have changed, irrevocably. So have the material conditions which shape and define our possible options. Arthur Scargill's 1984 analysis of what was wrong and what should be done might have been right, but now we are on a different planet. Things have moved on. Liberated imaginations, nourished not knackered, by history, are what we in our communities need now to envision and construct our new futures.

What this means for such as me is that we have to engage in intellectual peace-talks with ourselves. This involves being prepared to rise above and beyond old suspicions and enmities, mustering some faith in the belief that mechanisms of 'partnership' can indeed be made to work for some definition or other of community betterment. This does not imply swallowing an entire agenda but it does necessitate giving the benefit of the doubt to those who opt in to partnership structures, and judging them ultimately not by who or what they represent, but by their conduct, their actions and by their accomplishments.

For his last decade Peter Bowler shared his boyish enthusiasm and wide knowledge with readers of the Guardian Country Diary which he contributed fortnightly on Saturdays from his home in Rotherham South Yorkshire. He delighted in explaining the almost rainforest scale of flora and fauna which flourish in an area wrongly perceived as bleak and industrial.
Martin Wainwright, Guardian, September 2005

DOWN BY THE RIVERSIDE

My hero Ebenezer Elliott, Rotherham's great Corn Law Rhymer, lambaster of poverty and the wealthy, was born in the New Foundry in Masborough in 1781 while it belonged to the Walkers, the town's first great iron masters. They built on an iron and steel tradition that went back to the Roman iron founding at the camp in Templeborough and to the Wincobank smiths who serviced Athelstan's army at the battle of Brunanburgh (937), and were well established when Samuel Walker reached the Riverside in 1746. He had his own private 'goit' cut across to the canal to sluice water directly into the works and brought an efficient transport system to an industrialised empire that revolutionised the scope and scale of manufacture in the area.

In the course of ninety years a rural landscape was transformed and ravaged inexorably. Walkers became known internationally for the quality of its iron, and most particularly for the effectiveness of its armaments. Walkers cannons aboard Nelson's *Victory* helped sink Bonaparte's fleet at Trafalgar. Into Holmes and Masborough was sucked a veritable pandemonium of allied trades, ancillary industries, a chaotic and unplanned infrastructure, to support its growth. Inevitably in its wake came an exponentially increased population of incomers, from every corner of the land and beyond, to make it all work. Waves of migrant workers arriving later on in the mid to late twentieth century simply travelled greater distances. The Jemia Mosque on Hall Street, once the Ebenezer Wesleyan Reform church, seems only to emphasise the point.

Walkers though was much more than a factory. It was an arsenal of ideas. At the height of its fame the company played host to Tom Paine in 1788. The strategist of both the American and French revolutions, Paine's legacy in South Yorkshire was long lasting. In *Common Sense* he appealed to idealists and to those interested in economic advancement, as he worked for a powerful change in the minds of men not only in France and the USA, but here in Britain too. Joe Mather, balladeer of the poor and impoverished just up the street in Sheffield, captured the spirit of Paine in a dangerously seditious song, 'God Save Great Thomas Paine', which he set to the tune of the national anthem.

Walkers made a fortune out of the Napoleonic wars and lost much of it in the slump that followed the precarious peace. The huge single entity that was the family firm was finally broken up in 1833 and sold off in segments to numbers of other local entrepreneurs, engineers and mechanics who had grown up in or had been drawn into, its shadows. The poet Ebenezer Elliott bought himself a small foundry which eventually went bust also, driving him away from Masborough towards Sheffield.

Elliott's father, known locally as 'The Devil Elliott' was a strident Jacobin, Painite and supporter of the French Revolution. Many of the father's sentiments, though tempered by an occasionally awkward strain of nonviolent, moral force Christian piety, transferred themselves to the son. Ebenezer saw himself as an 'avenger' of the 'plundered poor', flailing his 'whip of words' in the bloated faces of 'palaced worms' and 'propertied knaves'.

An advocate of political change, he was also a poet who understood the demands of new environments. Elliott's best works include marvellous evocations of the changing, darkening local landscape, and its rapid succumbing to the brutish imperatives of industry. Side by side however with what we might now describe as South Yorkshire 'environmentalist' rhapsodies, there is a classic liberal ambiguity. Elliott was awe-struck by the power and potential of the newly released energies epitomised by steam technology. Furthermore, as a foundry-owner, he was complicit in the expansion and management of such forces. Keenly aware of the impacts upon his beloved 'Nature', nevertheless Elliott came to believe almost religiously that the new technologies would bring about redemption. Mastered and developed properly by that new class of men such as himself, God-fearing and free trade operating, 'industry' would not only abolish poverty and hardship, but would save, literally, the world and all its peoples.

In 1838 the first ever train left Rotherham for Sheffield from Rotherham's new Westgate Station. To view it Elliott made his way up to the top of 'war mark'd' Wincobank and watched the procession cutting right through the heart of what would be later the SRB Riverside area. He wrote one of his finest works in which the train becomes a rarefied, and in retrospect slightly poignant, symbol of liberation and regeneration, bearing the weight of such promise, so much potential, so many radiant words

> '…that shall wither, in despair,
> The tyrants of all lands.'

There'll be a broad corridor of hi-tec business parks right through beyond Orgreave, employing more possibly than the steelworks ever did. Some of them will struggle for sure and some will go under but it will be much more manageable than in the past, peaks and troughs, rather than boom and bust.

From the brow of 'Winco' looking down over the town, Elliott would have been able to see looming beyond the confluence of the Don and Rother the dark outlines of what became known on twentieth century regeneration plans as New York.

No-one now seems to know when or why the name surfaced, though it is clearly marked on some maps dating back to the mid nineteenth century. It appears to describe that stretch of land along the riverside from Guest and Chrimes on Don Street down as far as Bow Bridge. All successful bids require a confident and aspirational name; this one was straightforward enough.

CHANTRY BRIDGE TO GUEST AND CHRIMES

Some part of the generally low level of recognition within the town for the Riverside Scheme and its achievements might well lie in different understandings of what is meant by 'Riverside'. Most people associate Riverside with that section of the town centre beginning at Chantry Bridge, moving southwards along both banks of the Don beyond Tesco, up the weir and curving around Guest and Chrimes as far back again as Bow Bridge. From the perspective of the town centre, the riverside looks the same today as it did ten years ago. That there has been no perceptible change is no fault of the SRB scheme itself. Ending up with the label 'Riverside' was perhaps a mixture of unfortunate timing and over-excited forward planning, but the original proposals for the site were sumptuous without a doubt.

The idea was that Tesco would transfer from their current Forge Island setting to the disused Guest and Chrimes site. This would have cleared the way for a huge new development right at the heart of the town, including a re-focused civic centre, arts complexes, residential and commercial premises, making best use of river and canal as both features and resources. These plans were scuppered when Tesco was refused planning permission for the move. The reasons behind that refusal still seem unclear. Rotherham Council blamed government legislation, though the suggestion in some quarters remains that the Council wanted to keep the Guest and Chrimes site within its own Renaissance plans. Tesco was offered other sites in the town but considered them all unsuitable. Today, several years on, Tesco still seems to be appealing against the planning decision.

For the SRB programme, at the very moment of its launch, this all meant that the New York Riverside scheme had little or no New York about it and even less Riverside. Clearly - and perhaps fortunately - the scheme deliverers let none of that bother them.

RIDO RIDO, IT'S OFF TO WORK WE GO

So much is in the language, and how it can alter perceptions. 'Business Parks' used to be 'Industrial Estates' when I first heard of them twenty years ago, a mere novice in the art of community involvement. Rotherham *Investment* and Development Office (RIDO) was once an *Industrial* Development Office. One aspect of RIDO's overarching strategy to secure that inward investment has been to try and change Rotherham's traditional image in the popular mind. It is no longer mucky, dour and smoke-enshrouded. It is practically post-industrial, a town with a future to set alongside its proud past.

I am reminded that one part of Walkers was reborn as the Phoenix Foundry. Later it became Yates and Haywood's, famed cast iron kitchen-range and stove-grate manufacturers. The 'Phoenix Rooms', sustaining that ever-so-symbolic appellation on Sheffield Road until British Steel's own recent dismemberment, housed the firm's first computer department, staff canteen and dance hall. Now the site is fully occupied by new custom-built high quality business units, and re-named 'Genesis'. Standing a few yards outside the SRB 4 boundary, its presence is declared testimony to the success of the model established and replicated within the scheme by RIDO, a bricks and mortar expression of that much sought 'synergy'. The explicit references to birth and rebirth, ('renaissance' as the new vernacular has it) in both the names, are clearly significant as confident, almost flamboyant, statements of intent in terms of future strategy, whether nineteenth or twenty-first century.

A bloke gave me a website address for cheap flights to North America. By mistake I found myself on a site looking at different ways of consulting communities of Aboriginal people in the Artic circle. It talked about highlighting and 'illuminating' the 'life-giving' forces in a community, focusing on community strengths, expanding 'the realm of the possible' and helping community members 'first to visualize and then implement a collectively desired future.' I thought, ni mind t'Artic Circle, we want some o' that here.
Jimmy Lallocks

These are important messages for businesses looking to put down roots and bring jobs to the town. RIDO's Tim O'Connell took me for a tour around those burgeoning Riverside business parks. Tim has a clear vision of that long-term strategy and of the inestimable role played by the New York Riverside scheme in setting it rolling. RIDO took a conscious decision to focus on high quality developments, pushing for example for high-spec buildings, as opposed to cheap and functional. 'We wanted forward-thinking businesses; here for the long haul. They have to be made to feel wanted.' Several of the buildings on both the Bradmarsh and Aspen Court sites make assertive physical statements in their own rights. The grey brick Orkot building with its atrium is a case in point. Orkot is a German firm that manufactures composite bearings for a range of marine and differing climatic applications. The post-modern laboratories of Dutch company Alcontrol are another original building but even the more sober traditional buildings look well considered, well constructed. The European headquarters of Toyoda Gosei are a case in point. Here they make specialist automotive parts; plastic seals and mouldings for doors, windows, and steering wheel columns. They employ dozens of semi-skilled to highly-skilled workers. None of them live locally. As we talked I wondered what Henry Hudd and Peter Hayden would have made of it all.

My guess is that they would have been impressed. They knew about high quality production. They might be saddened that locals were not acquiring the necessary skills to be part of that workforce but would know at the same time that towns like Rotherham have across the centuries imported workers. All they themselves had wished for was to continue to play their part in such processes, and to be reassured that opportunities would be available for their children and grandchildren to do the same if they skilled themselves to the necessary levels. For all its identified strategic and geographical weaknesses, my feeling is that Henry and Peter would have applauded the best efforts of the New York Riverside scheme to build and sustain a genuine future for the town's kids. If some of those broader questions of sustainability remain on the table then the scheme must, I think, be congratulated for placing them squarely before our eyes.

SOME COMMUNITY PERSPECTIVES

The New York Riverside scheme was dogged throughout its lifetime by sporadic personnel changes in key posts, which inevitably proved disruptive to its smooth development and the continuity of some projects.

The final evaluation report also highlights that its overall strategic coherence was weakened by the lack of a dedicated scheme manager. As we have seen elsewhere, and particularly in Ryedale and Hull, the presence of officers who are there for a long time is vital in the development of SRB projects. Careerism and the 'bobbing turd' phenomenon have been features of unfocused schemes which have dogged SRB. The latter is the senior officer who comes in with exciting ideas and pushes them forward on a base of rhetoric and bombast. In the wink of an eye he or she has moved on and appeared in a better job in an adjacent authority, having persuaded next door's appointments committee of their worth. Exhausted former colleagues are left to pick up the pieces. In all schemes, but especially those which touch the general public and have a need of community consultation, the presence of strong, permanent officers is very important. In that context it seems fair to say that in Rotherham the lack of a single responsible eye, overseeing things on a day to day basis, did allow gaps to appear between the strategic investors and the capacity builders. At that latter level, post-holders in community development, community safety and environmental programmes all moved on after short periods on the job. However in the case of Julie Barnett, the move proved serendipitous and clearly beneficial to the scheme. She succeeded to the post of community development worker after starting as an administrative worker in the same office.

Despite those occasional fits and starts, keen workers on the ground were able to rally grassroots support for a range of initiatives at key points. People in all three communities, Canklow, Ferham and Masborough, speak highly of SRB 4's environmental activities. Huge numbers turned out to the early meetings when the scheme's initial intentions were floated. Those gatherings are never easy to manage because people in the community who have been around for a long time have seen promises broken in the past as one initiative follows another. 'People still didn't believe anything would happen,' Julie recalls, 'and coping with the stick that you get at some meetings can be too much for some professionals. Some are not up to it.'

At first, outputs were driven by postcodes, so at the elderly Asian luncheon group dos you were supposed to ask at the door for their post-code. Course, it used to slip us minds.
Social worker

Julie for one stuck at it. Communities were consulted and changes planned. The area around James Street in Masborough is a good example.

Residents claimed that flowerbeds in the street were rat infested. Within two months they had been removed. Quick wins are important. That's how you begin to build credibility. From then on things bounced ahead, with improvements in street lighting, litter bins, dog bins, traffic calming measures, Masborough Community Centre and Canklow Pavilion both refurbished, better and safer play areas for kids in all three communities. Community safety initiatives were part of the strategic package with free locks, anti-burglary measures, new front doors whose panels might not be so easily kicked in.

Not everything however was that straightforward. Ted Sandland, one-time Community Safety Co-ordinator, recalls how the arbitrary boundaries defining the area of benefit could lead to explosive anomalies. If you lived at the wrong side of the street in parts of Henley or Thornhill then you might not be eligible for the safety measures enjoyed by your neighbours opposite. Those kinds of artificially imposed barriers can subvert a whole scheme. By the time SRB 6 came to Rotherham the principle of including 'natural communities' was built into the scheme's delivery.

Community Chest funds, which many small groups soon learned to exploit, were developed. Julie's classic community development tactic was to encourage the most dynamic, best-organised small groups to turn themselves into projects. This route made APWA, the All Pakistan Women's Association, a big SRB success in its own right.

Zenab Rasool is critical of many aspects of the overall SRB scheme, principally its failure to motivate greater involvement by the large Asian communities rooted in the localities, as well as its difficulties in overcoming some basic cultural barriers. Instead of a properly resourced community development approach in which informed people talked to community members, too much reliance was placed on mail-outs of letters in English. Zenab recalls also with a wry chuckle how many Asian men wanted their houses refurbishing but 'what they got instead was women's education.' That soon put an end to the men's involvement.

'In the end a too familiar pattern emerged. We were getting the same handful of people turning out to three and four meetings a week.' But for all its perceived failures, Zenab's view is that the SRB 4 scheme 'worked wonders' for APWA, as it did for Zenab herself. She is now employed full time by APWA's successor, UMCC, the United Multi-Cultural Centre, and sits on any number of borough-wide committees and partnerships, as well as on the magistrates' bench.

'When SRB 4 funded our Cultural Resource Project it was the first major bid we had submitted to anywhere.' The project was all about engaging women, 'though later we broadened it out to work with kids.' Working with local colleges and with the WEA - the Workers Education Association - women were able in the security of their own neighbourhoods, to learn English, sewing, keep fit; childcare courses were developed and providers brought lap-tops so the women could learn IT skills. Swimming classes for Asian women were also organised, which proved highly popular until, ironically enough, the Council was forced to close Sheffield Road Baths just across the river from New York itself, the key regeneration site.

APWA was a success but the most successful of all seems to have been the partnership developed at Millmoor, in the very heart of Masborough, with Rotherham United Football Club. Working against all the baggage of racism that football historically carries with it, the project was able to organise fifty to sixty kids at a time to play full pelt for an hour on the pitch proper at Millmoor. 'The kids were gobsmacked, but they were so disciplined, so focused for that hour. It's true they nicked the balls at first, but as the scheme went on, you couldn't keep them away. Even those who wouldn't go to school, even those with ASBOs against them, went. They loved it and they worked so hard. It was fantastic. The club made the effort and SRB paid the fees.' That footballing partnership continues still, as does an increased range of UMCC activities in the area. 'The SRB funding gave us the foothold. We were able to use it to apply for other funding and we've gone from strength to strength.'

In't old days, closing t'park of an evening, they used to ring a bell and does tha know - they used to go! Can thy imagine trying that now and where they'd stick thi bell?

Up the street from Millmoor, Ferham's own advice centre, FACE, was given a lift with funding for a co-ordinator post. The old park-keeper's hut in the middle of Ferham Park became a hub for local community activity. The former police hut a few yards along the road was smartened up to house the ACE team (Action in the Community for Employment, which became Action Team for Jobs). Smart new wrought iron railings also were fixed right around the park. Close working relationships were built via Julie with Surestart, resulting in many activities focused on young families and under-fives.

It seems clear that all this local ferment must have played its part in attracting Private Finance Initiatives (PFI) funding for the rebuilding of both Ferham and Thornhill schools. Whatever people feel about the iniquities of the principles behind Private Finance Initiatives the two new schools are up and functioning, rooted in the new local landscape, and impossible to ignore.

Julie describes how £2,500 was allocated to support Canklow Gala, and the same amount for Ferham Festival. The aim of both events was to promote the SRB scheme, but more importantly to engage the communities at a deeper level. As Julie acknowledges, that deeper engagement requires sustained development, and that is what the New York Riverside scheme was unable to deliver.

Partly because of that failure those many undeniable successes were short-lived. Despite the valiant endeavours of the West Central Community Partnership which was constituted in the wake of the SRB scheme to try to maintain the momentum, any sense of a Ferham and Masborough bounce has all but halted. Julie has moved on. There is no longer a community development worker in either area. The hut-cum-community centre was torched and later flooded. Its sunken roof now looks like it was sat upon by the Giant Despair. However, resilient kids still use the play areas and the railings look lovely yet.

HARRY ONE-OFF

A mile up the road in Bradgate Park that S-word, 'sustainability', is still a hot issue, but Bradgate has what Ferham did not, Harry Gresser. Harry has just won a community champion's award; deservedly so, for his efforts to sustain developments in the park; but whether the dawn to dusk omnipresence of a single dedicated unpaid volunteer amounts to a strategy is less clear.

38 SRB 4 & 5

Harry's story merits a book in itself. He worked in the park, employed by Rotherham Council, for thirty-nine years. When the work was put out to compulsory competitive tendering, contractors took over and Harry took early retirement. 'It were obvious what'd happen and it did.' Everything fell away. 'Apart from a bit of occasional grass-cutting, nothing got done.'

This coincided with the rapid disintegration of Henley Grove just across the dual carriageway from the park, towards the town. 'It really went downhill. It ended up like a ghetto.' The area around the underpass from the bottom of the park across to Robert Jenkins' factory became a virtual no-go area. It became a magnet for drug abusers and prostitutes, and the crime figures were sky high. 'They could break into Jenkinses or one of the other firms o'er there and then hop it back through the park and off.' So in those days nobody wanted to use the park either.

Harry decided he'd had enough and ended up forming 'Friends of Bradgate Park' and was elected to the Chair. Straight away the SRB 4 Community Safety Co-ordinator made contact with the group. Businesses around Henley and Midland Road were up in arms at being burgled so consistently. Some of them were even threatening to pack up and leave Rotherham. For that reason a bid was submitted to the New York Riverside scheme for 'reducing crime against businesses'. This included numerous methods of securing premises as well as sophisticated CCTV systems. In addition to these measures it was felt that something needed to be done to occupy the numbers of young people with nothing better to do than hang around the underpass. 'Keep them active, keep them out of trouble,' became something of a mantra. What was needed were 'energy-burners'.

Some o't kids wanted to paint a mural on that wall at t'top o' t'park. A bloke in one o' these houses objected, 'I'm not looking out at that!' Does tha know, to see it, he'd have had to stand on a pair o' step ladders and peep ovver t'trees through't upstairs bedroom window. 'Welcome to Bradgate Park' it says.
Harry Gresser

Harry was sceptical but reasoned that if they had their own areas then the young people might stay off the bowling greens. Even though Bradgate Park was geographically outside the SRB 4 area of benefit, the businesses under threat were located inside the boundary, so the bid went forward. Some partners are able to play the game better than others. Funding was allocated for a range of first-class play and multi-sport resources hand-in-hand with the installation of high-tech CCTV equipment, 'not much short of a quarter of a million quid.'

Our fathers were steel-backed, our mothers coal-wombed
In the cold slag of history untimely entombed.
Let their lives be our anthems, trustworthy hand-me-downs
To the People's Republic of Sweet Rotherham Town.

The People's Republic of Sweet Rotherham Town, Ray Hearne

Success was reported almost overnight. The kids' and young people's activities proved an instant hit attracting users of all ages. Furthermore, crime rates dropped to nigh-on zero. The park was transformed and became once more a vibrant focus for community activities. One unforeseen outcome of the experience was Harry's whetted appetite for securing funding. He quickly learned to match New York Riverside resources with any number of other pots, including Sure Start, WREN (Waste Recycling Environmental), Coalfield Regeneration Trust, Key Fund, Community Fund, and large amounts recently from the local Pathfinder. This has bought for the park everything including new gates, ornate iron fencing, paving and tarmacking, increased equipment for the play areas, high quality seating, a delightful garden for people with sensory impairments, and an un-burndownable resource centre with metal shutters, two sets of metal doors and thirteen locks. Harry got what it takes.

'All my life I've been a trouble-causer,' he says. In tandem with bloodymindedness clearly Harry has developed an uncommon capacity for strategic forward thinking. 'Not bad for a bloke wi' bad eyes, who can't spell and can hardly write!' Today the Friends' Group numbers nearly 400; in reality this boils down to five or six park key holders who fill in when Harry's not available.

Most likely people will have heard the word 'sustainability' misquoted. Because the concept is vague, there will probably be a perception that it is something complicated and beyond the scope of a local community, but a simple working definition can bring sustainability into focus for a community. The definition can be broadened, adapted, or abandoned as work progresses. The usual case is that, as understanding grows, there is no longer any need for a definition. As a project progresses and practical action gathers momentum, 'sustainability' becomes a household word, a way of thinking and a way of living.

For three years running, the 'Friends' organised an annual gala. The first year, courtesy of Julie, they received an SRB 4 grant. After that they raised their own money. Those galas were the biggest events the park had seen for generations, but they didn't run one this year. They couldn't get the requisite funding. 'Funders expect you to make money out of a community event. They're not on this planet. We had fifty-odd charity stalls last time and charged them a tenner apiece. They complained about that and said that they were not going to pay any more. Seven of us organised t'lot of it. Took us weeks. We were up all night. That whole hill over there were full of stuff. ' The 'stuff' of community, you might say.

The local environment has improved so significantly that estate agents are now eager to add 'overlooking Bradgate Park' as part of their sales pitch. The price of sustaining that status quo involves Harry, or a substitute on occasions, opening the park gates at 7.00 am on a summer morning and being around to lock them again at 8.00 in the evening. Harry thrives on it. Someone's done a marvellous cartoon of him in all his toothless glory and stuck it on the notice board of the resource centre. 'Some on 'em as use the park hate me but most on 'em speak as they pass.'

New York Riverside resources are the catalyst in this experiment in community managed green space. But how will it be sustained beyond Harry? There seems to be an assumption abroad that thousands of such characters are waiting in the wings. I am not so sure. Something is clearly missing here in terms of strategy. 'We do it 'cos we believe in it, but they forget, we do it all for nowt, and now they're wanting us to pay rent! But that's another story. How long has tha got?'

CASTLEFORD AND KNOTTINGLEY

Brian Lewis and Alison Seabrooke

In Monopoly the players who amass the most property including the 'utilities' usually win - in a game of chance with a Community Chest it is best to hoover up anything on offer when you can.

FRESHAIRE

FreshAire, *the Wakefield MDC led initiative, is aimed at regenerating the North East sector of the Wakefield district, specifically focusing on Airedale and Warwick housing estates, where the problems of multiple deprivation and social exclusion are being tackled. More specifically, it is addressing unemployment, low education standards, the crime situation, health and quality of life issues for the target group.*

FreshAire Partnership - SRB 4 - 1 April 1998 to 31 March 2005, £4.127 million, overall £20 million with match funding.

During major motorway roadworks two years ago archaeologists in the Five Towns to the east of Wakefield found the remains of a pre-Roman chariot, its driver and also a banquet of 250 bullocks in countryside between Castleford and Knottingley.

Historians were astounded. The find set their academic teeth on edge; the discovery implied that the Parisii, an aristocratic East Riding tribe given to chariot burials, lived much further west than had been suspected. The locals' enthusiasm was more prosaic, they merely wanted to know if he was Castleford's first man resident or if he came from Ferrybridge/Knottingley. People of a moderate disposition wanted him to belong to all of the towns but Castleford was not having this. They were on a roll. The Urban Renaissance and Channel 4 had come to 'Cas-Vegas' for a makeover. The cameras were there to record it so they were anxious to hold on to any newsworthy scrap. No one suggested that he should have been called the FreshAire charioteer, although judging from the place where he was found and the time when he was found it would have been a good name.

The FreshAire SRB 4 territory stretched from the ridge overlooking the River Aire in Castleford to the ridge overlooking the A1/M motorway in Knottingley. Two council house estates were involved: the Airedale estate, Castleford and Simpson's Lane/Warwick Estate, Knottingley. Physically they could not be regarded as an entity - a normal pre-requisite of an SRB programme - but if you ignored that, you could draw a perimeter line around them without much difficulty - they actually had a lot in common. People travelling by car from the Square, the heart of Airedale, to the Wallbottle Hotel, the centre of the Warwick, could be there in fifteen minutes but few made the journey. What they had in common was that both areas appeared as failing area in the *Index of Deprivation*.

The decision to apply for SRB money originated in Wakefield MDC's Housing Department. A Knottingley councillor, Councillor Graham Stokes, was in charge. When one of the officers pointed out that they might be able to bring in SRB to regenerate more houses on the Warwick and extend an existing programme in that way, he thought this a good idea. The wagon began to roll forward but it quickly got stuck in the mud. SRB 4 money could not be used in that way so they looked for a way around the situation. Someone recognised that from the air a casual observer could not see where Knottingley ended and Castleford began. There were good reasons for linking parts of the towns together. In both the Warwick and Airedale wards unemployment was high. There was a much bigger area to work in because partnerships already established in one area could be interpreted as being in both and the Council was prepared to lever in matching money. It was decided to draw a boundary line around the two and make them as one. FreshAire was born.

PRIDE OF PLACE KNOTTINGLEY

In small towns like the Five Towns of Wakefield - Castleford, Featherstone Knottingley, Normanton and Pontefract - pride of place matters. However this will vary from decade to decade. In 1500 Pontefract was the proud possessor of a castle, royal prison and monastery. From 1648 to the present it is a small market town which is famous for giving its name to flat liquorice cakes now made in Germany. In 1850 Normanton was a major railway junction. Today only the slow trains from Sheffield to Leeds stop at its overgrown railway station.

These days the government talks of 'localism' to describe the neighbourhood agenda. I hate the word - it is so bland - and prefer 'pride of place' it it suggests partisan emotion. What you call something matters.
Brian Lewis, writer

In the 1980s Featherstone was proud because it had a rugby team, Featherstone Rovers, and a major colliery. Twenty-odd years on the pit has gone. Castleford, which was little more than a hamlet when most of the others thrived ,is now speeding ahead and has transformed itself in the last five years. New houses, an attractive river front, shopping centres and a heritage culture are appearing. Knottingley/Ferrybridge – a trading and boatbuilding centre which once was the inn-stop half way between London and Edinburgh centre - has gone steadily downhill. It sometimes seems that Knottingley is Wakefield MDC's scapegoat, a sacrificial animal sent out into the wilderness - in this case the flatlands on the outer edge of the West Riding that stretch to the Humber estuary - with too little food or sustenance.

Some of the difficulties Knottingley people are facing are to do with town planning. Knottingley lacks a centre; this is partly because the town is cut in two by the Pontefract to Goole road. In the days when Knottingley's best known son, the architect John Poulson, had a lot of influence the Town Council had destroyed the totally adequate town centre in Aire Street. In the area close to the riverside they had ripped down adequate housing and replaced it with much poorer dwellings. Such had been the rush that on one occasion they had built some houses the wrong way round with their backs to the street. In this period they had also built an ugly promenade of flat roofed shops on the arterial road, and tried to make out that the town would be better served if its centre was built on this cross roads. This was an inelegant solution to population expansion in the fields on the ridge overlooking the A1. This new centre, with its few parking places and its location on the side of a road used by heavy lorries carrying coal, glass and chemicals to substantial factories to the east of Knottingley, was now supposed to cater for this population.

The Simpson's Lane Estate, often called the Warwick, dates from the early 1960s. After a period of 'rationalisation' when shallower mines to the west of the Limestone Ridge were culled, the National Coal Board (NCB) decided to open a series of 'super' pits to the east. Kellingley was less than a mile from Harker's boatyard, its traditional boundary; and four miles to the north was the Selby Coalfield complex of pits. The Warwick was built to serve Kellingley but inevitably its story is also tied into the growth and eventual demise of these other coal mines.

THE WARWICK - KNOTTINGLEY

When the local paper front page story is not about sending a sick child to Disneyland or about a young woman threatened by a wasting disease it is bashing the people who live on the Warwick Estate in Knottingley. Headlines, like 'Scum Must Go', and text such as, 'tormented residents on a Knottingley estate are urging community action against mindless scum' (8 April 04) have been commonplace for years. Knottingley can do without that sort of regular coverage.

One of the three local councillors recalls: 'I can remember the Warwick when it was much better. I think that it is on the turn again and is improving but in many ways it has seemed a disaster zone for so long that you do not tend to notice the small changes that are taking place.'

When you contrast it with Broomhill, a much older Knottingley council estate a mile to the east of Warwick, the difference is marked. Even today everyone you meet wants to live here although the buildings are much older. Warwick is new, Broomhill is old Knottingley. You'll find people here whose families built barges when the town was a boat building centre. They remember when the focus of the town was Aire Street and the curve at its end led to the shops in Racca Green. Old Knottingley was built on a diverse economy. Small engineering works, power stations, boat works, medium sized collieries, agricultural suppliers, canal trade, supermarkets and neighbourhood shops were all there. Broomhill served a more diverse economy and probably still does. The Warwick was built because it was close to what was a state of the art colliery, and there was a drive for coal which made men and women abandon older mining areas in Scotland, the North East, Wales and the Midlands and migrate to Yorkshire.

You'll have to change your banners lads
And join the exodus.
But leave your cares behind you
Your future has been planned.
And off you go to Nottingham
To Roben's Promised Land.
The Scotia Colliery
(Northumberland) Song 1965

The name of the working men's club on the Warwick Estate illustrates this. When it was built in the early 1960s there was a drive for coal. Until it was bulldozed away a few years ago after the majority of the local pits had closed it was the Scottish, Yorkshire, and Durham Miners' Club (SYD).

Geoffrey Lofthouse, the area's MP from 1978 - 1997, but in those days in charge of National Coal Board (NCB) recruitment for the area, remembers travelling to Fife, Northumberland and Durham and coming back a week later with bus loads of miners and their wives. It was 'up sticks and a job for life' time. The Warwick was sold as an estate fit for heroes, Kellingley pit as an Eldorado. When Geoffrey Lofthouse, living over the hill in Pontefract, was elected to Parliament fifteen years later he could still boast that there were over twenty pits in or within five miles of his constituency.

This period of growth ended dramatically in 1986. Following the 'Big Strike' of 1984/5 the pits went down like dominoes. Castleford lost Fryston, Wheldale, Allerton and Glasshoughton, followed in 2002 by the Prince of Wales, Pontefract. The Selby complex finally disappeared, after gradually rotting away, in 2003. Big K, Kellingley, hung on with great tenacity until it was the last pit in West Yorkshire, though with its workforce cut by half.

Associated with the demise of coal was the collapse of the coal burning power stations. Standing on the eastern ramparts of Pontefract Castle and looking north-east you can still see the cooling towers or the steam rising from Drax, Ferrybridge and Eggborough but none of them are working to their full capacity. They have been killed off by changing attitudes to emissions or the dash for gas. The development of Chinese and Indian chemical industries has seen off or reduced the labour force at Croda and Degussa. Three-generation unemployment is well known in Knottingley.

WHY THE WARWICK WENT DOWNHILL

The name Warwick Estate is now disliked by many. Vanda Dunachie, the publican at the Wallbottle, doesn't like it, nor does the woman who lives across from the Tin Bridge; she said, 'Top side of the Community Centre I should think, though I had never heard the phrase earlier than twenty years ago. All of this was Simpson's Lane when I first knew the area. That's what it says on the front of the bus that goes around the estate now and that is what it said when me and my husband came here from Cudworth so that he could work at the pit in 1962.'

Dr Terry Spencer, Knottingley's historian, a scholar who out of interest has tracked down all of the township's field and route-way names, says

that Warwick is not mentioned anywhere in the early place-name history: 'Simpson's Lane was always there from the nineteenth century onwards, it led to Simpson's Farm. The best I can say is that the name Warwick is probably part of a tendency that you notice all over the Five Towns area in the 1960s. In an attempt to make things seem more refined than they were, the Council started to invent upper-crust names for places and the name Warwick is one. They sometimes used poets' names such as Tennyson, Wordsworth or Shelley. All those are street names in what local people call 'The Poets' down in Ferrybridge. Councillors on the General Purposes or Transport Committee, as it was called in the 1960s, might be the culprits responsible for the name change.

'Warwick is a fanciful name. The area might have got it because a councillor's wife remembers reading the name in a novel or the chairman's family might have been there on holiday. Warwick Castle would have been becoming a tourist attraction in that period. These are silly but significant reasons. Remember there was little community consultation in that period. I would guess that they changed the name from the descriptive Simpson's Lane as part of a gentrification process.'

So that's it. When the area first got tarted up they tarted up the name as well but because people are not taken in by that sort of nonsense many of them have continued to dislike the new name from the beginning. The naming was part of a social manipulation process that came about when the estate was laid out. When it came to naming the place where they might live the full span of their lives, there was no reference to the people who lived there.

In the same way there was no reference back to local people about the way the estate was laid out. When they were not for high-rise, most town planning departments in the late 1950s and 1960s, the period when the estate was laid out, had a preference for semi-detached houses or short terraces of housing separated by great swathes of grass. The 'woman across from you' was 'not across the road', she might as well have been over on the next hill. That was because there was no shortage of building land on the edge of towns like Knottingley. Maintenance was cheap and so was public transport. As long as there was enough money in the

What are the neighbourhood issues?
Just about everything.
Community development officer

council kitty to buy the sort of industrial sized lawnmower that could be sent in to cut the grass on a regular basis they expected the residents to be happy. One man with a grass cutting machine needed a clean sweep if he was to get his bonus. For that reason there were no private defendable spaces, few trees, next to no flowers and fewer council workers. You see it at Bramhope in Hull, at Seacroft in Leeds and on Kendrey, Barnsley. In that period thirty years ago we 'designed-in' many of the social ills that rebound and upset us today.

ROZALYN IS A DOPEY BITCH

You learn more on an hour's walk with a councillor who knows his or her patch than you ever could sitting reading an evaluation report for half a day. It is partly because they respond to you and the answer drives you on to ask another question, but also partly because as the walk progresses you meet up with other characters who you get introduced to, and they in their turn suggest new lines of enquiry.

The first part of the journey was by car and then we walked. The car ride took us through areas that had been renovated on an earlier council scheme and then past a few hundred houses that had never had 'the treatment' before we came to a square of shops at the centre of the estate. As we approached the Wallbottle public house the councillor said, 'We get a lot of grumbles in those streets, for the people see neighbours getting something and we cannot give anything but vague promises in return, for although SRB levered in something approaching £6 million you cannot do everything.

'SRB 4 money was used to pave the square, put in CCTV cameras, get an artist to design the sheet metal screen and to open the community shop. It is a shame to see the community shop now. The sad truth is that after the treasurer ran off with the money a lot of people lost heart. Up to then they were doing okay. There were even plans to open up the empty shop opposite and run it as a community café.'

The shutters were still down on this empty building. These are well-graffitied in marker pen. 'Rozalyn' - no graffitist spells her name the same – 'is a dopey bitch' is in capital letters at the top. In lower case letters at the bottom it says somewhat plaintively: 'Nobody luvs me, nobody cares by Ros.'- 'Ros is a slag' and 'Lynchy is a chubby lad' end the tale.

There is a butcher, a baker and a Tandoori cook who shares the take-away shop with someone who bakes pizzas. Close by, two doors up and opposite Pound Stretcher, is Martin's, the newsagent's. There the specialities are rows and rows of sweets, cheap plastic toys and 'mucky books'. That day the covers of *FH2* and *Maxim* sported bondage pictures. Somewhat ironically the saleslady was complaining to a customer that it was a pity they had given a twelve year old no more than a care order for tying up a five year old in Dewsbury. There are no children's reading books. How we advance schemes like Surestart or the various early reading and story telling agendas in such areas needs serious debate. Books are expensive, and healthy eating only lurks in the sidelines. There is a fruit and vegetable shop but this is rivalled by the bakers-cum-sandwich shop. For £2.60 you can buy a 'Belly Buster' and for 40p less, 'Bol and Chips' - a carbohydrate sandwich enlivened by grease and salt. This could be swilled down with cheap beer from Booze Buster across the square. There is a post office and telephone box of the sort used if you want to contact a dealer. Oh Happy Hour, that we should live in times like these. Many of the local middle-aged walk with sticks or wander round on motorised mobility scooters.

Next door to the baker's is what remains of the Warwick Community Centre information shop. This was funded with SRB money and still bears the FreshAire logo. Unlike the other shops it had its protective shutters on the inside; therefore the shop front acted as a large display board. The windows are filthy. The most prominent sign reads, 'Due to severe lack of volunteers the shop will be closed until further notice.' Other notices report that this was where you could get car badges for the disabled and access the free prescription delivery service. There is information about classes and childcare.

Friendly faces
Well-heeled places
Chavs in prison
and community spaces.
A verse from a Community song

There is a time to be born and a time to die. I thought of this as I looked at what had been a few years ago a point of light in a difficult neighbourhood. Here SRB money had been invested, and invested wisely from what I could see, but the experiment had not worked. Now is the time to paint SRB and short-term solutions out of the environmental strategy and move on.

As Councillor Stokes and I walked on we talked a little about the man who had syphoned off money for himself and who had been treated leniently by the courts because up until the time when he had started diverting money he had given more to the community than he had taken from it. He was a relatively young man who was out of work - there were a lot of them on the estate at that time - and the temptation had been too much. He saw people from servicing agencies come into the community shop who had proper jobs, holiday pay and security, and he did not. The sadness of the situation was that he had not only stolen cash but had also taken away that most important ingredient in the regeneration mix: trust. After that it was difficult to repair the damage. 'One of the younger women, someone who with a bit of training would have made an excellent councillor, just lost interest. People stopped coming to meetings.'

In the Wallbottle public house all was quiet. There were two rooms; in one a group of older women were playing bingo and in the other four men in their fifties were talking. As we came in, the level of conversation was notched up and I heard Gordon Brown's name mentioned for they seemed to recognise that a local politician, Councillor Stokes, had entered the room. One was a well known union official in the days when the coal miners' union meant something in the area. In the old days they probably had more standing in the community than they do now. You see them all over the local area, men who had a reason to get up in the morning when Kellingley Pit or one of the mines in the Selby Coalfield were regularly breaking European records, but who these days have little to be proud of beyond their families. These experienced men had not taken much part in the SRB initiatives. Pensioners and women like the publican and her mother had driven FreshAire forward on the Warwick estate. Now they were tired and somewhat disillusioned and were thinking about other things. When there was some money there, they were pleased to be of use but again things had not worked out as they had been promised they would.

52 SRB 4 & 5

TIN BRIDGES, ALLOTMENTS AND FENCED GARDENS

When we left the Wallbottle we struck east because I wanted to see the area that had once held a skate park. Designed by local youths, it had later been stolen by men with a heavy loader who turned up one afternoon and took it away either to render it into scrap metal or to sell on to someone who wanted a used skate park.

A hundred yards on, we were leaning on the Tin Bridge and looking over towards the Warwick Community Centre. Tin wasn't the metal used in its construction but, in the Victorian sense, it described 'something done on the cheap with little purpose'. Graham explained, 'It once was a pedestrian underpass linking one section of about twenty houses to thirty houses on the other side but when the SRB group started to talk about ways we could improve the estate all agreed that it should go. The SRB gave us a chance to make that sort of adjustment to the landscape. People considered it an eyesore which was just used by kids who had nothing to do but muck around and intimidate older people, so we filled in the tunnel and left it as it is now. I suppose it seems a bit pointless unless you know the story.'

Then he pointed out to me that across the valley the houses had metal fences. 'They are not the best design on the market but they are cheap and stand up to a lot of battering.' I did not find them so bad. They seemed sturdy and I could imagine a dedicated group of workmen putting them up double quick once they had mastered the intricacies of bolting together these elaborate metal jigsaw puzzles.

Strategic organisations with large catchment areas can avoid intractable problems. Employment organisations shuffle 'people who don't want to work' into convenient holding patterns; health trusts bump-up patient treatment numbers by fast-tracking minor operations and allowing waiting lists to build up for more time-consuming complaints. Neighbourhood schemes, by comparison, must deal with the problems on their doorstep: they cannot cherry pick.

The Council have defended the allotment owners' space by surrounding it with eight foot high palisade fencing. This is stronger but the territory it defends is precious. Behind these bastions of steel are prize leeks, common vegetables and pigeon lofts.

As we were passing, a woman came out of the gate carrying a small child, two plastic chairs and a bag of vegetables. The easiest way to learn something about the fine grain of an area is to ask both pertinent, and occasionally impertinent, questions. 'Have you got your own allotment?'

I asked. She had, and for the next few minutes she told me of both the allotment's and her history.

The boy's father had left long ago, the plot had been her dad's but she had taken it over and loved it 'to bits', the defensive fence was a god-send, they had never had as much trouble as you might expect; but why should they? The bulk of the people were good to live amongst: 'The fair few bad-uns are all right after they are knocked back into line.' There was the usual division in this allotment's population, the gardeners were up at the top end and the pigeon men down at the bottom. I asked her what she thought of the estate gardens. She was more enthusiastic than I. Some were neglected, a lot weren't - I should look more closely.

Graham Stokes then introduced me to a man who had the healthy scepticism of an independent neighbourhood activist. He had written to Wakefield and District Housing about CCTV cameras. The cameras had been out of use for some time and this letter assured him that they were in working order. With that information he had gone up to the council offices and had the letter photocopied so that not only he but also his neighbours could monitor council promises given in the letter. He was now pushing it through people's doors and giving it to anyone who would listen. SRB money to the tune of £30,000 had been invested, he said.

Opposite the allotments was a cul de sac. Most of the occupants seemed elderly. At the bottom end, nearest the main road, there were some lovely gardens, most with hanging baskets. In my lifetime, England had ceased to be a nation of shopkeepers and had become a nation of gardeners. The corner shops had all but gone, a by-product of changing life styles, supermarkets and mass retailing, but new traditions had grown up in their place. Some of the plants on view had no doubt been grown from seed or been given by neighbours but the majority would have been purchased from garden centres. Few people seemed to grow vegetables. There were several reasons for this. Why grow when you can buy at Morrison's the cheap imports from developing countries; and without ample defendable space, why risk the fruits of your labour being stolen?

One of the reasons why this oasis survived was the new hooped fencing introduced when a new generation of planners took the opportunity to close off the ginnels and snickets that where in the original plan. In 1960, when more people were using public transport, quick movement onto bus routes was a priority. Now it was not. Designing out crime was now more important.

Of course not all space is easily defendable. For about four hundred yards beyond the allotments there are the remains of four civic sites which have in the last ten years been hit by arsonists. The first is SYD, the Scottish, Yorkshire, and Durham Miners' Club, built in the late 1960s. The next is Throstle Farm Infants' School, eventually burnt to the ground, as were the football ground changing rooms opposite. The Castleford Women's Centre Garden Project was another project which started with high hopes and failed to flourish. You can still see the foundations of their Youth Club and Community Centre.

One of the saddest stories regarding SRB 4 spending concerns the building and the subsequent removal of the adventure playground at the end of Simpson's Lane. In an attempt to lift the area, the SRB team brought together a group of young people and encouraged them to help design a children's playground. As more and more of the buildings on the lane were burnt down or demolished, this elegant and expensive play area became isolated.

It doesn't matter how many expensive treatments and appliances a bathroom cabinet is equipped with: there remain things (usually embarrassing things) for which only a pair of tweezers will do. When it comes to tackling social issues, neighbourhood projects are in effect the 'tweezers'. We can do something that other agencies can't - we can engage with people here where they live and where they are at in their lives. We can get them on that first rung.
Vic Allen

One afternoon, when no-one was looking, a low-loader backed into the lane and stole the skating ramp and the majority of the playground equipment. All that is left now is a battered community-designed gate and the remains of a rain shelter and still it goes on. Last year arsonists took out Simpson's Lane Junior School. The story is particularly sad, for every time the partners put in something that might lift that area of the estate a lad, or so the rumour goes, went in with matches. One sick child!

Up on some waste land a man was burning cable to get rid of the rubber and sell off the rest for scrap. A few yards on from this acrid smell there was a smell that was altogether different. When we turn a corner, a couple of kids, oblivious to all regulations about health and safety, are using their

mother's domestic cooker tray and some twigs to cook sausages. 'I like that,' I said, 'that is why you need defendable space, to grill half a pound of sausages.'
'Cremate them, more like,' said Graham.

As we walked on I began to notice what I think of as the 'five garden phenomenon'. If someone spends some time doing up their garden, the two neighbours on either side will take out a spade and do something themselves unless there is a void next door. If we lived in an ideal word the process would take you to the edge of the estate; we don't, so you rarely get beyond five houses. But it is the sort of start that restores your faith in human nature and in metal hooped fencing.

The 'Right to Buy' legislation did not immediately attract too many house-buyers but more recently in some streets the majority have bought their own houses. Even in the less popular 'prairie', open plan, areas of the estate people are buying from the Council or the stock company that has replaced it. In the original deed of sale there was a covenant that said that a buyer must not fence the surrounding land. As time has passed this ruling has been ignored, and now small plots of fenced land have appeared where once planners settled for 'open space'.

CONSULTATION AND THE COMMUNITY SHOP

Graham Stokes explains: 'So-called consultation is not seen to amount to much. This is pretty barren ground for consultation. Over a number of years people had been consulted by paid community workers but their views were ignored when agencies came in to bid for available resources. The people got what they were given, not what they requested.

'Local people have been let down too much and in an age when people do not generally go to meetings it is hard to create enthusiasm here. Consultation meetings can too easily become shouting matches; people want action to follow talk and usually they cannot get it. It is not easy for the officers. When I brought in a chief officer from the Council at the time of the Liveability Review he expected an easy ride. He didn't get it. One

woman got up and said pretty clearly, 'You think that you influence what goes off in this area. You don't. Drug barons influence life here. Sometimes they are better equipped. We have had a dealer working close to the shops, everyone knows his house but he has never been caught. That is because he has his own CCTV camera outside monitoring what is going off outside his front door. There's efficiency for you. When the woman next door got burgled it is said that he invited her in to see if she could spot the thief.'

'Everyone knew that he was dealing, catching him was the problem. Then early one morning the police turned up in numbers and smashed down the door. Still they found nothing. Immediately, as was his right, he demanded a new door for protection. Again understandably, for like everyone else's his property has to be protected, he got his new door. When it was in place he complained that it was fragile. A few days later the local authority came and fitted a stronger one. He got two doors in seven days!

'That happened at a time when good tenants were waiting months for repairs. Everything these days is supposed to be governed by joined up thinking, this wasn't. Housing, who were responsible, should have known better.

'SRB allowed us a temporary breathing space. We were grateful for that but it was short-lived. During that time we had five policemen in the area. Now we have one. Recently the police came in with a mobile cop-shop. That will ease things until they move on.'

I once attended a training session on European Social Fund audit requirements. The person delivering the training was the head of the audit team in London and was to be feared. Before I attended my boss instructed me not to put up my hand to ask any questions. If I did, it was likely that our college would be the next one to be audited.
Alison Seabrooke

THE WARWICK CAMPUS - KNOTTINGLEY

A local man, out walking his dog, stood chatting to the nursery worker through the large, green metal gates that greet you on the approach to Warwick Community Campus and Adventure Playground. The Jack Russell was happily yapping in protest at its interrupted walk but the youngster being held by the nursery nurse seemed unperturbed by the anxious animal.

I had woven my way with difficulty through the large and sprawling estate to find the Campus. The estate is made up mainly of row upon row of grey and beige semi-detached council houses, some well-tended and others down-at-heel. It is much the same as any privately-owned or rented residential estate that once belonged to a council. These houses were separated by swathes of grass where I imagined children would play, but now they were at school. I would have been worried about how to get into the fortress but the nursery worker swung open the gates to allow me to park and I entered a calmer world.

Mature trees, grassed and hard play areas and a range of play facilities - wooden fortresses, basketball courts, skate-board ramps, zip wire, swings and a large sand pit - made me feel as if I was entering some sort of haven. It was seemingly designed to stimulate children's imaginations in an otherwise characterless and colourless estate. Toddlers and 'tweenies' - those who will soon be at school - played happily outside, watched over by local playworkers. My only concern was for the two year-old who had ingeniously managed to take his trike up onto a sideless platform and looked like he was happily considering becoming a stuntman.

I was welcomed by Mandy, the administrator, who showed me around the Campus. The squat building had opened in 2001 and looked much like any community building from the outside. Inside, the large main room was littered with children's cheerful artwork. Children wandered in and out to get to their specially designed room at the back of the building, whilst four elderly people sat at laptops taking instruction on how to enter the technological age.

Mandy explained the purpose of the campus: 'There has been a play area on the Warwick estate for a number of years. In fact, children are at the heart of the Campus and are the reason why the building is now here. The crèche is open at the moment and whilst there are usually only 7 - 8 children in it, numbers can rise to 20 if their parents want to attend a class. There are 30 children attending the out-of-school club. The kids are picked up from home or are dropped off by parents for the breakfast club and then walked to school, and the same happens in reverse in the evening.' She explained that after school the Adventure Playground is open access to children from the estate and no adults are allowed into the Campus after 3pm. 'There are two schools on Warwick Estate, but the top end, which is thought of as the roughest area, don't venture down here. We cater for 5 - 12 year olds, although they tend to stop coming to the out-of-school club as they near secondary school age.'

I asked her how they managed to keep an eye on the children who were formally in their care while there were large numbers of kids dropping in informally. Mandy admitted that they had occasionally had some fun and games when the children forgot that they were booked into the out-of-school club that night and wandered off home to empty houses. Mistakes like this were rare, though, and it seemed on the whole a good arrangement - the kids turning up on an informal basis were able to play in a safe, and watched-over environment, even if they didn't realise it.

I commented on the artwork around the centre. Mandy explained, 'We have a specialist artworker, Claudia, who organises a range of projects for the children. These range from photography, batik, paintings, to dance performance. She recently involved the children in a graffiti project in Castleford. They were taught how to use the spray cans and produce designs that were displayed in the town. The committee was horrified when they found out. They thought the next step would be that the estate would be graffitied overnight. It simply wasn't the case, though because they were given an area and shown how to do it in a controlled environment.'

The playworkers had the luxury of a large office, which was used to plan children's activities, and prepare course-work for the playwork courses for which they had established a reputation. There was a chill-out area, where the older kids went to escape their younger siblings, and a soft-play area for the little ones. The centre seemed to want for nothing in children's facilities.

First man: *Sometimes I'd like to ask God why he allows poverty, famine and injustice to continue when he could do something about it.*
Second man: *What's stopping you?*
First man: *I'm afraid he might ask me the same question*
Anon

Mandy had her own office where she co-ordinated the wide range of children's and community activities. We sat down to chat and she explained that the centre had been without a manager for a few months and was just getting back on track. The new manager had started that week but was already out delivering a playwork course. Multi-tasking is not unfamiliar in a small community organisation where even the most senior employee has to earn their bread and butter, too.

She explained, 'Originally the site was an old quarry that our chairman, John Morton, acquired from the Council to convert to a children's play area. There was a portakabin alongside the play facilities which housed the volunteers and youth workers. The committee wanted something a bit more permanent and that was when they applied for SRB. We got a new building as a result and the adventure play area. The whole focus has been on providing something for the children on the estate, but things have evolved and we now have a range of community services and activities on offer.'

Mandy didn't live on the Warwick but she knew that the campus provided a lifeline to many of its residents. 'A lot of people never seem to leave the estate. There are many single parents on low incomes and all the problems associated with worklessness and low self-esteem, such as drug use. The estate has a terrible reputation around Castleford and Ferrybridge, but in the two years that I have been here nothing has gone missing.'

We had already swapped notes on the effectiveness of creating an anti-vandal building. My own community facility in Riccall had gone to lengths to ensure that there were no nooks and crannies where miscreants could hide. Our discussion on drainpipes had been interesting - Warwick Campus had hidden theirs internally, whereas at Riccall we had painted ours with anti-vandal paint to stop kids climbing on the roof.

ORIGINS

Mandy confessed that she had little knowledge of the intricacies of SRB funding, other than that it had paid for the new building and she had to continue to provide monitoring forms long after the funding had finished. Her main concern now was the ESF programme which had continued to ensure that local people could access activities free of charge. Again I empathised. Having applied for and monitored ESF programmes myself

I understood that no-one would go down that route unless they were desperate. Better sit in a bath of acid.

I had sympathy for Mandy. She was struggling without a manager for the last six months and there were several of the workers on long-term sick. You need a lot of support when you are managing finance. If she found SRB complex, I wondered how she had managed to cope with all the intricacies of the European Social Fund (ESF) grants. She could not be expected to behave like the manager without more training.

Having worked in the European unit of a local college I had been immersed in the complexities of ESF audit trails. They are complicated. Mandy had her work cut out and it was too easy to falter if you lacked the necessary experience and went unsupported. To keep her head above water she would have to know about apportionment of costs, complicated formulas relating to the percentage of the overheads and the staff time of those working at the Campus. These had to be clearly calculated and proven against the ESF project. Then there was knowledge of whether staff in other organisations, such as the local authority, had kept accurate time sheets to back up any contribution of time they had committed to the project at the application stage. This was part of the calculation on the acceptability of matchfunding. She also was required to know if this time/financial value had been calculated using the ESF formula and whether this came from a 'clean' source, one that didn't originate from the European Union.

I hoped that for Mandy's sake the centre would never be subjected to an ESF audit. Equally feared and disliked by delivery and finance staff, this is a horrendous experience. ESF audit teams descend at short notice and pick their way through the figures.

In 2004 the FreshAire programme had spent £4,126,969 of its SRB money. This money had attracted in a further £12,197,623 from the public sector and £1,362,367 from the private sector.

At such times in small organisations the absence of a key post can be critical. In a large organisation, such as the local council, there is usually someone else who will carry out essential tasks while a new or replacement member of staff is recruited. This does not happen in organisations like the Knottingley Community Campus. In small community sector organisations where the management committee members have to fit meetings around their day jobs, where there are few staff who can double-up on duties and where there is no dedicated personnel function, the unplanned loss or absence of a key member of staff can have a huge impact. Not only is there a loss of a pair of hands there is also a loss of knowledge.

Mandy told me that Terri Horvath, the previous manager, had recently retired to Spain: 'Lucky her, a place in the sun far away from grant programmes and interminable form-filling.'

I was pleased however to hear that she was still in regular contact with the Campus and after e-mailing her I found out a lot more about the history of the campus' venture into SRB.

Terri explained: 'Between 1977 and 1979 I ran the Wakefield Playbus and worked for Social Services as a community worker. At that time I was involved in a voluntary group called Tykesplay, which was just a group of playworkers and community workers trying to promote play for children as an end in itself - we did things like run play days. This group brought me into contact with the playworkers from Warwick Adventure Playground.

'Then between 1979 and 1990 I was employed as the Director of the Pontefract and District Council for Voluntary Services - now Voluntary Action - and as part of my remit I had the opportunity to work to further both children's play and play respite, including residential respite for children with learning difficulties. My association with Warwick Adventure Playground continued throughout those years and included a Manpower Services Commission team of workmen placed at Warwick who helped the local committee develop the playground and build its first building. I also worked in the evenings as a youth worker and occasionally worked the Warwick area. In that way I maintained my links with the group. On leaving CVS I worked as a tutor at Wakefield College and placed students at the Warwick Adventure Playground. As you see we go back a long way together.

'In 1993 I took the post of regional manager with NSF - now Rethink - and because I was working out of the area I did not have very much to do with the Adventure Playground. However, because I knew all the playworkers and the Chair they would ring me up occasionally for help with various issues.

'I was still working out of the area, at this point in Birmingham, when the Warwick committee decided to become involved in the SRB programme and in that way get a purpose-built facility for children's play. Because of the way modern partnerships are set up they had to acquire matchfunding and they had managed to pull in English Partnerships, Coalfields Regeneration Trust and the European Regional Development Funds. I was approached for help with form-filling and job descriptions by the playworker who was trying to get the deal together. Both the committee and workers were tearing their hair out as the documentation went backwards and forwards and so I began to get further involved. Like all voluntary committees with limited resources, the production of the paperwork and the time involved had worn everyone out.'

I could see where Terri was coming from. My organisation in a rural village had done a lot to prove to funders that there was no skills deficit amongst committee members - we had childcare specialists, bank workers, people experienced in construction - but nothing prepared us for the form-filling and politics of applying for government funding. We just wanted to get on with the job. A lot of this work, at least at the start, would be at no cost to government at all.

Terri continued: 'Eventually the Committee appointed a manager for 'Warwick Community Campus incorporating the Adventure Playground'. I became involved yet again in response to an SOS for help in managing the performance of the new manager who was not succeeding in meeting the targets set by the funders and in particular SRB who were threatening to pull out of the agreement. I was due to retire from NSF so I had my white charger at the ready. I waded back in, agreeing to become a member of the committee and support and line manage the manager.

English Partnerships is the national regeneration agency helping the Government to support high quality sustainable growth in England.

At this stage every mistake that a voluntary group could make had been made. The manager had raised 'a grievance' and had involved the union. Targets were not being met, the committee were under duress to perform and had had letters from SRB regarding targets. A plan of action was agreed which included more manageable targets and we went from there.

'To cut a long story short, I retired from NSF and the Campus Manager got a new job. The committee failed to re-appoint and I was asked to take the job on a temporary basis. This was supposed to be for three months - I had plans to retire to Spain - but ended up stretching to two years. There was no infrastructure in place either to manage workers or record targets. Of the £250,000 acquired by the Campus for the capital costs of the building, £98,000 was from SRB in 2004. This came in a one-off capital payment. The rest came from English Partnerships.'

Now there was a name that interested me. At the same time, thirteen miles to the east in the Selby Coalfield village of Riccall, the organisation I chaired, Riccall Regen 2000, was also part-funded by English Partnerships. We had been exasperated by their requirement to negotiate a formal contract which required solicitor's help and fees to the tune of £5,000. We were also required to complete a contract guarantee bond. This was a formal requirement for all the multi-million pound land investment deals they handled. However, they were alone in this practice. All of our other, often more significant, grant funders had been comfortable enough to trust us to simply sign grant agreements.

Life would become a lot easier if government, or quasi-government bodies, used 'joined-up thinking' and came to a consensus on the most efficient way of passing grants to community organisations. There are some interesting proposals on the horizon regarding 'clawback'. This means that public funders have the rights to the proportion of the community building project which they have funded. By relaxing the clawback clause community organisations may, in the future, be able to raise funds against, or sell, community assets, provided the purpose is to continue, or increase, public benefit. My big concern here is the inability of the funders to join up and reach mutual agreement on relaxing the terms of their individual claims. There is a tendency to talk about joined-up thinking rather than actively promote it.

Terri continued: 'The other amounts were from the Coalfields Regeneration Trust who revenue-funded 51% of the manager's salary and that of the out-of-school playworker. The revenue remainder of 49% came from the European Regional Development Fund. There was also a small revenue grant from the New Opportunities Fund in matchfunding for the out-of-school playworker assistant post and some running costs. Building running and maintenance costs were met by Wakefield Metropolitan District Council Young People's Service as payment for the placement of their team of three workers based at the Campus.'

To the enlightened, this cocktail of public and private grants is known as 'matchfunding'. No-one ever gets 100% for all of their capital and revenue costs from one single body. As an applicant you have to apply to very many grant bodies, most of them at the same time, in order to put together a jigsaw of different types of funding to remain functional. And each time you do this you have to alter the emphasis of your project just slightly, to meet their differing criteria. So, for example, if one funder's emphasis is on regenerating the physical appearance of a place or its infrastructure, you would apply to them with an emphasis on what the new buildings and roads would do to kick-start the social regeneration. Another funder might be interested in the skills and work elements of regeneration and another perhaps just in young people. In this instance you slant your application towards those features. The outcome is that many projects become skewed towards the funding, rather than the aims and objectives of the organisation.

The whole thrust from Government is that projects like these, if they provide a necessary local public service, should now become 'mainstream'. The local government agencies, such as the local authority, police, fire and health authorities, should start to include these community-based services within their annual budgeting of resources received from the central pot.

It is for this reason that more and more organisations with some savvy begin to operate a social enterprise model: they run on business principles but have social objectives. They begin to trade and take on contracts from a range of sources with distinctive objectives. In that way they become more self-supporting. Bit by bit they lose the grant funding element and replace it with other funding streams. They mix their income base so that it includes earned income, contracts, franchises and mainstream funding. This means that they become much more independent and sustainable.

However, this isn't everyone's cup of tea. There are many voluntary and community organisations that have one single purpose and would find it difficult to turn their project into a going concern without losing focus.

Terri went on to describe the relationships with all of these funding partners: 'There was a good relationship with the Young People's Management back at the Council, but there were many problems with the workers based at the Campus. These involved demarcation, territory and 'what's mine and what's yours' issues. These workers had been at the Adventure Playground for 20 years and were set in their ways. They did not like the new expansion or the new regime and were non co-operative. They hated SRB and it was difficult to get them to co-operate.'

Terri described their relationship with the Coalfields Regeneration Trust: 'They were always helpful and willing to work with us through the quagmire of monitoring and reporting. Their monitoring forms were simple, their targets realistic and related to the Campus objectives. We had a similar relationship with the people of the European Regional Development Fund. We enjoyed working with them. They were helpful but there were some problems with the clerks who received the quarterly reports. They seemed clueless if information deviated from their tick boxes. We eventually developed a good relationship with one of the managers and so, too, with the New Opportunities Fund; so there were no problems here. This fund was a straightforward grant based on a quarterly report. This money also totally fitted the objectives of the organisation and did not involve creating new initiatives. It supported the Coalfields Regeneration Trust revenue grant.

'Some of the targets overlapped or were duplicated with SRB's. SRB would not accept that an individual might come in and perform a variety of tasks. They have to have 'different' people. It was a real bureaucratic muddle.' At Riccall we, too, had been caught out by this ruling. European funds, for example, require you to count 'beneficiaries' which means individual people, as opposed to having a tick-box which records 'number of contacts'. Potentially the same person can be contacted more than once.

There was also that old matchfunding problem which centred on the timing for match monies and promises of awards called by some the 'I will if you will' and by others the 'you show me yours if I show you mine' paradox.

Terri again: 'Being around in a consultative role at the time of application, I was very aware of the difficulties. These were: mountains of paperwork, constant liaison rushes and last minute deadlines. There were time constraints, additional committee meetings with additional costs in expenses but above all, the cost of worker time in additional word processing hours and extra printing cost. This could lead to lack of confidence and more wear and tear on volunteers and young, often poorly paid, office workers.' Terri and I both felt strongly about this.

Terri: 'As a community worker with a lot of paid and unpaid experience, I have seen small committees destroyed by the roles forced on them by the short-term government funding mechanisms. Small committees are forced into a role for which they have no training, they are given very little meaningful help, they sign up to artificial, time-limited targets they do not really understand - and have no hope of achieving - they are encouraged to bend their objectives so everything becomes difficult, not enough time is given to allow for an infrastructure to be put in place to set up a company/business, or for meaningful recruitment. They lose sight of what they set out to achieve and just become harassed, feel inadequate and eventually stop coming to the meetings.

'There was no infrastructure in place for monitoring the grant, in particular financial controls, other than that held by the Chair. At one time they had nine different bank accounts and account holders, but as there were no human resources and operational policies or recording systems, monitoring was initially impossible. Wakefield Metropolitan District Council workers placed at the Campus had their own recording systems as they worked to the Council but these were 'confidential'. The WMDC workers resented the new project and saw it as a threat in some way. The local people felt that they could be obstructive and insular. This created a real jumble. Some of the work relating to the targets was done by them, some by the Campus officers. It was well-nigh impossible for the original

The children who live round here know next to nothing about real vegetables but then their mothers don't either. They ask me which is an onion and which is a cauliflower. That said, I still love the Warwick. I have lived here most of my life.

manager to record numbers. Under my regime I dealt with this through the committee and through introducing an infrastructure of policies and procedures which the District Council Management agreed to.'

I reflected on my own experiences of grant monitoring at Riccall after listening to Terri's accounts. By the time I left I had become a bit of an old lag when it came to form filling for a number of grants awarded through public funds and charitable trusts. But of all the regimes I came across I have to say that it was SRB that almost drove me to distraction.

Riccall's SRB funding had been managed by a different local government establishment from that which looked after the Warwick. In my case it was North Yorkshire County Council, in theirs, Wakefield Metropolitan District Council. As the accountable body for this Yorkshire Forward fund each devised monitoring systems so that they could provide detailed information on how the money had been spent. The monitoring returns were paid quarterly, in arrears. Eventually other funds were drawn in, but not always solely because of the SRB initiatives. There was other money out there that could be more important such as the European Regional Development Fund, Coalfields Regeneration Trust and New Opportunities Fund revenue funding. SRB and English Partnerships however did make significant money available for capital funds and without these funds the building would not have been there to house neighbourhood capacity building programmes. Yet this brought mixed blessings. Having a building is one thing - making it function effectively is another.

Terri: 'In the case of Warwick Community Campus, for the £98,000 SRB capital funds they received from SRB they were expected to fulfil impossible targets over a period of five years, which they did not really understand the significance of and which created major problems for the first manager and the Committee. They felt bullied by SRB which seemed intractable to them when they tried to alter the targets to some meaningful level. Despite meeting and exceeding the lifetime targets, SRB are still insisting on their quarterly returns to the end of the 5 year period which is additional work for the already overworked staff.'

LETTER FROM AFAR

Terri: 'During my time as manager, things were sorted with SRB and I did develop a good relationship. I realised that many were people I had known when I was at CVS, local authority officers who had just moved constantly sideways like crabs as each new government measure developed. They in their turn allowed me a certain amount of license, maybe because they saw the Campus developing in an acceptable way. We mellowed after many similar experiences in the area. Jointly we began to bring in new money. We developed accredited Playwork and Disability Training that helped their targets. In turn the committee became more knowledgeable and I was able to represent SRB to them not as something that was fundamentally alien but as a grouping of people who, like them, were trying to do the best they could for the people of the Warwick Estate whilst trying to reach government targets.

'I can't think of anything funny that happened in my actual dealings with SRB officers - they are not particularly humorous people. They asked us to host various prestigious events and I spent hours with my chair persuading him it was a good thing when he clearly did not think it was and then pretending to SRB that the committee 'welcomed them'. Devious or what?

'As I lie on my sun bed or on the beach I will try to let good thoughts come into my head and record the good things that have happened within the project.

There are hundreds, for example: The Playwork and Disability Training, which we developed from scratch because of the need to train volunteers and workers, was a great success. I still work on this with a colleague from Warwick. I e-mail lesson plans and conduct the odd training sessions when I am in England. I love to see enlightenment dawn on students' faces and to see them achieve their accreditation awards. Many of these students have not done any academic work since school. The training has also helped many other small groups - particularly volunteer parents trying to run playschemes - as we managed to get funding from Early Years Education and Sure Start. On the Warwick we are able to cover 80% and sometimes 100% of the cost.

You don't have to speak slowly or raise your voice when you talk to the average community activist. And you don't need minutes to cover your back. Leave 'back covering' to the officers. In my experience people remember quite nicely what went off at the 'last meeting'. Remember, they do not trail from one meeting to the next like professionals. They are focused and often have time to give local issues serious thought.
Chairman of the
Smawthorne Area meeting

'A small group of local first step learners at an art class have now formed their own self-help art group and have managed to obtain small funding grants, open bank accounts, visit art centres and craft shows; they are another success story. These people like to get off the estate and go to city art galleries. One of them is now off anti-depressants after 20 years and has recently got a place on a course at Wakefield College; that's got to be good news.

'In particular it is good to know that I helped in the development of members of the Campus Committee into assured and knowledgeable people.

'As you will have deduced nothing went to plan initially and there were quite a few casualties both among committee and staff before it began to go well. The problem with SRB - and this is the same for other short-term government initiatives which move in and move out - is that their programmes often do not reflect what the people within the community see themselves as needing. Community development work is a long-term educative process, and with each new generation that comes along the process of what needs to be done changes as the community presents a different set of issues.'

KNOTTINGLEY NOW

In Winter 2004 Wakefield MDC brought in some consultants to do a 'health check' on Knottingley. What was handed in was pretty perfunctory. There were three pages on the area and the most positive thing that they could come up with was the suggestion that a footpath be built to Morrison's new super store. There was no mention of Racca's Road, an area which is still regarded by many as a centre of sorts, or Ferrybridge. The fate of Aire Street was not in the document at all. They dare not present that sort of report on Castleford - ever the centre of a powerful political lobby - or Wakefield City, the local seat of municipal government.

It is generally thought by Knottingley people who are in the know that, compared with Airedale, Knottingley did not get its fair share of FreshAire SRB money. There are several reasons for this. One is size,

Knottingley is much smaller than Airedale, but the other is location and the strength of the local politicians. Knottingley sits across the boundary of Wakefield MDC, and border towns of an area are often treated with less respect than those at the centre of things. With the best will in the world it is difficult to stop that happening. A border town rarely gets what it requires or deserves. We can also see that in the chapter on Stocksbridge, a Sheffield border town.

A number of factors are influenced by density of population and by location. Serious political power rarely resides in a border town. Generally the local councillors have little to trade as an influential group. Castleford has three wards; Knottingley, one. As a Cabinet member Councillor Graham Stokes exerted some influence but even that could not outbalance the fact that Knottingley was out on a limb. There were four Castleford councillors on the Board, including the Chairman, compared with one from Knottingley. The Five Towns Centre, the operational headquarters of SRB, was in Castleford, councillors shopped and worked from there. Airedale started at the park, five minutes' walk from Castleford town centre, Knottingley was a car ride away.

SRB was about forming partnerships, and Castleford had a tradition of forming partnerships. In the recent past lots of money had gone into regeneration schemes in Airedale, therefore it was in a position to pick up more. On the Partnership Board there were representatives from the Employment Service, Eastern Primary Care Trust and Learning and Skills Council, all organisations that had worked in Castleford networks previously. The imbalance was particularly noticeable when we consider education. Airedale High School had two representatives, Knottingley did not have one. Subsequently when the Partnership had responsibility for a further SRB 6 programme this operated in Smawthorne, the Maltkins, Glasshoughton, Half Acres, Cutsyke and Ferrybridge. Only the last on the list was in the Knottingley area, the rest were in Castleford.

Castleford lasses must needs be fair.
They wash in the Calder
And rinse in the Aire.
Traditional rhyme

AIREDALE CASTLEFORD

Airedale stands to the east of Castleford on higher ground overlooking the town. The Airedale estate has around 6,000 houses with a population between 18,000 and 20,000. The whole of Castleford including the Airedale estate only has 40,000 people. Some of the estate is pre-war. Some old residents still remember when there was a copse of trees opposite the old Co-op. In the 1930s people first moved out from poor housing in the centre of Castleford and into houses on the Fryston Road. The main Airedale estate had appeared after the war. One of the older inhabitants said, 'It seemed to us as if in size Airedale would eventually rival Castleford itself.'

If Knottingley is still in decline Airedale is thriving, and some of the initiatives are to do with SRB investment through FreshAire. Others, like the earlier investment in the Kershaw Drive renewal programme, predate it, and were beneficiaries of European money. Many newly arrived Airedale inhabitants do not know of the poor reputation the area had fifteen years ago, and are impressed.

The postmaster at the little row of shops just off Fryston Road, close to the centre of an area that once had a very bad reputation, commented favourably on the improvements brought about by the FreshAire project. 'When we got here five years ago this row of shops was in decline. Several were boarded up. I suspect that some of the shopkeepers had given up the fight and were a bit like ostriches. We saw a real improvement in the area.'

THE SQUARE

Here the community consultation forums were well received. In Steve Truelove's *Airedale - As Told by the Natives,* written in 1998 - the year that programme started - an anonymous contributor tells about what happened when a group of local people came together to discuss the Square in Airedale:

'There's one thing that strikes me about the improvements to The Square, the hub of Airedale life. The people who live around here cannot say that they were not consulted about all the changes. We were invited to the planning meetings to discuss the proposals. But it is funny how the plans have changed over the months since then. I have to laugh.'

He then goes on to describe the first meeting when the plans were shown to the Airedale Community Forum meeting at the Castle School in the winter of 1998.

'A representative of the Highways Department came and brought along this fabulous plan, beautifully illustrated, with all of the shops drawn in detail; honestly, a work of art. The twenty people at the meeting loved it but when they got down to detail they had a number of concerns. One resident actually came straight out: 'It won't work.' It was then that we realised there were in fact obvious flaws in the design and began to look at the detail again.'

The story is told at length in the book. The plan comes back after two months and is sent back again and yet again, each time modified in light of residents' comments, until all that is being presented is 'stick men drawings with no detail at all'. Eventually the plan reaches a stage where it is acceptable and the writer is able to comment, 'I have to say to their credit the planners had almost got it right. Not perfect but almost right.'

Several years later the regeneration officer involved told the same story from the Council's side but with interesting additions. 'Ten years ago we would not have brought it back so often. Twenty years ago we probably would not have brought it back at all. It would have been assumed that the ward councillors would have had a chance to have seen it and that would have given the design enough community authority for us to get on with the work.

'My memory was that one of the shopkeepers was especially persistent and was constantly asking for modifications. Mostly they were right. In the end he pronounced himself fully satisfied. We had an ally from then on, a real community champion.'

The way SRB championed consultation is a feature of government policy that could easily be overlooked in 'Output' and 'Outcome' reports. From the beginning there was a desire on the part of the authorities to include the community in all of the decisions about their neighbourhoods. Even the over-glossy leaflets represent an attempt to communicate with local

You can teach a Yorkshire Man but you cannot teach him much.

people. The recognition that consultation matters is one of the keystones of SRB.

AN ENTHUSIASM FOR PARKS

Queens Park, close to Castleford town centre on the very edge of the FreshAire area, is much loved. When Stephen Hyde, the Chairman of the Friends of Queens Park, was young he was taken through the park by his granddad to feed the ponies at Wheldale Colliery. When his granddad was in his final years the roles reversed and he pushed the old miner's wheelchair along the same paths. From being a child up to the time when he and his wife Christine dedicated themselves to bringing the park back into good shape he regarded it, as many Airedale people did, as his park.

Queens Park, opened in 1897 to celebrate Victoria's Diamond Jubilee, is a natural lung of the town but by the end of the 1990s it was hardly used. Originally there had been greenhouses and a thriving band competition tradition, but no longer. Right up to the beginning of the 1990s it was in a reasonable state but local government cut-backs of that decade meant that the park became neglected.

Castleford is fortunate to have two organisations that did not need to obey the normal adult education practice. One is the Yorkshire Art Circus, founded in 1980, and the other is the Castleford Centre for Life Long Learning, (CCLLL) - once called the Women's Centre - founded four years later at the time of the Great Miners' Strike. In the early days they could offer people rooms without let or hindrance. This is what happened in 1998 when Steve and Christine Hyde decided to call a meeting to discuss the future of the park.

Over the years there have been fewer and fewer rooms where people can hold evening meetings without a caretaker hovering. On the surface this may seem a small thing, but it can be a great irritant for organisations in their seeding period; they have to either go to a public house or miss out. When Margaret Handforth, the Chief Executive of the CCLLL, heard that the embryonic Friends of Queens Park wanted a room for meetings she gave them one free of charge.

An advertising strategy in the local weekly newspaper and a few targeted letters produced a meeting of about 35 people. One was a councillor, though not the councillor for that ward. Representatives from the bowling club also made their one - and up to now only - visit. Out of necessity the talk was general, nostalgic and at times angry. The next meeting was quiet but then it was bound to be, for the subject was how to draw up a constitution. Five attended; one of them had been a senior officer with Wakefield Borough Council. He lived by the parkgates and regularly saw how the park was being used.

Committees usually flourish if they can find someone in the team who has experience of the workings of councils. At one time this person would have been a member of a chapel committee, a political party activist or a trade unionist. There were a lot of them around thirty years ago but the disappearance of non-conformist chapels, local government rationalisation in 1974 and the loss of trade union activists meant that this was no longer the case. Cyril Hoyle became Treasurer, Stephen Hyde, Chairman and Christine Hyde, Secretary. At this stage the group was small enough for the rest of the meeting to make up the committee. At that time there was a draft strategy but little else. There were no grants, but they opened a bank account, got a cheque book, designed an annual programme, worked up a constitution and decided that they would become Friends of Queens Park; a 'voluntary body not trading for profit and with charitable aims'. Their first group questionnaire was funded out of the Environment Unit's annual budget and was sent out in an edition of 7,000 across the Castleford district.

The price of the houses close to the park rose 6% above the Castleford norm in 2004. This contrasts significantly with the normal way in which such proximity to a park affects house prices. In an area where there is a park which is associated in the public mind with anti-social features such as drug taking, drunkenness and vandalism house prices are 20% below the average sale price for a town.

ENTER SRB

In April 1998 Wakefield MDC was awarded £4.127 million to deliver an SRB 4 programme called the 'FreshAire Regeneration Programme'. Started in October 1998 it was one of 38 projects. Several related to the environment. One in particular was important to Friends of Queens Park. It was called the Green Corridor Project, and its project officer was Bob Pipkin of Wakefield Council's Environmental Section.

Bob Pipkin was important in a number of ways. He gave advice during the embryonic stage and also recognised that the Friends would be eligible for SRB support. He had a plan which went well beyond the park itself but needed the Friends if any aspect of his vision was to come to fruition. His plan was to create a bridle path and cycle route which would run from the parkgates north towards the playing fields and then drop into the valley of the Aire. There it would cross the site of Wheldale Colliery - closed in 1986 - and strike east towards another pit village two miles up the valley. Ferry Fryston's railway bridge was intact though derelict. This was a natural route across the river to the nature reserve at Fairburn Ings. The names of the settlements which surround Castleford - Allerton Bywater, Whitwood Mere, Four Lane Ends, Wheldale, Fairburn - have a charm that makes the area seem like some proto-Cotswolds whereas until recently the area has been dominated by the dereliction brought about by chemical and glass factory pollution and coal extraction. The plan was to reinstate beauty.

Wakefield MDC had seen how successful such projects could be in the South Elmsall, South Kirkby and Upton (SESKU) area, a collection of ex-mining villages on the Doncaster side of Wakefield. There they had used SRB 1 money to plant sections of the old South Kirkby colliery site and to make a pathway which went deep into a rural environment. The creation of the SESKU Ringway is described in the first book of this series, *Theories at the Bottom of Our Jargon - The First Single Regeneration Budget Schemes.* Crushing the bricks from their derelict colliery site, ex-miners and other local people created an impressive country park, growing plants from seeds.

THE BOWLING GREEN CAFÉ AND MICRO SUSTAINABILTY

All of the Castleford volunteers agree that the grant to do up the hut on the edge of the bowling green was decisive to the group's story. As Stephen Hyde says, 'This gave us a base and without a base at the centre of your operation, you cannot do much at all.'

What is now the café is a small building and stands overlooking the bowling green at the centre of the formal part of the park. Close by and within easy reach are the children's play areas. They need to be close because each night when the children have finished on the tennis court volunteers bring the nets into the café.

A plaque on the back wall above the tombola table records that John Herron gave this building to the Castleford Corporation on the occasion of his eightieth birthday, 8 September 1970. Unlike the rest of the buildings in the park the café is a comparatively recent building, most of the others are a hundred years old. When they moved in, it already had two toilets. All they had to do to bring it up to current standards was to fit security shutters, a disabled toilet and ramp. Some of the SRB money was spent on this and was matched by the Council out of the annual parks budget.

Parks are used by young parents and their infants, teenagers and people walking dogs, hardly life's big spenders, and so the little earned income that comes their way is made in the café or from hiring out the marquee when it is not in use for summer band concerts.

Roundhay Park in Leeds charges £1 for a cup of tea, and in the swish café of the Botanical Gardens in Sheffield, a cup costs even more. Castleford Queen Park's pricing policy in the café is different. Management argue that since this is a 'working class' area, costs should be at a minimum. They cost a tea bag at 10p and sell tea in a plastic cup for 25p. Pop comes in at 20p and sells for 20p, crisps cost 20p wholesale and are retailed out at 20p. Both are loss-leaders. As Steve Hyde says, 'Our aim is not to make a profit but to bring mothers and children back to the park. Someone with children can buy herself and three children drinks for less than £1.' One childminder I talked with said that she always gave extra because she recognised that the staff were volunteers.

When I asked about the use of the miniature golf course, one of the Friends told me that it was not used as much as they would like it to be. 'You see you have to give a high level of supervision if you hand out golf clubs. If people start hitting each other with them you are probably liable. We just do not have enough people.'

The absence of labour costs is why this can be done. The profits from the tea money pay for small running costs and the purchase of prizes for the tombola. Tickets are 5 for a £1 and you win if one of them ends in a '0'. Together it brings in £150 a year.

These days the group meet once a month or as needed. In the early days they had met more frequently and formally. Now there is little need to because they are working together and the strategic policies worked out four years ago are being implemented. As the Chairman said, 'Obviously we need money to implement strategies but that is done without too much trouble. We know each other and unlike council departments our formal meetings are rare. We have an annual strategic plan and we know where we are going.'

FOUR TABLES AND SEVERAL HUNDRED RUBBER MATS

It is possible to reduce crime by design but when you look at some of the things SRB money was spent on, you are left wondering if some things were designed by the suppliers to be easily destroyed. The mats in the park's infants' playground are a case in point. It is good that they can be quickly taken up so they can be replaced if worn, but this led to many of them getting burnt last summer.

In the best tradition of English secondary schools some of the boys in the lower part of the town's two high schools arranged a fight in the park. There is some dispute over which side won but what is not in doubt is that when the fight was over, those left in control of the neutral ground decided to uproot the rubbish bins, fill them with playground mats, place the bins in the corner of the infants' play area and set them alight.

It is possible to blame the conflagration on too many film images of the Vietnam War, the policy which encouraged governors to sell off school playing fields or even on the Doctrine of Original Sin but you can also blame the playground design company. If a pensioner with a car key could lift the corner of a rubber mat then three testosterone charged thirteen year olds could have a patch up in a minute with little trouble. I would guess that rabid girls with little mischievous fingers could do it in less time.

The matting does not come cheap. At £60 each it must have taken £12,000 to floor the area. This was a lot of money's worth in squares that are vulnerable to acts of vandalism. It was the same with the equipment. When I looked at the climbing frame I found that I could remove some small but significant pieces by stooping and twisting the large nuts on the back of the slide with my fingers. When I questioned one of the volunteers he said that had been pointed out when the plans were on display in the community café 'for consultation' and no one had listened. As he said, 'After the slide was installed it would not have taken half an hour to have flattened those nuts and bolts with a hammer. I suppose, as in most things the profits come in selling the expendables and not in selling the main piece of equipment.'

Sometimes the Council is pound wise and penny foolish. This was especially evident in the settling in of the picnic tables in the area outside the café.

These are well designed. The four of them are made of heavy resin and stand four-square close to the bowling green café. Steve Hyde pointed out: 'If they are left here and settled in properly like the first one was then they are with us for ever. Of course they have to be brown. Light-coloured ones create their own disaster zone and attract the graffitist. They come from all over to write messages of love or filth. You can do the same thing on brown but the message gets lost. Green, red, blue and black marker pens do not show up on dark brown benches.

'The first one was settled in with a concrete block at each corner. When the Council put in the second they used one block of concrete to hold down two legs. That meant that someone intent on tipping the second table has half of the work to do.' To demonstrate he started rocking the table.

'We have tried out a lot of the prototypes. That is because we are on hand. A year after we had tested these tables their cousins were installed in Thornes Park, Wakefield and Hawes Park, Normanton. I think that they are also elsewhere.'

I had to give up work because of ill health. Because of the way I was brought up I felt that I could not take something from society without putting something back. I volunteered to work in the park. This was my way of paying society.
Barry Spence, FreshAire volunteer

PASTURE LAND

A resident in the Castleford Potteries said to me, 'We get a lot of overseas visitors to Castleford during the summer months. They are mainly from south of the Sahara and they come for the mating and food. This was the sort of environment where they thrive.' As I stood in the park's wild meadow area on the other side of the locked gate at the far end of the park close to the infant children's playground, her words came to me. This was where one of the team had found a fledgling blue tit that morning when I phoned. One of the school volunteers I talked to had gone to assist her grandson's teacher on a nature walk. 'You would never believe it,' she said, 'it is so unexpected and so wonderful.'

Pasture land the size of two football pitches stretched out in front of me. This must have been what the land around Castleford looked like when Thomas of Castleford, the medieval chronicler, wandered the area in the fourteenth century well before the coal owners started throwing up muck stacks and the chemists began polluting the Aire valley below us.

There is a great variety of trees and plant life around us. Daisies predominate but I was assured that close to me were yellow rattle, thistle, kidney vetch, clover and fifteen species of grasses. In the band of trees on the perimeter there were rowan and maple.

'When the children from Airedale Middle and Redhill Primary come we ask them to go out onto our lawn areas and look for a variety of plant species. They are lucky if the whole class can find more than eight species. Then we take them through the gates and we give them a square metre patch. There all of them manage to find in that comparatively small patch at least twenty species.'

When the volunteers got the SRB money it allowed them to think big and plan strategically. Up to 1990, when the first serious cut backs to park maintenance had occurred, this land had been covered with greenhouses and gardening-support buildings. Ten years later these had been vandalised and now in their place is a green portakabin. This is opened to reveal an exhibition of the history of the park and a small library of natural history books.

A SENSORY GARDEN

Over the years since the SRB grant was given, a good relationship has developed between the Friends and the Council. Both recognise each other's strengths. 'At first they seemed to resent any work we did. I remember that when we tried to bring the bowling green outside the café window up to its potential we were warned off in no uncertain way. One senior officer told us to stay in the shop and make cups of tea for that was what we were good at. That attitude has changed. They saw that we were here to stay and that our ambitions could improve one of their parks. Our determination reflected on the quality of the service they were charged to deliver. We helped make the healthy outputs every department needs at the end of the financial year.'

The building of the sensory garden near the car park illustrates the usefulness of this and other partnerships. Eleven sponsors are listed on the plaque on one of the pillars. I was told, 'Of course the main ones were the Council and SRB FreshAire. Some of the others made it onto the list because they were keen to be there and it cost us next to nothing for them to be there. Everyone wanted to get in on the act.' PR matters, especially when a volunteer group is doing this sort of project.

The idea of a sensory garden is part of the Victorian obsession with blind people. Most public parks in that time contained this sort of area. In those days there were more blind people around who wanted to sit in the park and smell roses. Today laser surgery, preventive medicine, home based gardens and television have made this corner of the average park redundant except for one thing. The idea of the provision has given the park's volunteers a focus for a worthwhile project.

Queens Park 'sensory garden' has three raised flowerbeds, ample seating and two tactile walls that contain tiles created by local people, a small fountain and five little reading lecterns on which are written words by local writers. Everything is well crafted. The quality of the fountain itself and the forged iron railings that surround it are particularly fine. These were made by Julian Wadsworth following a commission brief worked out by the Friends group.

Castleford is the birth place of Henry Moore and therefore its citizens have had their bellies filled with Modernism for half a century. Like many people who live in industrial towns the Friends have a keen respect for techniques and ideas they understand; and they understand craftsmanship. Julian Wadsworth was more than just 'an artist'.

They wanted a garden that could be heard and touched as well as seen. In line with the English pastoral tradition this suggested running water. Unfortunately all of the discussion group were aware of the Princess Diana Fountain fiasco in London and did want open access to the running water. The water should be heard but not seen, a bit like a Victorian child. In the end they took the advice of the Groundwork Trust and invited in a Huddersfield sculptor, Julian Wadsworth.

He was very well qualified for the work they wanted him to do. He had trained full-time as a blacksmith before going on to study Art and Design. Two years before, he had received second prize from the Right Worshipful Company of Blacksmiths at the Yorkshire Show and was a serious contender for the top prize in 2005. As someone who had struggled and eventually become a freelance businessman, he appealed to the group.

The Friends wanted symbols representing aspects of nature's passage through life and in the end they hit upon the title *Metamorphosis*. The sound of water was to be a feature but the water itself had to be enclosed in the elliptical shape about three feet high which stood on the ground and was the focus of the whole piece. The setting was a park and therefore 'life' meant more than human life. In the iron work there were bumble bees, flowers, plants and birds. Julian Wadsworth said, 'Once I got to making it I found myself becoming more adventurous as the work moved towards completion. I would sometimes close my eyes and see the landscape. The group enthusiasm for the project began to waken my own imagination.'

When it came to shaping metal he could do everything and if you look at the detail of the piece you can see the range of his skills. There is evidence of forge-work, modelling and the use of imprints, hot chisel work, repoussé, pattern making and casting. The commission as presented to him was to create a tactile handrail using forge metal. Because some casting was involved he had to out-source to a small foundry in Meltham.

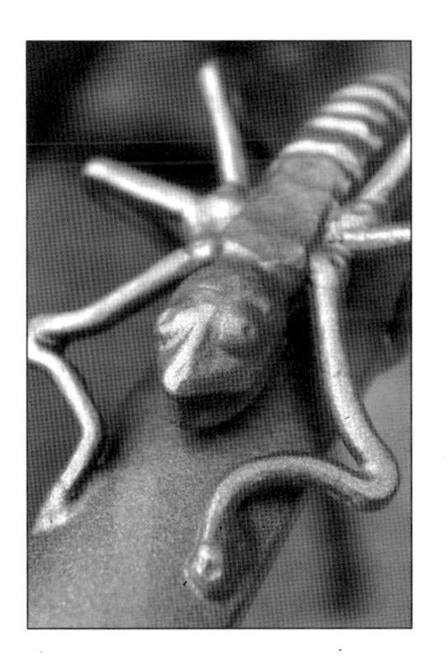

The professional life of a busy craftsman is precarious to say the least. The commission came at the end of a busy year because freelance craft workers cannot afford to be choosy, they often have to take work when it is on offer. He was forced to take on another worker. All the time the profit was diminishing. The fee was £5,000. Out of this came everything: materials, travel, wages and the castings. By the time he was finished he reckons that he worked full-time for a couple of months for about £2,000.

A consultant architect by comparison gets something in the region of £1,500 a day. The rubber mats in the park's children's play area cost £60 each and there are hundreds. We should keep those figures in mind when we think of artists' fees.

An upright hollow casting that hid a water source was intriguing. After a while wreckers came. They needed to smash it. They rode their motor bikes at it and eventually brought in a hammer to smash the polycarbonate windows. Julian Wadsworth was brought back and had to modify the design to thwart their ambitions - *Metamorphosis* survives.

Today the park looks and feels good.

THE CHRYSALIS PROJECT

The directions from Castleford to the Active Youth Project and the Chrysalis Project had been good: 'Turn right at the roundabout in Castleford, past the DSS building, past the chemical factory and the green energy plant, over the bad railway bridge,' the helpful receptionist at the FreshAire SRB 4 scheme had told me. The project was clearly marked from the road; this boded well. I was no stranger to interesting detours to find community-based projects.

When I turned off the road at the top of the rise that looked across the Aire and into Fairburn Ings there were two buildings to choose from. Both had Active emblazoned in white lettering on the ridged band of dark turquoise fascia that ran around the top of the building. Beneath this a brick façade gave a more homely feel to what was obviously an industrial building in design and build. I made the right choice and walked into the reception area of the organisation's main office. Everything was clean and tidy; a range of plaques - National Lottery Charities Board, Coalfields Regeneration Trust, Community Recycling and Economic Development (CRED) and Social Economic Environmental Development (SEED) - were ranged on the wall in front of Neil Kennedy's office.

A guesstimate given by the Friends of Queens Park is that 254 people used the park in 1999. There were only four effective members at this time so the figures are suspect. More recent figures suggest that in 2004 they had 40,000 visits.

Offices of this size and style intrigue me. It was very big. I always worry about the size of this sort of room and immediately glance around to see if it has been designed for a change of function. Sustainability has to be a watch-word and one day the chief executive's office might have to become a crêche or an IT training room. Was there a sink or a battery of electricity sockets around the room - cheap to put in when building, expensive later if you feel the need to adapt a room and give it a new focus?

I had wanted to ask Neil some detailed questions. Conceived by a church organisation called 'Chrysalis', how had the idea to start working with young people in a deprived area of West Yorkshire emerged from its cocoon and taken flight into a fully-fledged social enterprise? There was a huge expanse of tarmac and overgrown grassland in front of me with two impressive buildings but the sight of the plaques triggered thoughts about my own experiences seeking and monitoring grant aid, and the interview took a different direction.

The previous month I had interviewed staff at the Warwick Community Campus and Adventure Playground, Knottingley - a neighbouring FreshAire project - and this experience had brought back personal memories. Their administrative worker mentioned that although the funding had ended long ago she had only just finished sending in the required monitoring forms to Wakefield Metropolitan District Council. I knew the process. As Chief Executive of a community project which had received an SRB 6 grant in another Yorkshire sub-region, I had been ultimately responsible for applying for and monitoring the grant in the period 2002 to 2005. I must say that, although I had secured and managed funds from a number of sources including government awards, European monies and cash from charitable trusts, nothing had quite prepared me for the rigours of SRB regimes.

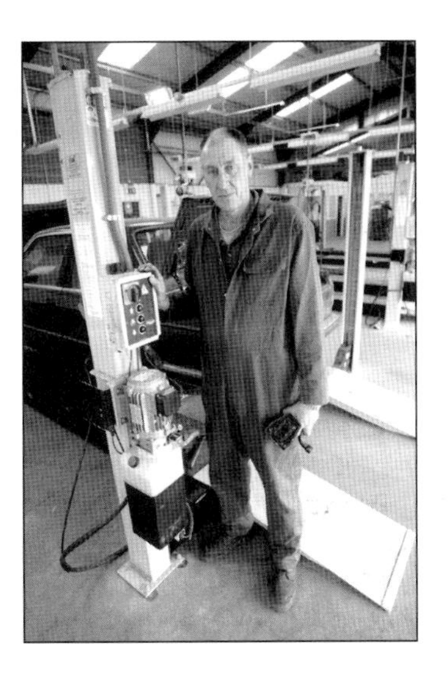

For that reason I asked Neil the date on which Chrysalis had accepted its first SRB award and whether he was still involved in monitoring the scheme. Within five minutes the boardroom table was covered with a selection of files, the six years of paperwork from the SRB archives. He confirmed that, although the grant had run from 2000 to 2003, they had only recently submitted the last monitoring form. As he spread them out I again experienced the sinking feeling that came to me as I started preparing my own SRB quarterly returns.

84 SRB 4 & 5

It is hard to explain the intricacies of SRB to a SRB virgin. The monitoring form was several sheets long and had to be returned to the local authority every three months. Each page covered a different subject; for example, outputs, funding, expenditure, milestones, existing assets and assets sold. Anything you have bought with government funds remains government property and has to be accounted for. On each page was a grid that represented a year of SRB funding. Vertical lines, or columns, broke the year up into four quarters - April to June, July to September and so on. Each of these quarters was split in half, with one side entitled 'Forecast' and the other 'Achieved'. At the end of these four quarters, at the right-hand side of the page, further columns captured the accumulative sums of 'Forecast' and 'Achieved' detailed as 'Total', 'Revised Total', 'Lifetime Total' and 'Revised Lifetime Total'. These columns were repeated for each year, for each subject heading.

And then there were the horizontal rows which broke the subjects down into more detail. On the 'Outputs' sheet these showed the activity Chrysalis had promised to deliver with the SRB funds: jobs preserved, construction jobs, people trained and qualified, young people and residents benefiting from social development, youth crime prevention initiative, land improved and so on. On 'Funding' SRB income was broken down into capital (buildings and equipment) and revenue (running costs) and also listed all the other bodies contributing to the project, such as English Partnerships and the National Lottery Charities Board. The same was repeated for the 'Expenditure' sheet. Each time the pages were split into the quarterly 'Forecast', and 'Achieved' columns and four variants of 'Total'. Numbers had to be inserted into each of these boxes on each of these pages before the monitoring form could be returned. Without the form there was no money.

Business survival rates are the same as the UK average but start-up rates are notably lower – 32 business starts/yr per 1,000 compared with 39 in the UK and lower still in deprived areas.
Regional Economic Strategy for Yorkshire and Humber 2006-2015

You may have entirely lost the thread of SRB monitoring systems by now. If so you will be able to understand why I, and many other veteran applicants and monitors of funds, began to feel anxious as the end of each quarter approached. During my SRB experience I became so frustrated by the process that I was compelled to write to anybody who might listen and point out the simple fact that SRB, designed to encourage community-driven activity, did exactly the opposite. Those of us that entered into the fray of community development because, momentarily blinded by our zeal and community spirit, we were anxious not to spend overmuch time on this sort of excessive bureaucracy. We would do anything to get our project off the ground and if that included prostituting our personal life to SRB so be it, but we all knew it to be a tedious and unnecessary testing ground. From what I can remember the officers thought so too.

There are two explanations of why this happens. Either the higher civil service cultures demanded it or alternatively a lower level of officers got overly bureaucratic because they did not have knowledge of the bigger picture to balance risks against outcomes and therefore failed to provide appropriate measurement.

My experience and that of Chrysalis were similar. The organisation had ended up jumping through these familiar hoops, seemingly put in place to iron out the perceived woolliness of the voluntary and community sector. What this failed to recognise was that organisations like Chrysalis or Warwick Community Campus did not have the luxury of specialist individuals and teams, who could dedicate their time to poring over these complex forms. This had also been my experience when I had become part of a community group after going to a mother-and-toddlers' group and seeing the possibility of getting rid of a leaking, ugly 1920s parish room and replacing it with something better.

Like Neil I had known that at each quarter's end all receipts and invoices had had to be copied and sent through to the SRB monitoring teams, to prove that we had spent their money appropriately. Most other grant-funders, such as the Community Fund or the Coalfield Regeneration Trust, worked on a principle of trust. During the application process, your organisation had to be able to prove internal finance systems would withstand a visit from the funder's audit team, but SRB was much stricter. Particularly in the first few months of a project, when you were finding your feet, you had to go through all sales and purchase files, and pull out three months' worth of invoices and receipts. There could be hundreds of items. Information about the purchase of chairs and tables and proof of staff wages were all fodder in this bureaucratic nightmare. Each

document had to be photocopied, re-filed and then passed on. What a waste of time!

In the end we are talking about lies, damned lies and statistics, about a belief that there is some value in attempting to measure the immeasurable. I'll admit that I have time for the senior civil servant who said that she would floor people who always asked for measurable outcomes. From an activist's perspective SRB 4 and SRB 5 - and it was still the same with SRB 6 as far as I can see - persisted in encouraging excessive monitoring and reliance on consultants' evaluations. There is something to be said about mechanisms which record the added value to healthy and sustainable communities and community cohesion - both lovely buzz phrases - but they are not found in excessive number crunching. The voluntary and community sector has to get better at evidencing key outputs in different ways and the public sector has to get better at recognising them.

Of course SRB wasn't the only over-bureaucratic programme. Neil Kennedy told me of a small grants scheme, worth £4,000, for which they had been encouraged to reapply, having successfully administered an earlier project. He had turned down the offer because in order meet the terms of the second grant he would need an extra £5,000 to employ someone to fill in the monitoring forms!

CHRYSALIS'S HISTORY

The project has been going since 1992, when the local Methodist Church got together to help young people on the Airedale Estate. They secured some funds from the Rank Foundation to employ a part-time youth worker and part-time information plus advice worker. Neil Kennedy worked at the Citizens' Advice Bureau. He had always wanted to work with young people and saw this as a good opportunity to enter a new field of work. I wondered what the motivation was for working with this challenging age group, particularly in such a deprived area. He told me.

In Ireland, Slovenia and Norway education for enterprise is often mainstreamed in schools. It is linked to teaching methods that support enterprising attitudes and confidence, as well as what is taught.

'I was in care from the age of thirteen to seventeen in Adel in Leeds. It was a community campus with a farm, fields, cows, and workshops where you could learn craft skills - mechanical, electrical and joinery. It was a very good place to live in care and I was very happy there. There were 40 kids and 25 staff who lived on site in semi-detached houses. Close personal relationships were developed with the kids and this is the principle that we apply at Chrysalis. It works, but it is very expensive; the home in Adel shut in the end because cheaper but less effective care could be provided. When I left I really wanted to use my own experiences to shape a career in youth work.'

'Eventually I got married and had kids of my own. In that time I went through a variety of jobs, but I always had set my mind on a career in youth work as my ultimate objective. I was driving buses when an opportunity came up. I had the chance to be made redundant and so, with my wife's backing and a couple of grand in my back pocket, I started to do some voluntary work. First of all this was with the Probation Service and Citizens' Advice Bureau. It lasted for two years but I saw that at last I was getting the experience I needed. I also felt like I was putting something back into society.

'From there I went to work for a private firm, Family Support Services, who contract to Social Services to run children's homes. We got all the kids that Social Services couldn't cope with. This was part-time paid work. Then the part-time job with Chrysalis was advertised and I started work on the Airedale Estate. I did 18 hours for the Family Support Service and 18 hours for Chrysalis.

'There was a desperate need for something for the kids to do. I was working with groups of fourteen and fifteen year old lads. We had a flat at 65A Fryston Road where we met at night. There were two rooms - a bedroom measuring 4m x 4m, a living room 5m x 4m and a kitchen 2m x 3m. We had around forty to fifty kids meet up there each night, so as you can imagine it was a tight fit.

'We began asking the kids what they wanted to see on the estate. The unanimous choice was a motorbike track. So we gathered together a meeting of all the important local people, such as councillors and police, and got them to sit at the table with the young people. The motorbike

track was turned down for noise and safety reasons, but they encouraged the kids to come back with other ideas. The next idea was an off-road go-kart track and that's the one we went with.

'Our original plans were to have three to four karts which the kids could both ride and get skills from maintaining. We estimated that this would cost around £80,000, but then we hit a hurdle because we couldn't find any suitable land. There was a piece at Ferry Fryston but although the Council wanted to use this, it was a bit too near to a residential area and there was a strong possibility that the neighbours would complain. The Council then came up with this piece, at Stansfield, where the buildings are today.

'By 1999 we had built the basics of the site up to what it is today. The building we are in went up in 2000 and the one that we will walk over to in a minute went up this year, in 2005. There's 8.8 hectares which needed clearing but as time passed the project grew and grew. We ended up with seventeen go-karts, four of which were adapted for disabled use. The go-kart project had multiplied; it was now hitting £120,000.

'We realised that we needed a business plan so I went and did an HND in Business and Finance at Wakefield College between 1996 and 1999. I was still only working part-time and I hoped that there might be a full-time job at the end of it. So the Chrysalis project became part of my course-work. It started to give us a sense of direction and prepared us for the form filling. It took us the three full years to put the package together.

'No-one else would commit to putting their funds in until the other funders did. SRB approved funding in theory but wouldn't provide an offer letter - required as proof by the other funders - until the other funders had provided their offer letters. Catch 22! They didn't expect the project to happen and weren't helping it to happen because of this over-cautious approach. The Lottery was the first grant-giver to put in big money.'

One of the sad things is that for all the SRB money that was invested in these six years and additional money coming in as SRB 6 support, both Airedale and Warwick estates have not moved down the Index of Deprivation.

Again this was a familiar tale. Everyone has 'good' and 'bad' funders, or at least those who are helpful and those who basically patronise you because they don't think that a bunch of community 'do-gooders' could be capable of running an ambitious project. This attitude completely overlooks the fact that do-gooders often have a range of business skills - such as Neil's HND - that match those of the officers responsible for issuing the offer letter. Enthusiasm, dedication and a commitment to the local community more than make up for any lack of so-called professional skills found at the 'Council'. Community activism is a personal investment in the community, which should be recognised, celebrated and factored in.

When the Active Centre opened in 2000 the final costs were £1.2m.

We agreed that whilst SRB was at one end of the scale for application and monitoring, at the other end of the 'gold star' spectrum was the National Lottery Charities Board - later the Community Fund and now known as the Big Lottery. The National Lottery Charities Board let you have 100% of your capital costs against each claim and gave you your revenue costs quarterly in advance. There was obviously monitoring to do, but this was straightforward and on an annual basis. 100% funding was very unusual. Where a project had a cocktail of funds from a range of sources the majority of the public funders would only provide a percentage of the overall costs each time a claim was put in. You had to estimate what this would be at the application stage - it was called the 'intervention rate'. So each time a claim was made you might get, say, 22.23% of the costs from one funder, 46.8% from another and so on. It was up to you, the applicant, to predict that you would have enough funding to make up the 100% to meet the project costs.

Neil and I decided that the Coalfields Regeneration Trust was pretty close to the National Lottery Charities Board when it came to a sensible monitoring and grant giving system. Although they still required quarterly monitoring forms they, too, provided up-front running costs. They also took a different approach to most funders when it came to assigning a regeneration manager to your project. They would help you work up an idea and give you a feel for whether it fell within their priorities before you spent too much time on it. Then they would stay in contact on and off for the duration and even after the project was finished.

Regeneration managers were assigned a coalfield regional or sub-regional area. West Yorkshire and South Yorkshire both had individual officers. The West Yorkshire manager, for instance, had learned his trade with the Lottery Board. They grew to know the local communities well and constantly spotted potential for local action. They developed a 'real' relationship with the community organisations such as Chrysalis and Warwick.

COAL AND THE COMMUNITY

The closure of the local pits, Fryston, Wheldale, Glasshoughton and the Prince, had had a big effect on the Airedale Estate. There were about 500 ex-Coalboard houses on the estate. Most pits had shut in the 1980s under 'Maggie's Axe' - before Chrysalis got going - although the running sore continued as the Prince of Wales Colliery closure had been as recent as 2002. However the main pit closures, although twenty years ago, still had an effect. Neil Kennedy and his colleagues were now working with a third generation of unemployed young people. It was clearly a long-term problem which required long-term funds and solutions. Neil explained: 'Not only did we need a sense of direction from the business plan, but we also needed to show that we could be sustainable, for the sake of the organisation which was serving the community.'

In the 2004 annual report, hot off the press on the day of my arrival and ready for the forthcoming Annual General Meeting, Neil had written as his opening line: 'Like all charities and community groups, Chrysalis are finding it more and more difficult to secure long-term funding from grant making bodies. New ways have to be found to remedy the shortfalls in income, to be able to continue the service that we provide. Self sufficiency and self sustainability are top of the Chrysalis agenda over the next year.'

When we took a tour around the site I began to make sense of the services that this organisation was providing to its community. We started with the go-kart track. This was an area at the back of the main building. There were red, white and black tyre buffers at the edge of overgrown grass verges. It was for this development, together with one of the industrial units, that Chrysalis had received the biggest part of the SRB award. Neil:

The prosperity of a people is proportionate to the number of hands and minds usefully employed.
Samuel Johnson - The Idler 1758

'The idea was to offer the track to the kids on the estate at £1.50 for a 20 minute session. Visitors from outside the area would have to pay the going rate, which was £6 for 20 minutes. This was there to help subsidise the local activities. If the estate kids volunteered to help out with the track, or went on some of our courses, they were rewarded with free sessions.

'Our biggest problem though, with this being an off-road track, was the land the track was built on. It was on limestone with a top-soil surface. After a few months the top-soil had been worn away and the track became cobbled. We refilled it, but the surface just shifted to the sides. So we got some road chippings and the same happened again, and then we got a tractor and shifted it all back on a daily basis. We could cope with this level of maintenance because we had entered into a contract with Wakefield Metropolitan District Council to deliver an Intermediate Labour Market scheme for them. This meant that we took a group of long-term unemployed people for twelve months and provided training for them whilst they were working for us for a wage. They carried out maintenance, marshalling and mechanical work and we taught them skills and provided support to help them into work. We got paid for the programme - the training element as well as their wages - so we could manage financially.

'Another problem was negotiating the lease for the land. Originally we were going to accept the lease that the Council had presented us with. This stated they could come in at any time, kick us off and sell off the land. Another funder, English Partnerships. was involved and their officer made us aware that this was unfavourable for us. Their help was important - we managed to get the contract changed. If the Council does decide it wants the land then they will have to find us something similar to replace it.

'In the first year the track brought in £12,000 and £23,000 in the second, but only £8,000 in the third year. Income had plummeted by £15,000 in just one year. We knew why. That was the year that Xscape opened.'

Xscape is the high profile leisure centre built on the old Glasshoughton Pit site and about two miles downhill from the go-kart track. Xscape offers an

indoor snowdome, with real snow for skiing, tobogganing and sledging. It also sports a climbing wall, overhead adventure trail, cinema and indoor skateboard and rollerblade park. Next door is a retail outlet - clearance shops for a number of high street brands and designer names - and a variety of fast-food outlets. Whether or not the Airedale kids could afford the activities on offer, or the cheap clothes, there was an obvious attraction in having somewhere warm to hang out, meet friends and pursue love conquests seven days a week.

'We couldn't compete with this,' Neil added, 'and the Council contract ended and so the track just stayed open in the school holidays. But the track was still causing us problems and that resulted in damaged karts. For every £1.50 income we estimated that it was costing us £8 worth of damage. The track closed in January 2005 and will stay shut until we have an alternative solution in place. The SRB 6 programme was not targeted at Airedale. We really want a multi-purpose area, tarmacked so that we can use it for proper karts, not the off-road type, and a range of other activities. We want to put in road markings and roundabouts and use it for driver training. It's got to be properly priced – we can't run it on £1.50 for 20 minutes any more. The local British School of Motoring is interested and so is Castleford and District's Driving Instructor Association. We hope that we can use the area at the weekends for fairs and car boot sales.'

The dormant go-kart track explained why the mechanics' workshop, at one end of the unit, no longer had go-karts in it. Instead there were four very old Metro and Fiesta cars, which were used to teach maintenance skills. This part of the youth work was still prospering.

The effects of the enlargement of the European Community and the effects of the outward flow of money from our deprived areas to the old eastern bloc countries will blow like a freezing wind across the old coalfield areas and their welfare services.We anit seen nothing yet.
Local political activist.

Neil: 'We were approached by a pilot Education Action Zone project and asked to work with kids who were having problems at school. In 2001 we put on a ten week course for twelve of them. They had problems, ranging from non-attendance to emotional problems and challenging behaviour. We ran a course of four days per week for twelve months. One lad moved out of the area soon after starting but the rest of the students averaged 85% attendance. This was a big success, given that their average attendance at school was about 33%. All of them came away with some qualification or other. Seven got jobs and two went to college. The next year we had fifteen students and it was a similar success story. Twelve went into employment, one into the army and one to college. Only one got lost along the way. We worked with them on a one-to-one basis, teaching them practical skills, making sure they could read and write properly, improving their self-esteem, confidence and life skills, such as getting up for work and what an employer expects. I knew it worked from my experience at Adel. The next year we had another group of fifteen with similar results at the end of the year.

'Money follows the kids through school, roughly £2,000 per student. So we had £30,000 for each course. We also had money from the Social Exclusion Unit of Wakefield Education Authority. But we needed £120,000 to run a course, to cover general overheads and the highly personalised support the kids needed - our funds were still far short of this. The Coalfields Regeneration Trust funded us for three years. They paid for six staff until March 2005 and we had to bank-roll these staff until June 2005 when we drew other funds in. This time £132,000 came from the European Regional Development Fund (Objective 2) and the European Social Fund (Objective 3) and £70,000, from the Esmee Fairbairn Foundation.'

'We have re-shaped what we offer to make it sustainable. Now we are going out and seek funding to support a successful project which should really be met from statutory funds and core budgets. This year we are selling directly to local education authorities, youth offending teams, schools and even outside the area to other education authorities. Liz, our Education Development Manager, develops these programmes. This year we will offer fifty places, forty of which will be two days per week and ten, one day per week. These students will bring with them £1,100 each so we hope that with the whole package we will be able to cover our full delivery costs.'

A SUSTAINBLE SRB SOCIAL ENTERPRISE

On the land leased from Wakefield Metropolitan District Council was a new industrial unit. The building we had just seen was the result of the SRB project investment. It came a bit later in 2005 and was mainly funded by the Coalfields Regeneration Trust. We entered through the 'shop front' end of the unit. An impressive range of computer equipment and peripherals, such as monitors, printers, cartridges, were on display. It was a very smart set-up but what was surprising was that most of the items on display were recycled product. In no way did the equipment look second-hand. I found this important as this often makes the purchaser, who is strapped for cash, feel like a second-class citizen because the goods look too much like what they are - used goods.

Neil: 'We started off with computer recycling in 2002 on an Intermediate Labour Market scheme working with Wakefield Council. This was SRB funding. It was specifically to get the over 50s long-term unemployed back into full-time employment after they had been on a twelve month project. Initially we started up in a shop on Kershaw Avenue upgrading and repairing computers donated by the Council. When they were refurbished and functioning we donated them to voluntary and community organisations. The project expanded quickly and because we were running out of storage space we decided to sell directly to the public.

Chrysalis has managed to get into the 'mainstream' market quite quickly compared to many community organisations. Mainstream funding refers to the resources local government agencies, such as Wakefield Education Authority, receive from central government to deliver local services. As a provider of these services Chrysalis can hope to deliver sustainable activity, rather than be dependent on grants. With its foot in the door Chrysalis should be able to develop a closer relationship with the public agency and continue to develop services according to local need and changing policies.
Alison Seabrooke

'Our turnover was impressive. We took £60,000 in 2003, £120,000 in 2004 and we predict £250,000 in 2005. The majority of equipment is donated and collected from businesses throughout the Wakefield area and we occasionally buy from asset-management companies. We refurbish as much as we can for resale and the rest is broken down for spare parts and recyclable materials. The metal goes to the scrap merchant and the plastic to a company that makes garden furniture.

'In 2004 Airedale Computer Recycling collected 2,600 computers and monitors. This amounts to over 62 tonnes of equipment. If we did nothing with it, it would go to a landfill site.' They have doubled the previous years' collections. More than 820 refurbished computer systems were sold on to the general public and 82 were donated to charitable causes. 'In 2004 we doubled the sales of new systems and consumables and increased our total turnover by 50%. In that year we won the Wakefield and District Environmental Services Award for services to the community.

'After a while we also began to stock new equipment. For example, customers would come and ask for a printer and we would send them away to Argos. So we started to stock peripherals. Other customers would start off with a basic computer to learn on and then come back six months later for a new, upgraded one. We now have this shop and another one in South Elmsall. The shop on Kershaw Avenue is used for storage.'

The shop up on the Airedale Estate was open and airy. Behind the counter was an array of printer cartridges and on a carousel was a display of books to help learners of all abilities. Customers could browse around the range of desk-top computers, laptops, traditional and flat screens. Behind a false wall there were the stores and an office which co-ordinated the training and sales activity. In the last couple of years they have employed two trainees from the scheme, one as a supervisor and another as a technician. They had gathered a range of accreditations, including Microsoft Authorised Refurbisher, and taken the chair of the Regional Electronics Initiative. They hope that they will be able to open up membership of this organisation to other non-profit computer recyclers and ease the way for them to gain similar accreditations.

'The Intermediate Labour Market programme meant that, until last year, we had six staff whose wages were paid for by the scheme and Chrysalis received a management fee. We initially had a cocktail of smaller funds to pay for our staff to train them, but since 2003 the project has been self-sustaining.

'Until the end of August 2005 the management body was still Chrysalis, but then we set up a separate trading company, Airedale Community Trading Limited (ACT). It is anticipated that the trading arm would become fully self-sufficient by March 2007. Chrysalis will be the only shareholder and profits will be divided between the Charity, to enable it to meet its aims, and the various enterprises to enable them to develop and grow.'

Beyond the sale room wall a grey breeze-block unit housed the 'car clinic'. The need for this separate trading arm became even more apparent. Still in its infancy, the clinic will soon be offering services, repairs and full

MOTs. This spacious area is fully equipped with three bays. Cars will soon be able to drive up the bright yellow ramps for examination. There are pneumatic hoists at all four corners to lift them, if needed. Red and blue metalwork cabinets run around the walls, fully equipped to carry out diagnostics and repairs, just as you would find at any garage or tyre replacement specialist. At the moment they were only carrying out small amounts of work by word of mouth advertising on the estate, but this is only a temporary measure until the trading identity is established. Part of the car clinic will be a training resource; if the revised karting scheme goes ahead it will become an aspect of the transition back to the work environment.

To the side of the car clinic is another section of the industrial unit. This one recycles white goods, such as washing machines and cookers. It is another aspect of the partnership between Chrysalis and Wakefield District Council. When households ring the Council asking them to collect these broken or out-of-date machines the Council notes addresses and the type of goods offered and then fax a weekly list to Chrysalis. They collect the sad-looking machines with their innards hanging out. Then the trainees work their magic on them and transform them for some family somewhere. As they work these young people learn mechanical and electrical skills. Chrysalis has plans to increase trading of all of these recycled goods throughout the region. Currently the shop on the Airedale Estate serves Castleford, Pontefract, and the Five Towns, the one in South Elmsall serves SESKU (South Elmsall, South Kirkby and Upton). There are plans for a Wakefield Town shop and possibly for a Selby shop too.

SRB output data collated by the FreshAire partnership in 2004 and collected over a five-and-a-half year period range from the obvious, such as the number of jobs created, to the obscure, such as kilometres of road improved. It recognises five qualitative elements: engaging the community, involving partners, influencing mainstream funding, providing different ways of working and shaping the future.

It was evident, as with many other SRB schemes, that a little investment in a project could go a long way. In this case the desire to provide local youths with a distraction through go-karting had enabled the organisation to purchase assets, develop skills in various fields of work and also expertise in running specialist programmes with the 'hard-to-reach individual' we are forever urged to seek out. They managed to develop into a trading organisation, or social enterprise. As these activities have grown new branches, they had increased their chance of sustainability and their ability to offer even more services to a wider range of people who needed them on the Airedale estate.

The Chrysalis project has grown up since its early church-based roots. Among other things they have changed the way in which they employ people. They had originally taken on qualified youth workers, but have replaced them with qualified teachers who can cover a range of roles within the programmes on offer. Over the last three years they have also received visitors from Holland, the Czech Republic and Russia, wanting to look at the projects and replicate the model back home. On the back of a United Nations directive urging people to recycle computers, Neil had also done a slot on local BBC radio. They had got fantastic free publicity from this, including calls from remote Scottish islands and someone driving from London to buy a £20 monitor! They managed new demand by making sure they knew how to contact similar organisations around the country and signposting people. Chrysalis now turn over £700,000 per year, employ fifteen staff and are registered to deliver accredited courses through the Open College Network, Edexcel and City and Guilds.

Is it possible that an organisation is more likely to survive after grant aid is withdrawn if that organisation has already existed before the grant was on offer? There is undoubtedly strength in the origins of such an organisation. By the time money is on offer it has had to rely on its own resources long enough not to be wasteful.

In contrast a community organisation that came into being at the behest of an officer or a councillor because the money is there, has only other people's experience to rely on. It begins to be trained to spend at the point when it has money to spend. It is too often driven by the style of the organisations that surround it. The organisation produces a glossy, generalised, brochure filled with jargon at the behest of officers without thinking about how to deliver it to their populations or how to market the ideas it contains. They are frequently working with officers who have not asked that question either. In too many cases style, not substance, drives initiatives.

FILEY

In the summer of 1991, Councillor Dave Murto told the Scarborough Evening Gazette
that he was highly delighted after we claimed that Kylie Minogue
was the owner of a six-berth static in the East Coast resort.
'Kylie can be sure of a neighbourly welcome at Filey - the gem of the Yorkshire coast.'

Chris Donald, *Rude Kids - The Unfeasible Story of Viz*

OH I DO LIKE TO BE BESIDE THE SEASIDE

The Coastal Tourism Initiative was a 4-year partnership scheme managed by the Yorkshire Tourist Board and coastal local authorities in the region. The SRB scheme covered all wards in a coastal strip covering Scarborough, East Yorkshire and North East Lincs, with the bulk of resources targeted in the Scarborough District. The overall objective of the scheme is to improve the economic performance of tourism businesses and to maximise the contribution coastal tourism makes to the economic well-being of the coastal communities in the Region. This was achieved primarily by the provision of grants to tourism businesses aimed at improving the facilities for tourists visiting the area, with the primary focus on accommodation-based businesses.

Coastal Tourism Initiative - SRB 5 - Final year 2003/04, SRB contribution £0.5m

Visitors arriving in winter by train to Filey could be forgiven for staying on the train and continuing to Scarborough or Bridlington. The station, a Grade II listed structure built around 1850, is more than shabby, it looks derelict. The café is closed; the waiting rooms appear gutted and the only ray of seaside sunshine is a homemade notice in the ticket office window advertising: 'Local honey for sale - Best tasting ever! Borage or Field n' Forest' and another which offers 'Free-range eggs - £1 a dozen.'

It is a far cry from the 1850s when Filey was a flourishing spa town and, according to the guide book of the day, 'omnibuses from Taylor's Hotel and Foords' Hotel meet every train.' Mind you, the guide book was written by the town's physician, Edward William Pritchard, the last man to be publicly hanged in Scotland in front of a capacity crowd of 50,000, having poisoned his wife, mother-in-law and probably at least one housemaid, though the latter was never proved. He was such a notorious liar that he was said 'to speak the truth only by accident', so you can't entirely rely on his glowing description of the resort.

Back in the present day, prospects for the visitor don't improve outside the station. Although SRB funds were apparently used to improve the forecourt and to rescue the station from English Heritage's Register of Buildings at Risk, the black and gold Victorian bollards and flower beds, now choked with weeds, do not really divert the visitor's attention from the boarded-up buildings which surround it. It is a pity that this railway station, together with the equally dismal bus station next-door, should be the gateway to Filey; because if your courage does not desert you and you venture further into town you find some of the most glorious scenery in England, immaculate golden beaches, elegant buildings equal to any in Bath or Harrogate and a history to rival that of York.

Look down at the blue sea sparkling in the bright winter sunshine, below the picturesque cliff-top houses, and you seem a million miles away from the sad old railway station. There is no obvious sign of deprivation here. And that is the problem with rural deprivation. It is hidden, out of sight, out of mind. Inner-city deprivation is in-yer-face; with its attendant high crime, vandalism and social unrest, it screams loudly at MPs and local government officers that something has to be done. But it is only too easy to ignore rural deprivation because those who suffer from it largely do so in silence. You can't see it and it doesn't cause any trouble in high places, so it is hard to get funding to put it right.

PROBLEMS AND PERCEPTIONS

Filey's problems ironically stem from the very things which make it such an ideal holiday destination. It is a small, sleepy, non-industrialised seaside resort, seven miles south of Scarborough, framed by cliffs, fields and sea. Of the 6,800 inhabitants, 40% are over sixty compared to an average of 18.8% in England as a whole, with over 53% of all households with a pensioner in residence compared to 33.5% nationally. 31% of households in Filey have one or more members of the household who are suffering from a long-term illness. The elderly are largely incomers; on retiring, they sell up their homes or their right-to-buy council houses in the industrial towns of Yorkshire and move to Filey for 'peace and quiet'. Here property is cheaper and they have fond memories of idyllic childhood holidays bathed in golden sunshine.

The Filey Bay project is very different from many SRB projects; you might say it's SRB with views.
John Burroughs, Economic Development Officer, Scarborough Borough Council

But summer doesn't last all year. Set high up on the east coast, for many months Filey can be windy, wet and bitingly cold. The hilly streets, which were such fun when you were a child, seem like mountains when you are not so sprightly. Spouses die and suddenly the remaining partner realises that there are very infrequent train or bus services to get them to hospital appointments or to any large shopping centre. As the summer tourist trade melts away, most amenities close for the winter. The sunny paradise turns into a cold, grey ghost town, one of God's bleaker waiting rooms. Little wonder then that many elderly people here suffer from depression.

Although crime or serious antisocial behaviour in Filey is low compared to towns such as Leeds or even Scarborough, between 1995 and 1996 reported crime increased by 20% and rose still higher in 1997. It mostly consisted of low-level antisocial behaviour, assaults, car crime and burglary. But perhaps more important than the actual number of incidents is the fear of crime, which is very high among the elderly. Even the sight of three youths talking on a street corner can be enough to make them afraid to venture out.

And the street corner is exactly where you are likely to find the youth of the town, for they have trouble finding anywhere else to go. The council can only afford to open the youth club two evenings a week. There are no shops selling clothes for teenagers. There are no cafés open in the evenings, no cinema, no all-weather sports facilities. One teenage mum said, 'There is nowhere to go. I just hang about in the house and sometimes go down the gaming arcade, that's all that's open.' If young people want to do anything they have to go to Scarborough, but because public transport stops early in the evening it means a taxi back which is expensive and can put vulnerable youngsters at risk, especially if at the end of the evening they find they can't raise the fare to get home.

Work in Filey is largely seasonal, unskilled and dependent on the tourist trade which, as in most places, has some of the poorest paid jobs in the employment market. Career progression is often non-existent and some local employers freely admit they are reluctant to train or skill their employees, in case the employees move on once trained. Though to be fair, it is much harder for a small family employer than a big company to spare the time to train an employee or send them on a course when they cannot afford to employ someone to cover for them. Unemployment in Filey in January 1997 was 9.9% against a county rate of 4.6%. Male unemployment in Filey was running at 12.9%, with well over half of these long-term unemployed. And it isn't easy to travel out of Filey to find work. The buses and trains servicing Filey do not operate at convenient times to get people into nine-to-five jobs in the bigger towns. This makes shift work impossible, unless you own your own car, and 36.6% of households in Filey do not. As one resident told me, 'Young people stay in Filey, despite the lack of work, because they don't have the confidence or the skills to move away to find work elsewhere.'

The holiday parks which are dotted around the town in the nearby countryside are both a lifeline and a curse for Filey. The lifeline is that they provide employment for people from Filey all year round, especially the trades such as electricians, plumbers and even bakeries which are needed to keep the camps running. The curse is that those who come to the camps have no reason to leave to use facilities in the town. Food, entertainment and all necessities are provided in the camp itself and so the local shops and pubs often don't benefit from these visitors.

THE VISION

Filey Ward covers the whole of Filey Town, Filey Bay, the promontory known as Filey Brigg, as well as an area of existing and former holiday campsites to the south, including a length of coastline measuring six miles. Filey Ward is ranked the fifth most deprived ward in North Yorkshire, the worst if measured against factors defining rural deprivation. It is also a PESCA eligible area, because of its dependency on fishing.

There is a huge barrier between Filey and Scarborough Borough Council. There are a lot of people in Filey who still get out the garlic if the Borough Council's name is mentioned.
Geoff Carline, Chamber of Commerce

In January 1998, with Scarborough Borough Council as the lead authority, the Filey Bay Regeneration Initiative Partnership (FBRIP) was formed to bid for £1.3 million under SRB 4 to tackle three key problem areas in the Filey Ward. The first was tourism and environmental projects, which were to include clearing and developing the 200 acre former Butlins' holiday camp site known as Amtree Park; to refurbish the promenade on the seafront; to build a new Tourist Information Centre and to improve coastal access including coastal walks, access to Filey Brigg and the Country Park. These projects were aimed at encouraging tourism back into the town, which would in turn help employment prospects.

The second area of FBRIP was to focus on employment issues themselves by providing start-up business units and skills training. They also wanted to improve the town centre area by smartening up shop fronts and improving signage to help retail businesses. The final strand of FBRIP was to work with the socially isolated, including elderly people, the youth and the unemployed. In particular, they wanted to help the community to become actively involved in regeneration through training and participation in the voluntary sector. It was hoped this would also help to reduce crime by taking off the streets the young people who were believed to be engaged in nuisance crime and also help reduce the fear of crime - probably the bigger factor - by making elderly people feel more secure and involved.

From April 1998 to March 2001, FBRIP drew £3,821,789 into Filey from SRB, private and public funding. SRB money has funded or part-funded 26 different projects ranging from massive schemes such as the Evron Centre to small projects such as helping the local sailing club to develop training facilities.

THE EVRON CENTRE

It would be hard to overestimate the historic hostility many Filey people feel towards Scarborough Borough Council. The trouble began when the borough was formed in the early 1970s. As several local people in the town independently told me: 'The Borough Council took all our buildings and amenities and gave us nothing back. We even had to buy back our own museum.' As with so many small towns and villages that find themselves lumped in with bigger towns, there was a general perception that 'Scarborough gets everything and we get nothing.' And it was in this climate of resentment that the idea of the Evron Centre was first conceived. The proposal heaped yet more coals upon the smouldering fire of suspicion. For the initial reaction of many Filey people was: 'They are taking yet another one of *our* buildings to turn it into *their* Borough

Council offices,' and there was the widespread belief that '*they* were using *our* SRB grant money to do it, money which belonged to the people of Filey.'

The building which is now the Evron Centre is a magnificent mansion, built around 1830, high above the sea in the centre of Filey with sweeping views over the bay to the cliffs on either side. Originally built as a family home, in 1904 it was taken over by The Sisters of Charity of Notre Dame d'Evron (Our Lady of Evron) who added a third storey to the building and turned it into a school for day pupils and boarders, educating girls aged four to eighteen. Both nuns and school were very popular and much loved, and even now many old girls still turn up for the annual reunions. The building briefly became Filey Town Hall, and then a community centre with the old school hall becoming Filey Concert Hall, but the building was badly in need of renovation. Despite this, it was regarded as one of the jewels of Filey's historic buildings, so there was much resentment at the idea of it becoming a home to Scarborough Borough Council Southern Area offices.

The idea, of course, was to try to help the people of Filey by creating a one-stop shop for council services which local people could use without having to trek into Scarborough. The planners hoped that this might help to change the perception that everything was run from Scarborough. But more importantly, the £1.5 million development was also intended to house a new Tourist Information Centre to promote the town; a community advice and resource centre with rooms that could be used by any local community group; and a drop-in base where social workers, the Citizen's Advice Bureau, bereavement counsellors and health visitors could meet clients. It was also proposed to include a number of start-up units for local businesses. But the idea stuck in the public mind that this was going to be Borough Council Offices, run by the Borough Council and as one lady in a café told me, 'We weren't going to set foot in it on principle.'

Sisters of Charity of Notre Dame D'Evron was founded in 1682 by a French widow, Perrine Thulard, to educate the poor and care for the sick. Many of the sisters were executed during the French Revolution, but despite that their numbers grew. They came to England in 1904 when, once again, a hostile French Government made it impossible for them to continue their work in France.
Karen Maitland

THE BATTLE FOR HEARTS AND MINDS

It takes a brave and imaginative diplomat to manage a centre surrounded by that much controversy but as it happens, Sharon Balding has all of those qualities and more. She left school and went into the catering trade before starting a family. At thirty she went back to college to do an HND in Hotel Management and took a degree in Business Management at forty. She worked on the Woolworth's management team for four years and then with the YMCA, training young people with social problems, before applying for the job as Manager of the Evron Centre five years ago. She was appointed in the January towards the end of the building work. The building opened to the public in June, so that when Sharon first took up her appointment it was in a hard hat and steel-capped boots.

Sharon had several major problems to deal with from day one. Firstly there was the town's hostility to the project and fierce local opposition to the proposed car park that was needed to serve the building. Then there was the problem of trying to create a centre that worked for the Borough Council Offices, community projects, Citizens' Advice and start-up business units all in the same building. As if that wasn't enough, just before the building was due to open she was told that the Council were closing the Sun Lounge, the only entertainment venue in Filey, because they couldn't afford to make the repairs. She was told, and she says she will never forget the words, 'We are going to put the entertainment centre in the Evron Centre, you'll be alright with that won't you?' Sharon had never managed an entertainment venue before - usually a highly specialised field - and the building was nearly complete so it was too late to make changes to the plans. The venue would have to be run from the old school hall in the Evron Centre, making do with the existing school stage and facilities as there was no money left to do it up.

DIVIDE AND GROW

A lesser woman might have resigned on the spot, but in a spirit of determination that the old Filey fishermen would have been proud of, Sharon rolled up her sleeves and got on with trying to solve the problems. First of all she created two different entrances for the Evron Centre - Community and Business. It is important for businesses that their entrance looks smart and professional, with no handwritten notices for jumble sales or advice about avoiding loan sharks. There are carpets on the floor and trendy lights that come on ahead of you as you walk along

the corridors. Everything is designed to make it look like the entrance to a professional business office. This entrance had to be shared with the Borough Council Offices, and Sharon had to work hard to persuade them that notices about fraud or benefits claims should be kept round the corner in their section, so that businesses clients would not be confronted by them as they walked in.

But the very elements that go into making an entrance area look professional are also those factors which can appear intimidating to ordinary members of the public by creating a barrier, so the community entrance on the other side of the building is deliberately designed to look different. Here we have a reception desk alongside notice boards advertising calligraphy classes, Weight Watchers, the playgroup, tabletop sales and courses for making Xmas cards. There is also a set of small offices near the entrance which were designed for people like health visitors and bereavement support counsellors to run drop-in surgeries, though uptake of these facilities by the professional agencies has so far been poor.

Just inside the entrance door from the car park there is an alcove containing two computers and a rack of leaflets, so that people can come in and look up information or search for jobs. Despite the perception that there is a high crime rate in Filey, there clearly isn't; every time I went in there, the reception was unstaffed and the computers were located next to the unlocked door, with members of the public wandering in and out to attend Weight Watchers or simply to use the inside toilets.

The hardest job is to get people from different organisations to work together on a big project. It is vital to have someone with leadership skills. You can't just toss in an inexperienced community development worker; you need someone with the skills to empower the people they are working with.
Borough Council officer

The community side is not run by Sharon. It is run and managed by Filey Community Advice Centre Trust, a group of volunteers and organisations who have the reception area and offices for free. This is proving a problem, for although the rooms are very well used by community groups, the reception office is hardly ever staffed because volunteers are tied up with their own community projects. Since a number of the 'community' organisations - such as Age Concern who run sessions in the Evron Centre - have a nationwide focus and are not based in Filey, it is hard to find people from the organisations to staff offices or reception desks, especially at times when they haven't got a session running.

This lack of reception staff not only presents a potential security problem, which fortunately so far has not become an issue. More importantly, first-time visitors who come to the centre through this entrance cannot find anyone to answer questions or direct them to the right room on this side of the building. A notice on the door to the corridor connecting the community area with the Borough Council reception desk says 'Staff only'. Those in the know ignore this notice and walk through the corridor to the main reception, but it undoubtedly puts a lot of newcomers off from venturing further into the building to seek help.

ALL THINGS TO ALL MEN (AND WOMEN)

The Evron Centre is a very versatile space, using folding doors to divide many rooms so that they can be made bigger or smaller to accommodate almost any group size. Upstairs is a huge, brightly decorated meeting room - once the former chapel - with the play group above that. Smaller rooms, with big picture windows overlooking the sea, are well used by groups such as the art society which has over a hundred members. Given the stunning views and the natural light coming into these rooms, they always have something to paint, just by looking out of the windows. There are dance classes, photography and calligraphy classes, clubs for older people and many other activities which are well attended during the day.

Two simple rates are charged for rooms in the Evron Centre. If the proceeds of the activity go back into the group, then the room is rented out at a community rate of £13 for three hours. If the takings go to one person, such as a tutor, then the room is rented out at a business rate of £19.50. So popular is the centre that they are struggling to find room for Yoga and Keep Fit. Organisations engaged in providing care in the community use rooms in the centre for training sessions. They also have an IT centre managed by Yorkshire College.

Sharon Balding, Evron Centre Manager, has put her office right next to the main entrance, so that she is always accessible, and judging by the number of members of the public walking in to ask questions, they obviously feel welcome to drop in. But it wasn't always like that. Sharon spent the first few weeks after the building opened standing outside grabbing passers-by and 'saying this is *your* building, come in and have a look at it. I'll take you round. What do you want it to be?'

It was a slow, hard battle, but it is being won and there is no doubt that many people in Filey now do regard it as *their* building once more. The biggest problem is the teenagers and early twenties age group who are hardest to reach in most towns. Several young people I spoke to, including some young mums, had never been in the Evron and didn't realise there was an advice centre in there, so there is still some way to go. But, having been flattened against the wall by a stampede of unruly pensioners trying to get into one meeting, I can safely say they at least now feel very much at home in *their* Evron Centre.

HARD BRASS

You have to have a good business head and be willing to take calculated risks to run a centre like the Evron. It receives an income from Scarborough Borough Council and the Tourist Information Centre. The salaries for managers and other permanent staff, including the caretaker, are paid by the Borough Council which allows some parts of the Evron Centre to be subsidised. Nevertheless an income must be generated from the business start-up units, and to do that you first have to get the businesses to base themselves in the centre.

There are two types of businesses in the units in the Evron. Complementary therapists such as reflexologists and osteopaths will probably stay long-term as they cannot really expand beyond the number of clients they can treat in one day. Then there are commercial businesses that may outgrow the units; they include a company trading with Japan, building surveyors, a removal firm and Global Bagtag, an innovative company providing an international tracing system for luggage via the internet.

Never let it be said that Filey business folk didn't offer their visitors the latest amenities. According to local historian, Kenneth Clark, visitors to Filey in 1828 could take a warm bath 'by applying to Mr Munroe, Surgeon, who processed a portable tin-bath. It could be lent out or used at Mr Munroe's house.'
Karen Maitland

The eighteen business start-up units in the Evron Centre were a great success from the first. They are so popular that there is a waiting list to move in. A unit rented by one firm who are moving out in three months' time has already been let. Several factors contribute to this popularity. The first is the central location in the town, in smart premises with convenient car parking but low rents are probably one of the main factors. Rent covers both lighting and heating with no additional overheads. Rents are set below the local market price for the first two years; then, after the business has been established for two years, they rise to match the current market price.

Another factor which makes these units so popular is that the businesses only have to commit to a month's lease, so in theory they could move in and give a month's notice on the same day. This is vital when people are starting up, for the risk of being tied into a year's lease can discourage budding entrepreneurs. Of course, the month's notice means a great risk for the Evron Centre Manager, for in a month's time all eighteen units could be empty, but so far the gamble has paid off; the units are fully occupied and seem likely to continue to be so.

Businesses are allowed to rent either one or two units, but if they are successful and find they need to expand, they are encouraged to move on. This isn't easy, because there is a shortage of next-stage-up units in the town. Hotels, when they close, tend to be converted into private residences, not into offices and business premises. Hopefully by redeveloping some of the old buildings around the station area there will be more business units. The last thing Filey needs is for those successful businesses which started in the Evron Centre to move out of Filey because of a lack of anywhere suitable to expand into. Perhaps this is a case where traditional thinking has to be overturned and you have to mix business with pleasure, allowing non-industrial businesses to be set up in residential or leisure areas.

Another potential problem for business development is that small businesses have received relief on their business rents for the last fifteen years. That relief is ending this year and the fear is that it could sound the death knell for a number of struggling businesses in the town.

THERE'S NO BUSINESS LIKE SHOW BUSINESS

Entertainment is synonymous with seaside resorts, but public taste has changed and the venues which traditionally hosted the old variety shows in Filey have closed. Yet, there still is a demand for some form of afternoon and evening entertainment both for holidaymakers and locals. So when Sharon Balding found herself running the one remaining entertainment venue, Filey Concert Hall, as part of the Evron Centre, she had quite a responsibility to keep people happy.

The name 'Filey Concert Hall' sounds much grander than it is. It is in fact a traditional old school hall with stacking chairs and a school stage at one end. The doors leading to the hall through the Tourist Information Centre have to be pinned closed with a stack of tables when not in use, because they rattle in the draught and set the alarm off. Despite this, a regular programme of summer concerts, winter pantomimes and events is put on at the venue.

If the Evron Centre commissioned the shows, events and concerts it could potentially run the risk of considerable losses if they didn't sell out. Artists and promoters book the hall on a shared-risk basis, with the centre taking a percentage of the takings. Although this scheme results in less profit for both centre and promoter if the show is successful, there is also less risk to both parties if the show does badly. This means that the Evron can host a wide range of shows and concerts, from regular afternoon tea-dances to tribute bands to see what works and what doesn't. They have recently hosted the Stephen Joseph Theatre Summer Tour which was a huge success. If the Evron Centre was standing the whole loss, then it is natural that they would opt for the safer events which were tried and tested, and they would not be able to take the risk of trying new ideas. They now hold 25 lunchtime concerts a year which regularly attract over 50 people; when they first started, only about a dozen people turned up. It takes time to build an audience base.

Evron Centre Manager Sharon Balding has big plans for the hall and aims to turn it into a modern arts space. She hopes to get it refurbished and install raked seating which can be folded up at the touch of a button, to leave a clear floor space for dances and other activities. She also wants to improve the staging area and make it into a flexible space which can be used by the whole range of arts events, attracting a wider cross-section of people into the venue. Since Filey doesn't have a cinema, she hopes too

The photographer marvelled at the flithergirls' efforts. He will soon be with them up to the waist, and then when they have got their baskets full they let him climb with them up a cliff some 500ft high. He will then think that women's work by daylight is even harder than the fishermen's toil and danger at seas by night.
Frank Meadow Sutcliffe, photographer, 1896

that the venue could also be used for a regular film club. The Evron Centre may be up and running, but it is still a work in progress and if Sharon has her way, it will continue to evolve to meet the needs of both visitors and residents. The trick, as Sharon says, 'is not only to give people what they want now, but to be able to predict what they might want in the future.'

LAUNCHING THE BOAT

Kath Wilkie is one of the few people who backed the Evron Centre from the first. She was a volunteer with a group called LEADER II, and at the rather stormy meeting to discuss the Evron Centre, the vote was split between a number of interest groups. The people of Filey wanted the building developed for the benefit of the community but most were very vague about exactly what they wanted. Kath decided to give the SRB proposal a chance and, as she puts it, 'went for it and has never regretted it since.' She feels that the opportunity the Evron Centre has created for start-up businesses and for the many community projects would never have been achieved without it. Even the analysis and evaluation of the Filey Town Plan was done by volunteers at the Evron.

Kath was forced to take early retirement from care work. She was trying to lift a patient to help a pregnant colleague but the bed suddenly rolled away, causing a permanent and very painful back injury. But although disabled, it hasn't stopped her being one of the most committed volunteers in Filey. As she said, 'I may be disabled, but there's nothing wrong with my mouth.' Kath was one of a number of volunteers who founded the Coble Preservation Society in 2000 to help save Filey's last remaining coble boats. The project, which has created training opportunities for over 180 people, has also led to four people obtaining full-time work. Kath said, 'When we applied for grants to restore the coble *Margaret*, we had to call it a floating study, because we couldn't get a grant for anything vehicular. It's a question of trying to make the things we want to do fit into the criteria of the various bids, and that takes a lot of imagination and creativity, but we're getting better at it.'

But the Coble Preservation Society would never have got off the launch ramp if it hadn't been for the Evron Centre. Kath was based at home with no computer and no office. Without IT facilities and a base at the Evron Centre, the fundraising for the project, the information website and all the organisation which the project involved could never have been achieved, for they had no money to buy the equipment or rent an office. Without access to a computer it is very difficult to compete with other organisations for grant funding or to raise money through appeals. You need money to be able to raise money.

THE YOUTH CENTRE

'Get the young people off the streets, but not into my back yard.' It's a common attitude among the not-so-young, which is why having a youth centre in a residential area occupied by many elderly people seems like a recipe for trouble.

Filey youth club has been open for forty years, but until the Filey Bay Initiative the numbers attending were declining year on year, despite there being precious little else for young people in Filey, with the result that residents were constantly complaining about them congregating on street corners or engaging in vandalism and nuisance crime.

It was hardly surprising the young people were not attracted to the youth club. About 25 to 30 years ago, it had been decorated in the style of a 1950s pub, with vinyl seating round the walls, velour wall paper, heavy red velvet curtains, brown ceiling and dark wood panelling and cheap plastic floor tiles. If the décor didn't put you off, the layout certainly did. The upper and lower floors were connected by an open staircase, so that youngsters had the run of the whole building, regularly bursting into rooms in which people were trying to hold meetings or engage in some arts or craft activity, just to annoy the people inside. Staff had no time to help with activities, they spent the whole time patrolling the building, trying to stop the youngsters wrecking the place or maiming each other. As Dee Heims, the Club's community leader, says, 'We were not youth leaders, we were policemen. The youth were frustrated and bored and the youth workers were having a collective nervous breakdown.'

'Do you have live drawing sessions with nude models in your art group?' I ask the art tutor at the Evron centre. 'It's becoming very popular in Lincoln.'
He looks aghast. 'I don't think Filey is quite ready for that sort of thing.'
Karen Maitland

Despite the problems, youth workers like Dee were determined not to give up on the centre. She started youth work as a volunteer in 1992 in Scarborough. She became so interested in it that she gave up her day job to work on a rural youth project, and through that she took a degree in Informal and Community Education. She has been a youth worker in Filey for the past seven years and was there at the beginning of the Filey Bay Initiative Project.

When the SRB Steering Committee met, community safety was a big issue and two things were needed to resolve it. First, that the youth should have a decent meeting place to call their own; second, that there should be outdoor facilities as well. The first step was to tackle the youth centre and with the help of the county architects, the building was remodelled. The kitchen was made into a self-contained unit. The stairs were moved, closed in and protected by a lockable door so that the youth workers could control who went upstairs to the meeting and activities rooms. Some of the rooms upstairs were converted into rehearsal rooms and IT rooms. The new design means that the four or five youth workers can now spend their time in activities with the young people, rather than policing the building.

The rooms downstairs were redecorated in lilac and silver, colours chosen by the young people themselves. They also chose the chrome tables and chairs. It is proof of the power of the sense of ownership that never once since the building has been refurbished has it been vandalised or damaged. This is even more remarkable when you learn that the young people using the rehearsal rooms for music and drama have their own key and let themselves in and out at times when the youth club is not open. They now have between forty and fifty young people between the ages of eleven and seventeen coming to the youth club. Unfortunately the council can only afford to open it two nights a week, leaving many of the young people back on the street corners for the other five nights.

HEART OF THE COMMUNITY

The youth club does not lie empty for the rest of the week. Since the refurbishment, it is used during the day for adult classes ranging from art to literacy and family learning. The Job Centre, Connexions, young mums' support groups and other organisations can use the youth club as a drop-in centre. The policy is open access for community groups without charge. Situated in the middle of a residential street, the club makes an ideal community base. Although the SRB grant money didn't stretch to redecorating upstairs, inspired by the changes downstairs several of the groups using the building have redecorated the rooms themselves in bright colours and graffiti artists have worked with the youngsters.

Through the Prince's Trust Excel programme ten young people who were excluded from school or who were disruptive are taking GSCEs at the youth centre. As Dee says, 'for young people who find it difficult to work in a classroom this is a perfect venue. They can do an hour's work and then when they find their concentration slipping, they can break off and have a coffee or play a game of pool and then go back to studying again. Unlike school they don't have to stay in their seats or have to work to a fixed timetable.'

The whole refurbishment has been the catalyst for the teenagers to fundraise themselves for equipment for a recording studio. They actually wrote their own bid for a grant for video recording equipment. They want to turn the first floor into a multi-media centre including a video editing suite and community resources. They have also applied for a lottery bid, but don't know yet if they have been successful. Part of this project would be a community radio station based at the youth centre. Eight young people are already being skilled-up to run the station and are being trained in the technical side of broadcasting as well as communications skills, while the youth centre tries to look for funding. This may seem premature but they must be able to convince the licensing authorities they can run the station. It costs £600 pounds just to send in the licence application and over £ 1,000 per year for the licence itself, so they must be ready to broadcast as soon as they get the go-ahead. No wonder some groups set up pirate radio stations.

Here's me casually throwing funding terms around like a government officer. I wouldn't have been doing that before SRB.
Community volunteer, Filey

COMMUNITY RELATIONS

On the third floor of the youth centre is a twenty bed dormitory style residential unit, which groups can use as a base for week-long activities. A number of groups have used it in the past to bring young people with social problems and young carers to Filey from towns all over North Yorkshire, to take part in visual arts, music including drumming, computer art, performing arts or outdoor pursuits. Again these groups have their own keys, and their own staff are expected to supervise their students.

Unfortunately this can create problems for the youth club. As any parent or teacher knows, a group of youngsters away from home and sharing a room have a natural tendency to go mad and stay up half the night laughing, creating noise and generally annoying every adult within earshot. Despite the fact that we all did it when we were young, there have been complaints from residents living around the centre. The staff now have to be very selective about who they let the residential accommodation out to, because too many complaints could put the future of the youth club itself in danger.

And that is the problem with the location of the youth club. Although being in a residential area makes it ideal for a community base for all ages, it also means that neighbours are subjected to noise and music from the centre itself and from young people coming to and from the centre in groups. Youth worker Dee Heim's policy is to try and bring the complainants and the young people together in face to face meetings to try to reach an understanding. She says that often people who complain the loudest refuse to come to the meetings. Other residents do and start by voicing their complaints, but by the time they leave they are saying that the youth club should be open every night of the week, not just two nights. It is, Dee says, 'often a question of perception about young people not reality, and once this perception is challenged and they have the chance to sit down and talk to them face to face, their attitude changes.'

Young people need more healthy exercise, that's what the government tells us, and most people would probably agree with that. The question is, where are they going to get it? You try playing football in the average residential street and see how encouraging adults are then about the idea of exercise. There are no sports facilities in Filey except a golf course and an outdoor bowls green, neither of which are exactly appealing sports to most youngsters nor, let's be honest, would the majority of golf or bowls players welcome hoards of teenagers invading their facilities.

Unfortunately this is one instance where, unlike in the case of the youth centre, SRB grant money may have made things worse not better. They did have an existing skate board park, but SRB grant money was used to relocate it to a site which had been earmarked for a kick-about site for ball games. The skate board ramps had been made of wood and had been exposed to the wind and rain of the seaside town already. When they were relocated the pieces wouldn't fit properly back together again. There was no funding for maintenance so the ramps stopped being used, and then the park was vandalised by a gang of youngsters from outside Filey. The one good thing to come out of it was that the controversy surrounding the project raised awareness of the need to provide some sports facilities for young people, and with a site already allocated it is hoped that something might eventually be achieved.

DOWNTOWN

You would think, wouldn't you, that any shopkeeper would be delighted if someone came along and offered to renovate their shop front for free - once, of course, they overcame the natural Yorkshire suspicion about getting 'owt for nowt'. In Filey, nineteen out of twenty shopkeepers in the main shopping area welcomed the opportunity to have their shop fronts made smart and elegant. But there was one dissenter. He said he did not want his shop front smartened. He operated a discount shop and argued that if his shop looked smart and elegant, then people would think the goods inside were expensive and wouldn't come in.

Filey shopping area was a sad remnant of the declining fortunes of a seaside town. At the time of the SRB bid, 20% of the shops were either boarded-up or only opened during the summer tourist season. There was a mixture of charity shops, discount shops, cheap souvenir shops and a number of old family-owned stationers, bakers and butchers. The shop fronts were scruffy and neglected, not a place that would tempt you to browse.

Private companies don't invest in charm.
John Burroughs, Economic Development Officer, Scarborough Borough Council

SRB funding refurbished some of the shop fronts on the main streets. They also introduced new signage pointing visitors towards the tourist attractions, and also huge skip-size blue metal planters. It was a bit unfortunate that when the blue metal planters arrived they were at first assumed to be rubbish skips which civic-minded people obediently filled with rubbish. Now, moved to new locations and planted up, they make a big bold splash of colour in the summer.

The traffic calming measures have also proved popular, though perhaps not quite in the way the planners envisaged. Sections of the pavement extended out into the road in a curve to create alternating single lanes at regular intervals along the road, so that traffic would have to slow down to filter through. One enterprising publican used the new pavement area in front of his pub to lay out tables and chairs, continental style, in the summer. Some local people admired his initiative and were most annoyed when he was ordered to remove them.

CCTV in Filey has proved the bugbear it is in most towns. As always in any regeneration scheme, local residents and shop keepers demand it, convinced it will be the magic wand to solve their crime problems. With little money to spend on it, a compromise solution was found to provide six mobile CCTV units to serve both Scarborough and Filey, with two based permanently in Filey. One of the problems with fixed CCTV has always been that rather than preventing crime and antisocial behaviour it can simply move criminals on to areas without cameras. With mobile units, the cameras can follow the trouble, giving it no hiding place. This innovative project was jointly funded by Castle Pride and the Filey Bay Regeneration Initiative.

But it was almost inevitable that this solution would not please everyone. There were complaints to Scarborough Borough Council that the promised number of units had not materialised and those that had were situated in the wrong place and were not working or were not being monitored. Even today in 2005, the CCTV issue is still dominating the local paper, the *Filey and Hunmanby Mercury.* But the reality is that although the anti-crime measures were small, CCTV and a project called 'Safe and Secure', which helped 100 households in Filey to increase awareness of personal safety, do seem to have had a positive effect on reducing crime. The police are reporting that the number of incidents of all types of crime has fallen since these measures were introduced but unfortunately this has not had much effect on reducing the fear of crime.

And we are here as on a darkling plain
Swept with confused alarms of struggle and flight,
Where ignorant armies clash by night.

Matthew Arnold, *Dover Beach*

The improvements to the town have certainly helped. For the first time, business people like Geoff Carline who runs a baker's shop, have noticed a difference: 'This is the first year that our profits have been up both summer and winter.' But they do need to get the word out. Even in the run-up to Christmas, I found the streets of Filey almost deserted as if some national emergency had been declared. There are still too many discount shops and too few good quality gifts or clothes shops and nowhere at all selling the kinds of clothes and gadgets teenagers or young people might want. As one rather critical visitor to Filey pointed out in a letter to the local newspaper in November 2005, ' the only thing I can see going on in Filey is the certainty of being run over by an older person and his dog on a mobility scooter.'

'I DO LIKE TO STROLL ALONG THE PROM, PROM, PROM'

In complete contrast, the newly renovated Filey promenade is one of the most interesting and imaginative regeneration building projects in SRB history and certainly one that every visitor will immediately notice. Yorkshire Water Services undertook extensive waste water improvements to the seafront, and on one of those rare occasions when a good plan comes together, SRB funds were made available at the same time to redevelop the promenade and surrounding seafront area. A series of pretty slate-roofed sandstone buildings are dotted along the newly paved promenade housing lavatories, shops and ticket booths, although they are all closed in winter. There is a crazy golf park which looks at first glance like a sculpture park. Each hole is outlined by a length of ship's rope and inside each roped area are lobster pots, rocks with sculpted metal limpets attached, sculpted shells, starfish, eels, fish and a giant lobster. Not only is this design practical, because the stone and metal will weather beautifully, but when it is not in use for a crazy golf game it makes an attractive little park where people can stroll around.

There are new information boards pointing out interesting historical and natural features. At intervals along the promenade, picked out in cobbles on the pavement, are the names of all the boats, yawls and cobles that Filey men have crewed - *Guiding Star, Energy, Girl Annie* - some of which came safely home and too many, tragically, which did not, such as the *Trio*

which went down with all hands. Also hidden at intervals along the promenade are tiny metal sculptures of limpets known locally as flithers, which children take great delight in discovering and counting. The shells are a tribute to the flithergirls of Filey. During the nineteenth century, flithergirls, aged between about eleven and sixty, would climb down the perilous rocks and cliffs into the sea in wintertime to prise the flithers off the rocks. Flithers were used to bait the long-lines of the fishermen catching herring in the bay. Without the flithergirls there would have been no winter fishing and many Filey fishing families would have starved.

The formal Northcliff and Town Hall Gardens have been restored to their former glory with new seating and resurfaced pathways, redesigned planted areas and restoration of the tiled floor of the upper terrace of Northcliff Gardens. Now it is possible to imagine those Victorian and Edwardian ladies, their health and nerves fully restored by the spa water, strolling among the terraces under their parasols, perhaps on their way to pleasant dalliance with a young rake or even an old roué.

COMPASS AND COBLES

Perhaps one of the most important SRB renovations was Coble Landing at the north end of the promenade. The coble boats are kept high above the sea on an area at the end of the walkway and are pulled by tractor down a steep ramp and across the wide stretch of sand to the water were they are launched. Coble boats, direct descendants of the Viking longboats, have flat-bottomed keels with two iron runners so they can be dragged across the sand like sledges, making them capable of being launched at both low and high tide. They are extremely versatile boats used for long-line fishing in the winter, lobster pots in the spring and herring fishing with nets for the remainder of the year. Much prized catches are lobsters, crabs and Filey Bay salmon, otherwise known as sea trout.

Filey's spa spring was discovered in 1625 by Mistress Farrow, and was said to taste like sea water. By the 1850s it was claimed to cure skin diseases, scrofula, dyspepsia, hypochondijasis and torpid liver especially when brought on by immoderate use of wine and opium and a 'too constant application to severe studies'.
Karen Maitland

In the 1880s there were 190 cobles in Filey used for fishing and as pleasure boats; now only five cobles remain and one of those was burned by vandals in 2003. But thanks to the Coble Preservation Society founded in 2000, a sixth coble, the *Margaret*, was fully restored, helping to train young volunteers in the ancient art of ship-building in the process. The *Margaret* is now used as a floating school for the mandatory training of fishermen and for taking children and young people out to study bird and marine life and the fossils on the cliff, including the famous plesiosaur.

But not every improvement has been welcomed locally. The smart new fountain on the promenade bubbles out of a giant sculpture of a marine compass and points to all the names radio listeners will be familiar with from the shipping forecast - *Tyne, Fisher, Dogger, Viking, Cromarty, North Utshire*. It is great fun and you can watch visitors walking around it, reciting the list and seeing how many they can remember. Unfortunately, the fountain was built over a dilapidated but much loved shallow pool, on which some people claim they used to sail toy boats as children, though others say that is just another of the Filey myths. Nevertheless many locals resent the loss of something which was part of their childhood, fact or fiction. What is true is that children and adults used the pool to wash the sand off their feet before trudging up the hill to their homes or boarding house suppers. The design of this fountain means it doesn't accommodate feet so people have go home with sand between their toes. But isn't that why hotels have bidets?

The environmental improvements have not just been limited to the promenade. At Carr Naze, now designated as the Borough's first local nature reserve, a new carpark and footpath have opened up this area to disabled visitors. New information boards up on the cliff tops in the country park and at the Brigg show the way to various walks and inform the visitor about points of wildlife and geological interest. Grants to the Sailing Club, Filey Brigg Ornithological Group and others have enabled small but significant areas to be improved, and walks were developed which, with assistance from LEADER II, are helping to promote green tourism in Filey.

THE SINKING OF THE SRB FLAGSHIP

Say 'Filey' to most people in the North East and the one thing they associate with the town is Butlins Holiday Camp which opened in 1939 on a 200 acre site just to the south of Filey. In its heyday 100,000 campers stayed there each season, and despite having everything they could possibly want on the site, most campers were thought to visit Filey town at least once during their holiday. Indeed, Filey continues to attract summer visitors and people retiring to Filey, because of their memories of childhood holidays at Butlins. Equally important to the town, Butlins employed over 1,000 people, many of whom were local.

With growth in cheap package holidays to Spanish holiday resorts, demand for British holiday-camps declined and no-one was really surprised when Butlins finally closed in 1983. With the decline of the fishing industry already underway, the people of Filey were devastated by the closure, not only for the loss of the jobs in the camp itself, but for the knock-on effect it would have on the tourist industry in Filey which, like Butlins, was already suffering adversely from package holiday competition. The abandoned site rapidly became derelict and stood out like a rusting hulk among the green fields, an eyesore which could be seen from Filey itself.

The former Butlins site, known as Amtree, was intended to become the flagship in the SRB Filey Bay Project. They planned to clear it and turn it into a commercial leisure park to create employment and revive the tourist attractions of the area. But after they secured the funding, the plans ran into trouble. In a tit for tat move, the owners had already been refused planning permission to turn the site into residential housing and would not release the site to the Borough Council to cooperate with their vision. So the Filey Bay Steering Group had just one meeting to decide if they should try to pursue the original plans by seeking a compulsory purchase order and risk losing the grant money because of the time factor, or if they should abandon the project and divert the reserve of £300,000 they had put aside for Amtree into projects within Filey town. They diverted.

In the Filey bay area 7,000 bed spaces currently exist, the majority of which are out of town in camping and caravan sites. 9.1% of homes in Filey are now used as second homes.
FBRIP Project Bid document, 1998

But that wasn't quite the end of Scarborough Borough Council's problems with Amtree. When they still thought the plans would go ahead, the derelict site was surveyed in preparation for clearance and development. As well as badgers, protected birds and bee orchids, they discovered a colony of a rare protected species, the Great Crested Newts. Apparently these newts regard derelict sites and rubble as the perfect des.res. With hindsight Amtree should have been declared an SSSI - Site of Special Scientific Interest - but it wasn't and despite the presence of the newts it was still legal to clear the site for development, but only under licence from DEFRA who would have supervised the careful collection and removal of the newts to a safe location.

In October 2001, Scarborough Borough Council were forced to call in PC Graham Bilton of Eastern Area Wildlife Liaison Division when they discovered that the landowners had gone ahead without safeguarding the newts and had already cleared half the site. Despite police warnings, the company went ahead and finished clearing the site destroying the newts and other wildlife species. In January 2002, the Director of the company, Wayne Low, was arrested and subsequently convicted on 16 counts including the destruction of habitat, and killing and injuring a protected species and was fined £6,800 pounds plus costs. It was something of a landmark case because it was the first time a successful prosecution had been brought under these charges.

The site is now a peaceful English pasture, blending in seamlessly with the surrounding farmland and cliff tops, no longer an eyesore. But in removing the blot on Filey's landscape, rare species of plants and animals have been destroyed forever. The irony is that the ugly derelict site was teeming with wildlife, while the green field offers little protection to rare birds or animals.

Despite all the problems, the question remains: If the original proposals for the Amtree site had gone forward under SRB, would it really have benefited the people of Filey? Clearly, in the short-term many local young people could have found employment in the construction of the site. It was suggested that up to 4,000 construction jobs could have been created, but given a population of only 6,800 with 40% of those being over sixty, many of the workforce would have had to be brought in from outside. And those jobs would have had a limited time span with no obvious place to move onto. Early bid documents admitted that the planners were 'not able to be specific about the precise nature of the leisure development' and therefore presumably did not know who the potential clients might be - holiday makers, locals travelling out from Scarborough, summer visitors to Filey - or indeed whether these 'facilities' would be aimed at day-trippers, people looking for a good night out or even people staying in accommodation on site. So how much long-term benefit it might have brought to Filey is impossible to guess.

The heritage of Butlins, once the pearl of Filey, could easily become the bad oyster which incapacitates the town. Though fond memories of Butlins do bring parents and grandparents back to Filey with their children to recapture their lost youth, it is also the holiday-camp image which sticks in the minds of people who have never been to Filey, forever conjuring up a 1950s picture of the knobbly-knees contests, chips and whelks, candyfloss and saucy postcards. Unfortunately, the new generation who want that kind of organised fun holiday have now gone elsewhere - it is cheaper to go to Benidorm than to stay in Britain - but it puts off the kind of tourist who would adore the charm, stunning scenery and the peace of Filey, but just doesn't associate that with the town because it is so famous for Butlins. Filey needs to do some serious remarketing of itself if it is to attract a new client base.

Plans are once again afoot to convert Amtree into a leisure complex using private investment, and certainly the new owners are showing themselves very willing to commit to projects within the town itself, so perhaps it may once again ring with the sound of people enjoying themselves as it did back in 1938. Will this help to restore the fortunes of the town? Perhaps - but only if the town itself is willing to embrace change.

FILEY IS CLOSED

In 1867, Filey was described as a very fashionable resort. One writer claimed to have seen Earl Russell, Cardinal Wiseman and the Archbishop of York on the Brigg in one day.
Kenneth Clark, local writer and historian, 1998

The lavatories on the seafront are closed; though it doesn't actually say so on the door. The new Tourist Information Centre has lights blazing and looks colourful and inviting on a cold winter's day, but try to walk through the automatic door and you'll find that it too is closed. It only opens at weekends in the winter, though that is a step in the right direction, since for several years it didn't open at all in winter. But never mind, according to the twenty-four hour interactive electronic board

outside the TIC the town museum is open, just the place to spend a cold afternoon. But having walked all the way round several streets to find it - yes, you've guessed it - a notice on the door informs the visitor that the museum too is closed until April.
The couple I found staring at the notice were not amused.
'Will you be coming back when it re-opens in the summer?' I ask them.
The man shakes his head. 'No. It's supposed to be open today, according to the tourist office, but it isn't. How do we know it will be open in the summer, if we come back? Not worth the risk, coming all this way for nothing.'
'What are you going to do now?'
'Push on to Scarborough or Whitby. We were thinking of finding a nice little B&B and spending a few days here, but everything's shut. We've had a lovely walk along the promenade, but you can't do that all day, not when it's cold.'

There you have Filey's problem in a cockleshell. Filey is like a divorcee who refuses to believe the marriage is irretrievably over. In its own mind it is still wedded to its Butlins past. To some extent it does continue to attract the summer visitor wanting the traditional bucket and spade seaside holiday. But it has yet to recognise that tourism has moved on. More and more people, especially retired couples or people without school-aged children, now take midweek or weekend winter breaks. With the start of two spectacular walks in Filey, the Cleveland Way and the Wolds Way, with wildlife and birdlife in abundance and a history and heritage that many other towns would sell their own town councillors for, Filey has everything to attract the winter break visitor. It could equally offer special activity holidays such as bird-watching, fishing, painting, creative writing, golf or sailing. But it is going to have to get to grips with the idea that it has two entirely different potential client bases.

The winter visitors or special activity holidaymakers expect good quality restaurants and cafés which are open when they want to eat, not at the convenience of staff. They will come to the seaside in the autumn, winter and spring, as they do in Norfolk, Suffolk, Devon and Cornwall precisely because they want to avoid the crowds of grockles and their noisy little ankle-biters. They have money to spend and they will expect good modernised accommodation with ensuite facilities, not old-style boarding houses, and they want art and craft galleries, museums, heritage and information centres to be open midweek in the winter, not just so there is something to do to in wet or cold weather, but because history and heritage is what they are interested in. It is difficult for facilities such as the museums to stay open all year round when they are being staffed by volunteers, but perhaps they shouldn't be and should instead be treated according to their potential, as future revenue earners for the town. Come winter, Filey must not switch *off*, but switch *over*.

PROMOTING FILEY

The large impressive Tourist Information Centre (TIC) is a new-build added on to the front of the Evron building. It was intended to be an all-weather visitors' centre, providing not only tourist information, but also a display area and shop, an amenity which people could use in wet or cold weather. It is very popular during the summer, with 12,000 people per year coming through the doors. In May, schools bringing children to Filey for history and nature trips often book rooms in the Evron Centre to work in or eat their sandwiches in, in case the weather is wet.

In its first year, the Tourist Information Centre was open all year, but they didn't get enough visitors in during that first winter, so they took the decision to close during the winter months. You may say that is understandable; if there isn't the demand why provide the service? The trouble is that it is also a self-fulfilling prophecy. If people find it shut, word spreads and nobody comes because it isn't open. If it isn't open, how can you tell the visitor what Filey has to offer?

The town consists of two parts: the old town comprising the residences of the tradesmen and fishermen; the number of its inhabitants being about fourteen hundred. The New Town, the chief resort of visitors, has been built entirely with the last fifteen years.
Edward William Pritchard, 1853,
'Filey: a Guide for Visitors'

Inside the TIC are arresting photos of the area and an interesting display with exhibits from the local museum, together with a notice informing the visitor the museum is closed until Easter. But could someone please tell them that displaying a notice *inside* the Information Centre telling visitors that the museum is closed, is not awfully useful when the Information Centre is also closed, so no-one can get in to read it?

But as I was to find out, when I was kindly allowed a peek inside the closed TIC, even when it is open it seems that Filey is not keen to promote itself. Visitors to the TIC report that the staff are welcoming, friendly and helpful, doubtless doing their best to promote Filey and its attractions. There is a video of Filey for sale, a good start, although most people are now switching to DVDs. However, I had to hunt to find two duplicated little booklets on the history of Filey, hidden on the bottom shelf of a big display of glossy books on Scarborough, Whitby and Bridlington. All of the souvenirs on display were mass-produced of the kind made in China and overstamped with 'Present from….' There were no local crafts or souvenirs, no flithergirl dolls or models of coble boats that I could see, not even some of that 'best tasting' local honey as advertised at the railway station. In fact everything seemed to say to the visitor: 'Leave Filey as rapidly as possible and go to other towns which are more interesting.' I know TICs have a remit to advertise the whole area but come on, Filey, advertise yourselves first, not Scarborough or Whitby. Where are your books, your crafts, your souvenirs? Come on, Filey where is your pride?

THE LATE TRAIN

According to one community worker, 'Filey has a split personality. The indigenous people are disillusioned. They resent the outsiders coming in and therefore also any ideas they may have to change things. The people coming in often don't feel part of the community and therefore don't get involved.'

There are some very active and dynamic people and organisations in Filey but that lack of agreement in the town has a paralysing effect on many projects. For example, plans were put forward to have a land train in Filey long before it was ever thought of in Scarborough. The train would take residents and visitors alike on a circuit of the town, helping people to get up and down the steep hills and hopefully significantly reducing Filey's parking problem. But endless discussions over the route and other minor niggles have meant that Scarborough's train is out of the station and running while Filey's is still stuck in the sidings.

Another project which has fallen because of the lack of local agreement is the conversion of a boarded-up shop on the local council estate, empty for ten years, which was earmarked for a £96,000 makeover with SRB money with the idea of turning it into an IT centre. The project was proposed at a local meeting between council officers and residents. After the concept of the IT centre was outlined, one community worker stood up and said to the residents, 'but it doesn't have to be an IT centre; what do you want it to be?' One resident turned round in surprise and said, 'But I thought it had to be an IT centre because the Council said so. I didn't know we could choose.' The trouble is that so far nothing has been chosen and the shop remains boarded-up.

There is no reason why Filey can't take off in the same way as Whitby which is attracting lots of private investment. It certainly has as much, if not more, to offer. The difference, as one local government officer put it, was that 'Whitby has a streak of independence. It is less insular, connecting better with its hinterland. Filey will only achieve what Whitby has if it can change its attitude.'

SCALING THE FUNDING CLIFF

Geoff Carline, Leader of the local Chamber of Commerce who runs a bakery in the town, says that SRB and the Filey Bay Project created a steep learning curve for all concerned. 'We had never undertaken anything like that before.' The process was made more difficult by the fact that advisors on Scarborough Borough Council were on short-term contracts, so that as soon as one advisor had got to know the projects and problems they seemed to be moved on, leaving the Filey Steering group to deal with another new face who had no idea of the background and was therefore not in the best position to offer advice. Other people on the Steering Group felt that the support structure was patchy. As one said, 'Even for officers who spend their life doing it, managing a group composed of representatives of different, and often conflicting organisations requires considerable people-skills. Such groups need a lot of external guidance, particularly if they have never worked together before.'

There is a lack of private investment in Filey, which is not surprising because Filey is forever talking itself down.
Incomer to Filey

Many local people commented that too much of the SRB funding went on feasibility studies which led nowhere, and not enough on projects that were ready to go, if they had got the funding. The professionals' fee demands on small groups trying to get a share of grant money can bleed them dry before they even get to the starting line. Accountancy fees alone for projects that never get up and running can amount to £2,000. It cost £1,028 for an audit to allow the Coble Preservation Society to obtain charitable status. A limited company set up for one of the projects was charged £220 to get the accounts done when they only had £15 in the bank.

One community worker said that 'you quickly lose trust in the Council when they try to talk down your bid. We had to spend money we didn't have on things like professional surveys and estimates of building works in order to even be able to put in a bid. Then when you ask for £20,000 and they turn round and say, 'put in for eight and you might get it,' you have to be very strong and say, 'no, I'm going for twenty.' All of these costs suck the life blood out of small groups, using up the precious amounts of money they raise and probably doing more to strangle projects at birth than any other factor. And as two volunteers, Kath Wilkie and Geoff Carline, have found, while there are ways of getting money by learning to use the system, all of the effort required to do so rests on a few volunteers who rapidly become exhausted.

Geoff and Kath and other volunteers have a brave vision for Filey: a decent heritage centre open all year round; a multifunctional centre on the seafront offering all-weather activities; upmarket restaurants where people can enjoy the seafood Filey is famous for; quality shops that cater for all ages providing everything from clothes for children to quality gifts for tourists; a craft centre selling locally made crafts and gifts and a reintroduction of proper apprenticeships to skill young people. They also recognise that if the tourists are to come back in any numbers they need good quality hotels. A lot of small guest houses in Filey have closed and the biggest hotel that remains only has 30 rooms.

They both agree that the SRB grant funding was the push that Filey needed and that it has made an enormous impact in terms of the seafront improvements and the Evron Centre. Filey Chamber of Commerce won 'Best in Yorkshire' this year, so there are plenty of success stories in the town. What's needed now is more co-operation between the Town and Borough Councils, TIC and all the other organisations, to keep this momentum going. For example, the Chamber of Commerce would dearly love representatives from the Tourist Board to attend their meetings.

The projects that are moving ahead are mainly those that have been generated from the community itself but they do need the support of the statutory authorities. Filey is currently hoping to twin with Calvert County in the USA to encourage American tourists to come here. Filey has long claimed that the American War of Independence was fought in Filey Bay. In September 1779 John Paul Jones, a Scotsman who fought for the Americans, set sail in his ship *Bonhomme Richard* to attack a British convoy lead by Captain Pearson in the *Serapis*. After a long battle, Captain Pearson surrendered to Jones to prevent further loss of life, having bought time for the British convoy to escape to safety, but Jones's ship was already sinking so he transferred his crew to the *Serapis* and returned to France. After years of searching, the wreck of the *Bonhomme Richard*, the first American fighting ship, may have been located and in the future might be raised from its watery grave, so there seems reason to hope that some Americans at least will want to include Filey on their history trail.

SUIT-LED

The feeling from both project officers and local people in Filey was that the FBRIP was suit-led. This, more than anything, has contributed to the difficulty in getting local people to take part in the various regeneration projects. It has also in many cases reinforced the hostility in the town towards what they perceive is a Borough Council led initiative. The frequently expressed view is that '*they* assumed what we wanted.' Some people felt that the expectations of officers were very narrow but the funding potential was immense, given some imagination.

Writing a bid is the equivalent of writing a master's thesis. It takes considerable time and skill just to get a few thousand pounds for a project. Community groups need much more support to do it effectively.
Dee Heim, youth worker.

Although the Borough Council were the lead organisation in this project, this perception of the FBRIP as being suit-led is surprising, for one of the key elements in the bid was the involvement of the Filey LEADER II Steering Group. LEADER II is an EC project which tries to involve rural communities in exploring their own needs and finding ways to tackle the problem. The Filey LEADER Steering Group did undertake a community appraisal at the very beginning of the bid process which involved local residents. Most of the needs which were identified by the residents were the very ones the bid tried to tackle. So what went wrong in the public perception?

One of the problems is that although local people and the Borough Council might agree - for example that there is a need to reduce crime - they may have very different ideas about the steps needed to tackle this. If local people firmly believe that CCTV on every street corner and a greater police presence provide the only way to cut down on crime, then it doesn't matter how many initiatives you take to get the youth off the streets or improve street lighting; that will not be seen as tackling crime. And however successful it proves to be in actually cutting crime, it will not reduce the fear of crime.

To be fair, although many solutions did seem to be imposed from the top down, a case in point being the Evron Centre, one of the major problems the FBRIP had to deal with was the reluctance of local people to get involved. Therefore the project managers really didn't have much option but to get things moving by pushing down from the top, otherwise nothing would have got done at all. The Youth Centre project, for example, was a multi-agency project with representatives from the Sea Scouts, police, youth workers and residents' associations on the committee, so on paper it did appear to be community-led, but as one youth worker said: 'In practice it was still professionally led by the representatives of the authorities and organisations on the committee and we couldn't get little Johnny's mum and dad interested or involved. Only when the ordinary man and woman in the street gets involved does it truly become a community project.'

Visitors or those who have holiday homes in Filey may grumble and complain, but they obviously don't want to spend their holidays solving Filey's problems. In parts of Norfolk, the retired incomers often move up from London and come from a professional or arts background where throughout their working life they have been movers and shakers, so it is this group rather than the locals who set up the museums, art centres, music concerts, clubs and societies, because they have long experience in doing so. To some extent this is also true in Filey. For example the current

Mayor, Aileen Newbury, is an incomer and everyone agrees she tries her best to get things rolling in the town. But the majority of incomers in Filey are people who haven't had that background in organisation, management or arts in their working lives and have come here for a bit of peace and quiet in their retirement after a hard working life, and who can blame them?

The elderly clearly do want to be occupied, as the many signing up for the clubs and groups testify, and by the end of the SRB funding in 2001, twenty-four people from community groups and voluntary organisations had undergone a ten week course to develop skills in voluntary work, which has certainly helped. But it is going to take time to get others from the stage of simply attending an art class to active volunteering and getting sufficiently involved with the community to have a voice.

Until they feel safe to go out, until they feel listened to, until they feel that their opinions matter, they will not come forward for training or even to attend community meetings. But as long as solutions are imposed top-down they won't feel they are being listened to. It is a chicken and egg situation. As one resident said, 'If you are a part of a small community and you don't feel part of the bigger plan, but you know there is a bigger plan in the hands of the professionals, you don't even bother putting forward your ideas.'

WHAT DID SRB DO FOR FILEY?

The original FBRIP plan had to change due to problems over the Amtree site but brave decisions were taken, the nettle was grasped and the changes were, on the whole, good. Many small projects got funding that would not otherwise have done so if the money had been spent on Amtree, and those projects have done far more to empower the community than the Amtree Park project would have done. Though the projects were small, they were not scatter-gun, and collectively they have made a huge difference to the appearance and the potential of Filey, encouraging local people to move forward and aim higher. Evron and the Youth Centre have created two great community resources which can be used as springboards for future community projects. But major progress

Change is hard to manage, especially if it comes from change in government policy. Before we can move on, all development stops while people talk to decide what it all means.
Dee Heim, youth worker

will need big and bold thinking and it will need the community on board. Filey must come up with a creative solution which will maintain what people love about Filey, but use those same resources to make Filey work for all the residents.

SRB funding in Filey became the catalyst without which many projects funded from other sources would never have been conceived or achieved. That, I think, is the real achievement of the Filey Bay Initiative, to shake people out of the paralysis of depression into which they had sunk, demonstrate that things can be achieved and to give them the confidence and skills to do it. Though perhaps 'give them' is not strictly correct. As one volunteer said, 'There has been more community consultation in the past five years than we had in fifty years before. We are now at the jumping off point. We've learnt how not to do it and people have gained the confidence to challenge the professionals and force them to consult for real.'

But if the people of Filey are beginning to change and move forward, there still remains the problem of how you change perceptions of the rest of Britain towards Filey. How do you convince tourists that Filey is ditching its tacky, shabby, kiss-me-quick image? How do you persuade American tour companies to include Filey in the tourist circuit of London, York and Scotland? It's not an easy one to solve, but I am going to do my bit - if you haven't been to Filey for a few years, give it another chance, you'll find it's changed for the better. It is one of the loveliest little corners of Britain and I for one will certainly be going back for a holiday, and you never know, on my next visit I might finally get inside that museum.

BEESTON HILL AND HOLBECK

Dee Grijak, Vic Allen

A grey, rainy morning on the Leeds Ring Road. Feral pigeons shelter on their favourite south-east facing ledge, above the roundabout traffic on a motorway bridge. More surprising is a flock of Lapwings, at least a hundred of them, wheeling above an industrial unit. Somewhere in Beeston, in this ringroad landscape, there must be an open green space.

Richard Bell on www.wildyorkshire.co.uk

A MOVING EXPERIENCE

Beeston Hill and Holbeck - Investing in the Community *saw 54 projects initiated in Beeston Hill and Holbeck through the Leeds Initiative Regeneration Partnership between 1 April 1998 and 31 March 2005. Its aim was to develop a sustainable regeneration strategy for the area that would provide local communities with an improvement to the quality of their lives, a positive change in the perceptions of the area, and an increase in the confidence of these communities, making the area one in which people feel safe and want to live.*

A key part of the strategy was to involve the community as far as possible in deciding on how to target SRB money so that it had maximum and sustained impact. A Community Involvement Unit was conceived in order to speed up and deliver this aspiration. If successful it was intended that the Community Involvement Unit should present a model for stimulating and supporting community-centred, sustainable regeneration that might be adapted and used elsewhere in the city.

SRB total: £7.4m, Scheme Total: £20.4m

The garage owner in salubrious Otley didn't pull his punches. 'Beeston,' he said, when he heard where we going, 'I really hate that place.' A second generation Pakistani immigrant, he'd lived in the Leeds suburb for a short time in the 90s after leaving home - but got out as quickly as he could.

A more substantial but no less vernacular opinion of Beeston can be read on the 'Chavtowns' website, which invites web users to submit brief essays of the area they think is most deserving of the title 'Chavtown'.

Beeston is nominated by a certain James Hull. He describes the route from the 'filthy' Dewsbury Road to Cross Flatts Park which is 'reputedly the most murderous park in West Yorkshire', thence to the Tommy Wass public house - said to be full of 'rednecks' and surrounded by a minefield of 'trollops' who throw out a 'blizzard of obscenities' when their services are declined.

Mr Hull focuses briefly on the 'evil' Cardinal Estate with its 'overgrown gardens and alarmingly untethered Rottweilers', before concluding his Beeston snapshot at the White Rose Centre - 'packed to the rafters with cut-price sports stores, shit jewellers and burger bars.'

The 'Chavtowns' website *www.chavtowns.co.uk* invites reader responses; and one resident attempted to defend his town, only to be slapped down by yet another ex-denizen who comments: 'Beeston = rubbish. Just accept it, and move on.'

Beeston is not the sort of place that many people wish to identify with. A significant number of Leeds citizens take a delight in actively condemning it. Nor are they wholly wrong. Research has shown that most of the area covered by the SRB 4 awards is among the top 5% of deprived places in the UK. Just to be clear what this means: 'Deprivation' is measured by low income and low employment; by poor health, education and skills; by rotten housing, air quality and road safety; and, of course, by high crime levels.

A supplementary investment of £7.4m made over seven years in an area as deprived as this is not going to create - to borrow William Blake's phrase - 'a heaven in hell's despite'. The hope could only ever be that this money would generate social hubs, centres and groups with aspirations to improve and with the ability to draw down more established funding.

There remains, though, a significant and additional problem that faces Beeston Hill. It is something that both the Otley garage owner and the 'Chavtowns' correspondent bear out: Beeston is the sort of place that people 'move on' from as soon as they can.

'My son had a choice of either Leeds or Middlesex for his psychology degree. Someone told me that Leeds had the highest rate of venereal disease in the UK,
so we subtly persuaded him to go to Middlesex.'
London mother

This was confirmed by a housing study commissioned from Sheffield Hallam University in 1999/2000 by Leeds Partnership Homes. The report has influenced many of the agencies operating in the area, and has in turn been reinforced by a separate study into the Leeds housing market published in 2003 (The Leeds Housing Market: Perceptions of Change, published by the Centre for Regional Economic and Social Research, Sheffield Hallam Uniersity).

In a city where on average 66% of people have stayed at the same address for more than ten years, it was discovered that in Beeston only 44% had achieved this feat. There is a great deal more that can be said - good and bad - about Beeston: but this volatile population weakens the area's identity and its communal sense of ownership. It is perhaps the major challenge to any scheme that seeks, as 'Investing in the Community' has done, to set up sustainable social projects.

IS BEESTON'S FUTURE LEEDS' FUTURE?

According to the Council, Leeds is 'the UK's favourite city' - as distinct from the UK's favourite capital city. So successfully has it surfed the wave of fiscal and retail activity that began in the mid 80s that leaflets and local media alike boast the presence of 'Harvey Nicks' as if it were a universal token of sophistication. The Council's website glitters with words like 'vibrant', 'successful', 'thriving', 'invigorating', 'dynamic' and - of course - 'vision'.

How to measure this success? The Annual Business Inquiry records that nearly 38,000 jobs have been created in Leeds since 1996. This compares with, say, Sheffield that has created only 8,300 jobs in the same period.

Unlike its erstwhile rival in South Yorkshire, Leeds has managed to catch the balloon of its nineteenth century prosperity before it touched the floor. The very nearly iconic Town Hall, The Grand Theatre and Opera House, St Paul's House, elegant arcades and numerous other instances of Victorian, Edwardian and Georgian architecture, all testify to its sustained success. The Corn Exchange, County Arcade and Leeds Market buildings have all undergone recent facelifts.

The Council website carols the latest dawn: 'Alongside the restoration and preservation of the Leeds heritage, exciting and flourishing new developments such as pedestrian precincts, the Playhouse Theatre and superb new office accommodation have been built. In conjunction with the new developments, the Leeds Waterfront has exploded into life with a mixture of business and housing supported by shops, restaurants and hotels; all of which epitomise the city's growing status as a European centre.'

Beeston and Holbeck is a single electoral ward, and Beeston Hill and Holbeck are both classed as neighbourhood renewal priority areas. They are pre-eminent - for the wrong reasons - in the ring of urban decay that surrounds the city's feted centre. Beeston, East End Park, East Leeds, Harehills, Chapeltown, Headingley, Armley and Holbeck were all described by one Leeds City officer as 'a doughnut of crap'. He probably ought to have known better, but we should be grateful to him. It is always useful to hear the real images that underlie 'gov. speak'.

So just how much at odds with Leeds' current and glorious incarnation are the residents of Beeston and Holbeck? At one time you would have turned to the 'Index of Multiple Deprivation'. But that was always a crude tool. This was partly because the political wards it was based on were too big for the information to be of use. Deprived streets could stand close to quite affluent ones, and especially so, it seems, in Leeds. 'The Leeds housing market was characterized by sharp spatial contrasts…' reports the 2003 Sheffield Hallam University Housing Report. 'Problem areas seem to be quite contained geographically. Just look at Beeston Hill,' one private developer told the researchers, 'people want to live above the park, but no one wants to touch the other side of the park.'

In the SRB4 area of Beeston, 47% of all households are in receipt of council administered benefits (city average of 27%); all recorded crime rates are at 220 per thousand households (city average of 181), teenage pregnancy rates are significantly higher than the city average, 37% of households lack central heating (City average of 21%), 22% of households are private rented (City average is 13%), and 99% of properties are in the lowest Council Tax band.
Inner South Leeds Area Profile and Priorities Document 2004/05

Fortunately, the latest *National Index of Deprivation* (2004) is based on what are termed Super Output Areas (SOAs). These areas cover the country and have a minimum of 1,000 residents and 400 households, although the average population is 1,500. There are 32,482 covering England. The top of the list (1) means the most deprived and the least deprived is 32,482. This makes it easy to tell whether a particular SOA is in the worst 1% (324 or lower); worst 2% (649 or lower); worst 3% (974 or lower); worst 5% (1,624 or lower) or the worst 10% (3,248 or lower).

The overall deprivation 'score' is generated through seven indicators. These are: income deprivation; employment deprivation; health deprivation and disability; education, skills and training deprivation; barriers to housing and services; living environment deprivation; and crime.

When we look in detail at the indicators, the Beeston Hill and Holbeck area has two SOAs in the worst 1% for income deprivation and three in the worst 2%

for employment deprivation. There are two in the worst 3% for health, three in the worst 3% for crime and eight in the worst 3% when we consider education.

When we look at what is currently called the 'Living Environment Domain' a bad picture gets worse. Most houses lack central heating, the air is of poor quality and road traffic accidents involving injury to pedestrians or cyclists are very common. Only in barriers to housing and services do they score well. This is because of the relatively close proximity of services.

Overall the statistics show Beeston Hill and Holbeck to be very poor indeed. There are three SOAs in the worst national 1%, six in the worst 2%, seven in the worst 3%, and ten in the worst 5%. The odd one out is still in the worst 20% nationally.

Housing officers seem to have long ago decided that Beeston's array of streets can be categorised by their group names. Beverley View, Beverley Terrace, Beverley Avenue and Beverley Mount don't just share a name: they share a reputation. So it is that the SOAs reveal the poorest streets to be the Garnets, Trenthams, Woodviews, Runswicks, Recreations, Bartons, Cleveleys and Beverleys, Westbournes, Clovellys.

Thanks to its metropolitan borough status Leeds now claims ownership of, rather than mere propinquity to, the rural delights of Otley, Wetherby and Georgian Harewood. And it is worth remarking that a major landowner in Arthington which abuts Harewood is the man whose name, Quarmby, is emblazoned across the futuristic constructions now encroaching on Holbeck.

The main difference between Beeston and Holbeck is that the latter lies on the right side of the M621 for the city centre. As a result the intricate warren of buildings that comprised Leeds Foundry in Holbeck, the erstwhile source of Range Rover engine blocks, has been resurrected as a frankly 'twee' collation of design and web oriented start-up businesses.

This part of Holbeck is an area where the remnants of a community have been swept away by charismatic commercial office development, by 'urban village' developments, and by chrome-kitchened flats.

The impression that one end of Holbeck has been sluiced of residents was reinforced when we spoke to Methodist minister, Reverend Neil Bishop. He stayed on in Beeston Hill, despite a failing congregation, and piloted through to completion the SRB 4-assisted Building Blocks Centre. 'We were conscious of what happened in Holbeck, where all the different denominations pulled out simultaneously,' he told us. 'We were very conscious of that.'

Quite how secure the smoked glass and mirror-windowed future will prove for this supercharged portion of Holbeck remains to be seen. Had it cared more about history and less about 'vision', the Council website might have mentioned that Leeds has been a 'European Centre' before. In the first half of the twentieth century the Corbusier-inspired Quarry Hill Flats attracted admiration. Today the flats have been ignominiously erased, and replaced by the West Yorkshire Playhouse, the new music college, a modest music venue, a fragment of the BBC, and by the Orwellian DHSS building.

Of course, architectural megafauna like the DHSS building is not going to stray onto Beeston Hill in the near future. Essentially, like Chapeltown Beeston was strangled in the 60s by road developments that isolated it from the centre. The old Ringtons Tea factory, now studded with mobile phone masts, might make a fine casino but Beeston Hill is not going to attract the kind of radical change that is happening around Holbeck's old foundries. And there's an irony in this. This is an area where only 6% of residents (see Sheffield Hallam University's report) will admit to being 'very satisfied' with their environment. That presumably means that Beeston's transient population would have been only too willing to be 'moved on' by compulsory purchase agreements and the impact of commercial property lust. But, while the Council Housing Department aspires to pull down the Beverleys, it is not going to happen on a large scale and they are going to be restored to residential use.

Which means that somehow a population needs to be found that will learn to love the place.

'The high levels of deprivation in the area and the relatively low level of investment by the SRB4 programme in comparison to the scale of issues meant that the community didn't see widespread or large scale improvements following their engagement efforts.'
Evaluation of Community Involvement Projects in Beeston Hill and Holbeck during the SRB4 programme 1999-2005 (FWA Consulting)

WAS BEESTON HILL EVER LOVED?

Now there's a question. Once Beeston was the home of the poet Tony Harrison (born 1937) and Holbeck was where the playwright Alan Bennett (born 1934) lived. Both grew up in working class neighbourhoods that were close to the centre of Leeds but were not divided from it in quite the same way that they are now. Today anyone going into the centre of the city has to walk through a sad landscape that has been sacrificed to the car. When these two grammar school boys went across the city they went past factories and streets with little corner shops. A cyclist who now comes down the Tempest Road meets a dislocated urban landscape after passing the shops on Dewsbury Road: a sweep of motorways-manquées protected by palisades that are designed to keep pedestrians from bothering the traffic.

Tony Harrison writes with famously conflicted nostalgia about his childhood. There's an especially vivid passage about him cowering with his mother on Tempest Road as bombs fall in the Second World War; and of how, on VJ Day, huge bonfires were lit on Beeston's wide, and at the time cobbled, streets. The fires burned the telephone wires and left heaps of ash that had to be carted away in tea chests.

In 2003, the West Yorkshire Playhouse premiered a play called 'Sunbeam Terrace' by a young dramatist called Mark Catley. Sunbeam Terrace is a street at the top of the Beverleys.

More recently stil, during the Summer of 2005, the Film Four director Penny Wilcock produced 'Mischief Night', described as 'a multi-character, multi-ethnic and exuberant story set in the build up to Bonfire Night in Beeston, Leeds'. It cost £2 million. It was tough in Beeston the producer Abi Bach said, but she added: 'I'm really proud of Leeds and have really enjoyed filming here. The people are so friendly and it is easy to get around, which definitely isn't the case in London.'

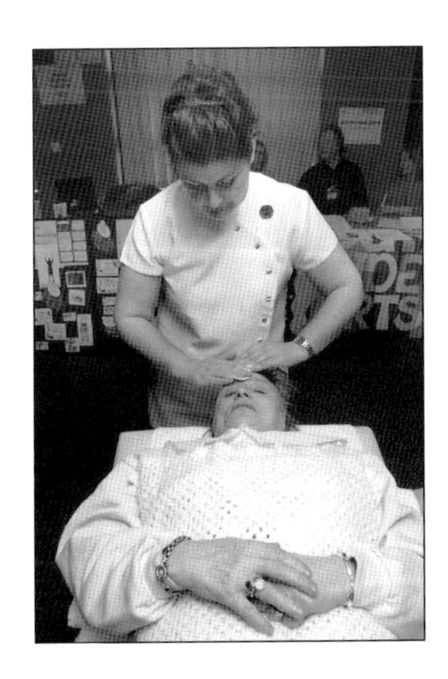

We've already said that only 6% of the Beeston population declare themselves to be 'very satisfied' with their area. But we might have said that at least 6% like the place. We could also point out that in a 2003

survey to find the most unpopular part of Leeds, Beeston actually came sixth - with 12% of people saying that they would refuse to move there. Chapeltown won the 'least popular' vote with a sizeable 25% of interviewees refusing to live there outright.

There is no doubt that the housing stock in Beeston falls a long way short of the government's definition of 'decent housing'. And yet in at least two surveys the residents there say they are only marginally more unsatisfied with their own homes than the rest of the Leeds populace.

That doesn't, however, mean that people want to stay in Beeston. In the 2003 Sheffield Hallam University survey, the area had the highest percentage of Leeds homeowners who felt 'trapped' by their inability to move, 6.6%. What this seems to mean is that the misgivings residents have about Beeston are encountered outside their front doors, not inside them.

Meanwhile it is curious that no-one offers to date the point at which Beeston's 'problem status' became officially apparent. The current writer knew the area in the early 70s when it was grubbier than it is now… but then, so was the rest of Leeds! Perhaps the sense of outrage evident in Tony Harrison's famously televised poem 'V' (1985), where the poet returns to Leeds and finds his parents' grave has been spray-painted with obscenities, is a salient moment.

BEESTON HILLS PRESENT

If the South Leeds Information Pack, put together by Leeds Council's Neighbourhood and Housing Department in 2005, had an advertising slogan, it would be the one used by British Rail just before the Tories privatised it. It would be: 'We're getting there.'

The information pack tells how partnership between community groups, politicians, voluntary and statutory agencies and the private sector has delivered 'significant improvements' in Beeston Hill and Holbeck 'over the last few years'. Says the pack: 'We now have falling crime, improving school attendance and attainment, slowly improving health and many exciting community building projects completed or coming to fruition.'

'I can't remember it exactly, but about five years ago The Headrow had three banners across it proclaiming Leeds to be 'City of Sport', 'City of Music' and 'City of summat else'. It was plain daft. It's just a 'City of People' really. But they'd never put that up.'
Leeds resident

Optimism in this kind of information pack is, on balance, more virtue than vice. But things that are 'slowly improving' and 'coming to fruition' have the muffled cheep of chickens still wearing their eggshells. Any notion that the £7.4m of SRB 4 funding (not to mention the matching £13m from private and other public sources) has 'done its job' is clearly premature.

The information pack does, though, acknowledge the SRB 4 programme as a 'significant catalyst' in regeneration. It claims that by 2007 there will have been nearly £90m invested from public and private resources in Beeston Hill and Holbeck since the start of the Millennium.

This £90m converts into projects such as new schools (£25m), new public sector housing (£20m), a swimming centre (£16m), two health centres (£8.5m), private sector housing (£4.2m), a new road link (£4m) and an FE College (£2.2m).

It's noteworthy that the 2003 Leeds Housing Report by Sheffield Hallam University found a good school to be the major common factor in people's decision to move house. And while one might quibble about the catchment area (will the new schools directly benefit Beeston Hill's predominantly BME population or was it a lure to encourage Barratt Homes' new 'urban village' in Holbeck?) the decision to invest in schooling is surely the right one.

Also 'right' is the effort that has gone into dealing with crime. The reason that Chapeltown topped the list of undesirable parts of Leeds is that it is perceived to have - and actually has - a problem with organised drug dealing. In Beeston, as distinct from Beeston Hill, the incidence of robbery, drugs and burglary is below the city's average. The figures suggest that you would still not be wise to park your car in Cross Flatts and jog the rest of your journey into work at a graphic design studio in 'The Foundry'... but the focus on crime prevention remains impressive.

And it turns out that the 'South Leeds Information Pack' is quite right. This focus is down to partnerships. The Council's consultative policy was described in 2003 by the Sheffield Hallam University Housing Report, which noted a commitment by statutory agencies in Beeston to provide decent homes, community safety and environmental management 'based on genuine rather than gestural partnership involvement'.

This initiative by Leeds City Council became, in Summer 2005, the 'Area Management Scheme'. It is an attempt to create a decentralised level of management led by ward councillors that will co-ordinate the relevant departments of the Council in a way that best suits local needs. The Area Management Team addresses issues as diverse as health, traffic, environment, housing and crime, and is charged to 'consult widely with the community'.

It is, if course, too early to judge the success of the Area Management Scheme. Councillors are not guarantors of unprejudiced local commitment. You still hear the story of the fitness-obsessed councillor who was 'disciplined' when it was discovered that he had allocated thousands of pounds to a cycle-lane that stretched from his home in Horsforth to the Town Hall. However, it has to be said that the 'profile document' produced by the Inner South Leeds Area Committee, which incorporates Beeston Hill and Holbeck, is an impressive read.

The 'Inner South Leeds Area Profile' talks repeatedly of 'hotspots', issues or locales that need attention. A six month rise in forced entry burglaries in Beeston Hill becomes a 'hotspot' for the local police; a corner of a park is a 'hotspot' for weeds; alleygateing - blocking off ginnels to make life harder for criminals - was a 'hotspot' that has been solved, now alleys are more likely to be a 'hotspot' for dog dirt.

You start to see an active link between administration and local concerns. For instance, a household survey in 2002 carried out by the Community Involvement Team found that 73% of respondents in Beeston felt that street cleaning was a priority. Now no-one would pretend that Bramhope isn't far prettier and healthier; but Beeston Hill in August 2005 has got cleaner streets and less graffiti and fewer abandoned cars than you would encounter in many deprived London suburbs. Was the SRB 4 programme - as the Neighbourhood and Housing Department Information Pack claims - a 'catalyst' for this? The answer is a simple yes. In a sense even the SRB 3 programme played a part.

'The graveyards of Leeds 2
Were hardly love-nests but they had to do –
Through clammy mackintosh and winter vest
And rumpled jumper for a touch of breast'
'Allotments' - Tony Harrison

CATALYTIC CONVERSION

The point about catalysts is that they help a reaction take place, without themselves being changed in the process. Beeston Hill and Holbeck did not get an SRB 3 award, but the process of bidding at least brought interested parties together. In fact, even before SRB 3 Leeds had expected a City Challenge award for the Beeston Hill and Holbeck area in the early 1990s but had not received one. Failure has its spin-offs, and one of these was the Cross Flatts Forum, an 'advocacy neighbourhood group' who went on to focus on LS11.

The original City Council bid for SRB 4 asked for £14 million. In the event they were given £7.4 million. On hearing the news a small community delivery team of three officers and an administrative support worker was appointed to take the reduced programme forward. This was the Community Involvement Team, whose collaborative 'new way of working' has directly influenced the creation of the Council's Area Management Scheme. When looking for evidence of an SRB 'legacy' it is conventional to cite sustainable buildings or successful community groups. In the case of Beeston Hill and Holbeck it could be that the major legacy is an administrative structure that has increased people's sense of influence over their own environment and enhanced their community pride.

But this is an issue for the future. After the award was announced the appointment of the Community Involvement Team proved arduous. By the time it was 'up and ready' in September 1999 it found that it was committed to spending a significant portion of its budget before the end of the financial year in March 2000. This regrettable symptom has been encountered before: there was a similar delay in appointing officers, with identical consequences, when Barton-upon-Humber won its SRB 3 bid.

It is an irony that winning only half of a bid, as often happens with Single Regeneration Awards, can lead to wastage. Even though scaled-down SRB projects might take less time than originally envisaged, the need to spend money to a timetable is still imposed. A halved budget doesn't mean you spend 'less of the same'; it usually means you spend differently; and time pressure can lead to reckless decisions. There is not the luxury of going back to the considered rubric of the original bid. Meanwhile, once it is realised that there won't be as much money to go around, the community politics can become invidious. People horse-trade or even totally cut the cherished visions of one section of the community so that the vision of another group of people can go forward.

Reverend Neil Bishop from the Building Blocks Centre remembers that many people 'took their bat home' when Beeston and Holbeck's SRB 4 award was halved, and lamented the professional planning and voluntary effort that was effectively squandered. The impact of this could be at least diminished if an interregnum between the announcement of the reduced award and the start of the programme was allowed.

Meanwhile the Community Involvement Team had to hit the ground running and immediately entered into a partnership with the Groundwork Trust, a charity which takes a community development approach to environmental projects and is highly active in Inner South Leeds; and Vera Media, a community video consultation company with a long working knowledge of the area. Vera Media's logo at the time seemed especially symbolic. It was a caryatid bearing a fragmentary pediment, all that remained of a once glorious roof.

A 'vox pop' video was commissioned from Vera Media, and at the same time the Community Involvement Team used a written questionnaire to find out about the community's priorities. This was distributed through the usual channels: libraries, community centres, church groups, one-stop-shops, housing offices, and fish-and-chip shops. A £50 prize draw was offered to encourage a response. A newsletter was also devised and distributed.

'If you don't improve the worse areas you will find you are sitting on a time bomb, like Bradford or Oldham. Outbreaks of crime and unrest will cost the city more in the long term.'
A private developer cited in 'The Leeds Housing Market: Perceptions of Change' (CRESC), Sheffield Hallam University June 2003

Recognising that they were an 'all white' group, the Community Involvement Team appointed four young people from the BME population on three-month contracts. This team was effective, and all have found further work in caring agencies as a result of improving their CVs. This is good news, although it is worth pointing out that 75% of the Beeston/ Holbeck population has a non-Asian lineage. Women and men who have left school over-early, but with a thirst for education and a mission in life, are found everywhere. The disadvantaged are not only found in one group.

By January 2000 the results of the questionnaire were in. Community safety was at the top of people's agenda, the environment was second, followed by housing and employment. In February 2000 a number of community meetings was called to refine these priorities, and the SRB 4 programme began in earnest.

We have taken three of the 54 projects that went on to benefit from SRB 4 funding and subjected them to closer scrutiny: the Building Blocks Centre, the Hamara Healthy Living Centre and the Canopy Project. The last of these is an admirable project that benefits the housing stock, the homeless and provides skills for young volunteers.

The first two projects take advantage of the 25% of SRB 4 funds available for capital investment but they are not simply 'prestigious building projects'. Instead they have helped to characterise a community whose character is especially fugitive.

THE BUILDING BLOCKS CENTRE

Any five-year old engineer will tell you that the frustrating thing about traditional wooden building blocks is that the buildings you can make don't have windows. Which is appropriate, because while Beeston's Building Blocks Centre has got windows, they are about as discreet as is possible for windows. This is a building that cradles its occupants and turns its back, protectively, to the street. The front door is like a back door, where an unblinking video camera hunkers down on visitors.

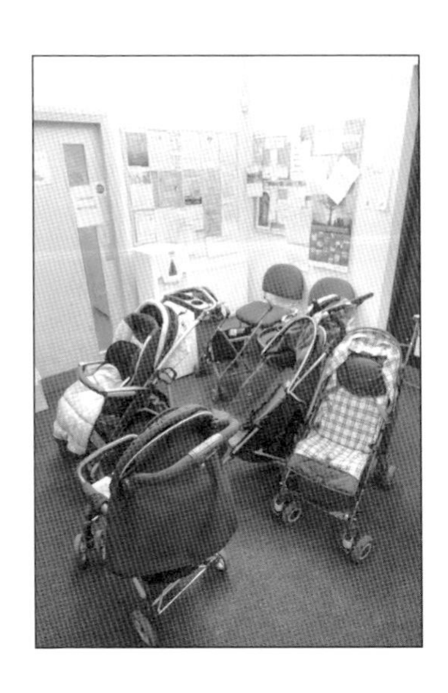

If the half-million pound 'community hall and parents resource centre' had been a municipal showcase project it would surely have exuded an alternative, transparently insincere architectural warmth. Indeed, the local Planning Department subjected the architect's proposals to close scrutiny, and absolutely insisted that the brick fascia should be lightened to match the stonework of the grade-2 listed 'parish church' next door.

'We actually didn't want light coloured bricks as they might attract graffiti,' explains the Reverend Neil A Bishop. The previous building on the site had been an 80 year-old parish hall with 'concrete disease' that was a graffiti magnet. 'Free Kashmir!' says Neil with a wry smile, but he notes that 'the new building has never had a problem with graffiti in fact.'

Twenty years ago Neil's Methodist Church and the Anglican Church next to it would together have commanded a congregation of some 300 souls. Now it is around the 30 mark. The number is small but he is glad that they have hung on.

'In the end you have to decide what you're going to do in an area where churches are declining and Muslim society is growing,' says Neil. 'There was a discussion and some people said we should just move out. In the light of what happened on 7 July with the suicide bombers' attack in London it's a good job that we didn't. We were conscious of what happened in Holbeck, where all the different denominations pulled out simultaneously.'

In 1997, prior to any talk of SRB 4, the Methodist Chapel was being used as a base for working with the elderly; in particular Bangladeshi and Pakistani groups were both using the building. The Methodists actually invested £8,000 of their own money to refurbish the Trinity Church building to make it more suitable for care of the elderly. 'But even then we couldn't disguise the fact it wasn't designed to be used as a community centre,' says Neil, 'it was warren of different rooms.'

'The local Muslim community had no public spaces, beyond the Hardy Street Mosque and a couple of houses tied together further up the hill,' says Neil. 'From our point of view the project arose out of embarrassment at having all this space and being unable to sustain it properly.'

It was against this background of misaligned resources and interests that 'Faith Together in Leeds 11' was born. The registered charity comprises nine member organisations including Muslim, Christian and non-religious groups, and serves the health and community needs of disadvantaged groups in the Leeds 11 postcode area. Neil is the company secretary of 'FtinLS11'. The quietly celebrated organisation lies behind the

'The SRB project was set up to spawn bureaucracy! We'd often say how 'a lot fewer people achieved just as much.'
Rev Neil A Bishop

creation of both the Building Blocks Centre and the Hamara Healthy Living Centre which eventually took over the Trinity Church site.

The Building Blocks Centre cost approximately half a million pounds to build, the bulk of which, £205,000, came from the Community Fund. Leeds Council and various Methodist Church funds accounted for another £60 - £70,000 each, and a private trust furnished another £50,000.

A further £150,000 came from the sale of the Trinity Methodist Church to Hamara. This purchase demonstrates the close affiliation between the Building Blocks Centre and the Hamara Centre, since it was made possible by persuading a charitable foundation to purchase the church on Hamara's behalf.

'We entered into a mini-agreement with them whereby we undertook to use our best efforts to encourage Hamara to redevelop the church into a Healthy Living Centre - which they duly did without the need for much encouragement,' says Neil. 'Our solicitor described it as a curious little document.'

To manage the construction of a new building is not easy; to worry at the same time about raising funds and meeting the protocols of a dozen trusts and statutory funding schemes, is a nightmare. To handle all this while delivering community services such as childcare invokes a level of personal commitment that 'professionals' routinely undervalue, or acknowledge only with glib phrases.

'The complexity of the project was horrendous,' says Neil, who cites a £16,000 legal bill that had to be met by the FtinLS11 – in addition to the significant legal costs incurred by the two churches. He was fortunate that one of his congregation worked for the Bradford and Bingley Building Society and was willing to do the very substantial 'number crunching'.

This raises the issue of 'sweat equity' that is attached to any 'match funding' scheme. If organisations such as Yorkshire Forward are happy to seek out and pay consultants to review and advise on projects, they must also accept with equanimity any claims made for the services of such volunteers and claims for the advocacy and networking skills of the Neil Bishops of this world.

After some initial hesitation the Regeneration Partnership Unit did recognise the importance of the Bradford and Bingley volunteer. She was eventually given a salary for 18 months because her intimate knowledge of the project became vital. As Neil points out: 'It became difficult to engage even experts unless they knew the whole story.'

The Building Blocks Project took six years to bring to fruition. Volunteers worked in the knowledge that their efforts might achieve nothing; and yet many stayed the course. Over the same period the management of SRB funding moved from the Government Office to Yorkshire Forward, and 'FtinLS11' had to engage with four different SRB project managers.

The impact of these 'professional' adjustments on the volunteers of 'FtinLS11' was not remunerated. 'The SRB process was set up to spawn bureaucracy,' says Neil plainly, 'we'd often say how a lot fewer people achieved just as much.'

Volunteer morale was given a major blow when the original bid was halved from £14 million to £7.4 million. The original application had involved a great deal of excellent work by individuals from a variety of backgrounds. These included government departments, research and community action groups.

'When it was turned down, rather than say, what shall we cut? - we said, let's start again,' recalls Neil. 'And a lot of people took their bat home. Me and Hanif Malik, the Director of the Hamara Healthy Living Centre, persevered.'

Not surprisingly one of Neil's criticisms of the SRB application process was the misaligned attitude of guidance officers and assessment officers: 'We'd say, 'Are you sure we're okay with this?' and guidance officers would say, 'Don't worry,' but they weren't the same people who monitored the project.'

'Some Council officers bent over backwards to help us. There were things people had done that we couldn't acknowledge in the Opening Ceremony.'
Rev Neil A Bishop

He is, on the other hand, quick to pay dues to the council-funded 'Regeneration Partnership Group', who helped 'FtinLS11' with tasks such as comparing their project with other SRB projects - 'We had no idea where to start that!' - and he candidly remarks on how some officials had 'bent over backwards' to help in ways that often stretched the rubric.

It is not unusual to find officers in the SRB landscape who have gone native. Yesterday's community activists become today's government employees, and many have had experience of social projects from Neil and Hanif Malik's perspective. As we recognise in the section on FreshAire, officers subvert processes. It is not that anything illegal happens; but they duck, dodge and body-swerve on behalf of the community they serve, bending rules and offering advice with a wink. 'There were things people had done that we couldn't acknowledge in the opening ceremony!' says Neil.

The Building Blocks Centre obtained several different SRB 4 grants, some relating to the building - eg the CCTV camera which is part of a security package recommended by the Home Office - and some relating to the delivery of parent support services. Neil was particularly pleased with an initial, modest grant of SRB money that helped establish whether the project was applicable for development.

Given the Methodist leadership for the new Centre, it was never in doubt that it would be used for worship (on Sundays and weekday evenings) and for traditional church/community activities. These presently include a Chinese exercise class, community form filling support, activities for asylum seekers and their children, and a 'Read It' club for primary school children.

The decision to adopt 'parent support' as a social remit for the centre came about because one of the church members was also a childcare professional. 'She felt that better childcare was a crying need in the locality. I picked her concern up and ran with it, very much at her instigation.'

That Beeston Hill needed parent support was also illustrated by high social service referral rates. There was, however, a great deal of confusion at the time about the intentions of the government child development agency, SureStart. This seemed to have been resolved once the Building Blocks Centre was operating under the SRB 4 programme. At this stage the centre was offering a wide scope of activities that were 'free to the service user'; for instance, special activities for teenage mothers, IT courses and community safety events.

SureStart courses were offered in conjunction with these activities; baby massage, for instance, or special support for asylum seeker mothers. And then the agency withdrew. 'They claimed our centre was too expensive to use compared to various unregenerated church halls and a portacabin they had erected,' says Neil. As the Building Blocks Centre moves further away from its heady, grant-aided status and wrestles with financial sustainability, it seems that this is one instance where the centralised directives of a government initiative have failed to embrace the expression of a local need.

If there were dissenters within 'FtinLS11' regarding the Building Blocks Centre - and there were - there was also suspicion in the community at large. 'Once the building work started here there was a lot of local hostility because people didn't know what it was going to be,' says Neil. 'I was threatened outside the building late one night. Muslim young people would see the very small cross on top of the building and say, 'That isn't going to be there long, we'll soon get that down'.'

The design of both buildings, observes Neil, discourages entry by battering ram! He also notes that once people started using them any conflict subsided. This could be read as an expression of the way both 'FtinLS11' projects have helped to mediate the character of the area. 'We exceeded all of our targets. In no time at all, the place was heaving.'

Monitoring the building's performance has been time-consuming and often tedious work. From the first 'FtinLS11' was advised not to over-egg its targets in the hope of impressing grant-giving bodies. This is a trap that the early SRB bids often fell into, and this advice is an encouraging sign that the system is maturing. It's easy to promise too many community safety events, for instance. 'While 60 people might turn up for the first talk on domestic fire alarms,' says Neil, 'it tends to diminish thereafter.'

'Every night before we go to bed, we must ask ourselves how much good have we done?'
Hilary Benn MP

One of the strengths of the Building Blocks Centre is that it has been designed to evolve. Neil met us in a room which had hip-level plug sockets, enabling it to be used as an IT room without compromising its potential as a nursery space. This rightly suggests that thought was given to sustaining the building after the glamour of the launch, although there can never be guarantees about revenue. The Centre is currently operating at an annual cost of just over £100,000.

The Autumn 2005 programme features regular courses at the Centre on four days of the week. These range from English as a Second Language, to Computers, to Crochet, and most now charge participants. The Centre has also taken over the only remaining playgroup in Leeds 11, although this is run from a different location. Inevitably, though, the daily crèche and nursery provision are regarded as the building's most sustained revenue point.

'The shortfall for this year is down to £5,000,' says Neil when we question him about sustainability. 'That's assuming that the nursery continues to grow in line with the projections in our business plan.' The Building Blocks Centre seems to be squaring up honestly to the task of balancing its books; and that was, after all, part of the SRB 4 bargain but in the climate of Beeston Hill it still seems like 'a big ask'.

The Evaluation Document (produced in May 2005 by FWA Consulting) on the Beeston Hill and Holbeck programme is generally very positive, but makes several references to the need to continue supporting these initiatives 'in the medium to long term'. It makes special mention of the increasingly sophisticated support needed by 'flagship projects' thus: 'It is vital that these projects do not fail for lack of support, as the consequence of crashing could be profound on community confidence and external perceptions about the area.'

It is telling that Neil, who has an attractive ability to convey a cynical appraisal without dropping the optimism that is a requisite of faith, used the word 'flagship' only once. The Building Blocks Centre, he said, was seen as a flagship project for the erstwhile Labour-controlled council. There was no doubt in his mind that interest in the Centre's achievements waned after political control changed hands. But the weather-cock turned again when Beeston was identified as the home of two of the London bombers: 'Now we're an example of a multi-ethnic project, because 70% of our users are Muslims and 30% are not.'

This identification of the Building Blocks Centre as an 'ethnic' project made us uncomfortable. Neil, however, cited research commissioned from Sheffield Hallam University that recommended that the Asian population should be the one that was encouraged to put down roots. 'Some of the people in our group said that too much was being spent on the ethnic families. But that was the whole reason we got the money. I had to remind some of the white people that we wouldn't have got the building without it.'

And while the ethnic and inter-faith emphases of the project might have been prompted by pragmatic funding reasons, Neil is keen to stress that they have come to play a more pro-active role. 'All the partners in the project now believe community cohesion – and faith cohesion – are vital to what the project has achieved.'

He cited research commissioned from Sheffield Hallam University that showed how over 40% of Beeston Hill's population had changed between 1990 and 2000; and he remarked how the survey recommended that the Asian population should be the one that was encouraged to put down roots.

The challenge now facing the Centre is to stay focused on its community targets while meeting its 'social enterprise', or revenue, expectations. 'The trouble is that the commercial impetus takes over,' Neil says; which made us think he was contemplating opening a burger bar. Instead he mentions the OFSTED restrictions that prevent children under 3 sharing a nursery room with older children. The Centre has to meet this restriction to stay in the 'marketplace'; yet it seriously diminishes the value of the Centre to families who, say, have a two-year old child and a four-year old child.
Neil takes us on a final tour of the Centre, and we remark again how the building manages to pack itself into such a small 'footprint'. Particularly arresting is the room used for worship: a slim, pomegranate-coloured atrium with an almost discreet cross. Our last act is to give Neil £35 to

'Holbeck Urban Village isn't just about the business side of the creative industries, it's also about building the relationship with the surrounding community through arts, education and improved high quality public space provisions.'
Vanessa Allen, Holbeck Urban Village Project Manager for Leeds City Council

remunerate the Centre for the time he has spent with us. Now there is enterprise and commitment to sustainability.

The external evaluation of the project was carried out by Barnardos and is unabashedly positive: '...it was evident that the support offered to families is invaluable,' it concludes. At the opening ceremony on 7 November 2003, The Rt Hon Hilary Benn MP told the press: 'Every night before we go to bed we must ask ourselves how much good have we done?' It is probably the ultimate testament to the Building Blocks Centre that it can vindicate such a question.

THE HAMARA HEALTHY LIVING CENTRE

Hanif Malik takes some tracking down. He's a man who seems to be permanently in meeting mode. I am in the Hamara Healthy Living Centre Café admiring the carpet which, while it must be comparatively new, looks as stained as a sea full of jellyfish. At the table opposite me, an affable, professional bloke is holding a formal interview with a mother and child in Urdu. The kitchen staff are bantering with some late-lunchers. But I'm more absorbed with the flock of community notices that must have waited for years like transatlantic albatrosses for somewhere to roost.

- Dealing with cancer? Getting to hospital shouldn't be your biggest worry.
- Leeds, a city uniting against racist crime
- Do you have diabetes?

There's also a poster in Urdu that shows a woman in a red head scarf cooking with butter and ghee. Here too is the 'Londonbombvictims.co.uk' poster, which I have seen several times: but only in Beeston.

Hanif appears and we go into a room marked 'Surgery'. 'I used to be a Beeston resident. I lived here for nine years, and moved out seven years ago…' he begins.

Originally he worked in the private sector: for BT, then HSBC, and then spent two years working for himself. In 1997 he took a job as a development worker for the South Leeds Elderly and Development Group solely to do something more in line with his Muslim faith. 'For me it was an attempt to get away from 'capitalist society',' he says happily. You don't hear that sort of talk too often these days.

'Then, we were addressing a serious void in statutory service provision. People like my dad came here in their 20s and worked hard in order to bring their young families over. There are people we've discovered who have never, ever taken a holiday. Now they are all in their 60s and 70s, but we don't have in this country a system for coping with an aging population that gives regard to their own culture and faith.'

Hanif acknowledges that things have got better in recent years, but at the time direct action was required. He and his co-workers hired the room in Trinity Methodist Church, where they immediately found in the Reverend Neil Bishop 'a like-minded individual keen to improve the lot of the community as a whole.'

'SRB was the catalyst that brought us together. We went to the initial meeting and like everyone else we wanted to see if we could get a slice of the cake. We were told quite clearly that the key to accessing the funding is partnerships. So we came out and formed a partnership that mushroomed into 'Faith Together in Leeds 11'.'

'The most wonderful thing about 'FtinLS11' is not only that it created these two buildings, the Hamara Healthy Living Centre and the Building Blocks Centre, which together cost in excess of £2.5 million: it's that it's been driven by local people. It was a very strange mix. A couple of reverends, me, some elderly local folk: to my way of thinking it's about the best example of what local people can achieve.'

'People like my dad came here in their 20s and worked hard in order to bring their young families over. There are people we've discovered who have never ever taken a holiday.'
Hanif Malik

It's hard not to like Hanif, or what he says. But, we ask him, didn't the Leeds Urban Initiative 'poach' him? In the way that councils and government agencies do, when they want to 'prove' to an electorate that they are taking an interest in real people's lives, by co-opting a grass roots worker? The worker exchanges his integrity for a civil service pension, and the grass roots project that helped establish him is temporarily or permanently derailed.

Hanif saw the paradox. 'When I plucked up the courage to tell my Chair I was leaving, I suggested I was going to pick up skills and bring them back here,' he says. 'I reminded him of that 18 months later when I returned. The point is that in those 18 months 'FtinLS11' had moved from an idea - somebody said a dream - to actually having some potential.'

'Here in Beeston was a once in a lifetime opportunity. But it was only going to happen with a full time commitment. 'Making a Difference' is now a very over-used term: but that was absolutely what it was about. It's always been my motto that if you're going to bring about change you've got to get off your backside and do something about it. The vast majority of people don't have the time because of children or other commitments. I don't want to sound like Mahatma Gandhi, but somehow I felt myself almost inadvertently responsible for these people.'

Hanif's work with Leeds Urban Initiative was in the Chapeltown/Harehills area: historically the part of Leeds most identified with racial tension. It offered an interesting comparison. 'They had a Polish Centre, a Pakistani Centre, an Irish Centre, the Northern School of Contemporary Dance. It was wonderfully well resourced. I came back to Beeston and it was like a time warp. There wasn't a single community resource.'

It was a condition of the SRB 4 award that only 25% of the money could be spent on capital schemes. While historically it is surely the case that renewal schemes place too much emphasis on buildings; there might have been a case for reviewing this restriction in Beeston. It's a place that needs communal areas. At least the stark contrast with Chapeltown's plethora of ethnic and activity-based buildings meant that Hamara attracted an urgent and diverse range of activities: Health Information, Exercise, Counselling, Skill Courses, Welfare and Benefits Surgeries, Translation Services, Respite Care.

It might seem at odds with the geriatric mission that inspired the building, but when Hanif and his co-workers asked the elderly what worried them most, they would usually respond with the concerns that their grandchildren were facing.

'In Chapeltown I was given a database of 180 care organisations which highlighted the enormous level of activity there, including a certain degree of duplication. There was competition! In Beeston when we went to tackle a particular service area, we found that nobody else was doing it.'

Hanif endorses the history of 'FtinLS11' put forward by Neil Bishop, including the times when the whole initiative seemed to have died. But he's resolutely sanguine about it: 'The bottom line is, without SRB 4 none of this would have happened. I'm very reluctant to criticise the initiative.'

'My criticism would be at the government. Time and again these three, four and seven year regeneration schemes like Leeds Urban Initiative - a three year programme - create very good institutions that close down because of problems with sustainability. The argument is that 'grant culture' creates a climate of dependency in the local community. I see where it's coming from, but I would argue with that to some extent.'

And so would we. Bureaucrats delight in the process of drawing up bids, visiting new projects, meeting people who might advance their careers, and launching new projects; but they also gain employment from stop-gap measures and protracted post mortems. And they are less than disappointed when the bidding process has to start all over again in order to redress a community need that has remained unsolved. Bureaucrats make a secure living from projects that are not sustainable. This should never be forgotten.

The SRB scheme is characterised as a 'pump priming' initiative. The metaphor refers to the need to fill the chamber of a pump with a little water, in order to create the suction necessary to pull up a lot of water. This will only happen, of course, if the pump is linked to a well with a lot of water in it.

'Chapeltown was wonderfully well-resourced. I came back to Beeston and it was like a time warp. There wasn't a single community resource.'
Hanif Malik

The Hamara Centre seems always to be buzzing with life. Its societal and social success is inescapable: but is it sustainable? Had 'FtinLS11' reckoned up all the public grant schemes, all the council initiatives, all the private trust resources, and all the commercial revenue points - and pieced together a set of balanced accounts that would come into effect once the grant-aided honeymoon finished?

'If I'm honest, it wasn't high up on our priorities at the time we received our SRB money,' says Hanif, swallowing the cyanide pill of honesty, 'seven years seemed a long time ahead.'

'I think that there's a case to be made for looking at how statutory services can become more involved in sustaining key initiatives. This is a centre for all, but its majority use is for the Asian community. Most of them use it several times a week. But it's for others to decide what criteria denote a key initiative.'

The Evaluation Document (produced in May 2005 by FWA Consulting) on the SRB projects in the Beeston Hilll and Holbeck programme argues for sustained support rather than what is currently an unrealistic insistence on sustainability. This is because projects like Hamara make the area attractive for other investors but they also have identifiable effects on the community. 'The community has demonstrated an appetite for making things happen itself...' say the consultants behind the Evaluation Document. 'The community is increasingly prepared to take risks with innovation... the area can produce able and willing community leaders who have proved ready to take up positions of governance and influence.'

An analysis like this should have meant that men in smart suits popped around to see Hanif to tell him to keep up the good work and 'not to worry about money for a while.' They didn't, of course. He is still chasing the sustainable ideal.

'We were very quickly aware that our funding income was lop-sided,' he says, '90% of it was coming from trusts and statutory sources: there wasn't any that was timeless. In the next 3 - 5 years our ambitious target is balancing that to 50:50. In terms of 'social enterprise' we thought of this 3 - 4 years ago. We designed the building so that we could hire out the hall; looked at the kitchen to potentially contract out a meals-on-wheels service.'

Perhaps Hanif and the project officers need faulting for a lack of rigour. But the regeneration of Beeston Hill and Holbeck is a deep well; and the pump was always going to need priming more than once. We push him a little further and Hanif finally shows a little of the radicalism that nipped in the bud his career as an HSBC middle manager. 'We care about sustainability, but to be honest I'm more aware that it would become easy to lose the ethos of what we are here to do. You have to meet the ethos of a community voluntary organisation.

'The feedback we've had about this centre is absolutely fantastic. The number of people we've had through the door justifies all the hard work. We still have challenges: I would like to see the building used by the wider community…'

He's aware that there have been criticisms about ethnic exclusivity, then?

'Yes, but it's not about issues. It's about perceptions. It's about the feeling people have that they can't drop in and have a cup of tea or take a course in IT Training. But anyone can do that.'

We had previously visited the Hamara Centre on the day of a community health fair. Here in the main hall you could apparently 'buy' any disease you wanted - from cataracts to chlamydia to acne; but what was most evident was that the throng milling between the stalls was in no way exclusively ethnic.

That's not to say that Hamara won't always need to work at its image. Its Urdu name was chosen after community consultation, but it is still not calculated to appease the understandably uncertain white community living on the other side of Cross Flatts Park, even if Hamara does mean 'ours'. 'We thought of putting a 'T' in front of the sign on the building,' quips Hanif. 'In Urdu, 'Thamara' means 'yours'!'

The most wonderful thing about FtinLS11 is not only that it created these two buildings that together cost in excess of £2.5m: it's that it's been driven by local people.

It was never part of their aim, says Hanif, but the success of Hamara has put Beeston on the map. 'Even prior to the events of 7 July people in Leeds had heard of Hamara. It's played a major part in the regeneration of the locality - which is what SRB is all about. It makes all the difference to people coming into the area and thinking they wouldn't mind living here.'

The evidence we've seen suggests this is a slightly optimistic assessment; but Hanif will not brook our caution. 'It's changed,' he says. 'Not least because of the housing boom. There are terraced properties opposite Hamara that used to go for £20,000, that now go for £100,000. I think there is more of a community feel. I think that the £7.4m that has come in here has contributed to that. This community needed an injection of cash.

'I dread to think what the community would be without that SRB 4 initiative. There is more work required, but there's much more of a sense of optimism. There used to be a great sense of pessimism, but there seems to be a greater degree of optimism.'

THE BEESTON CANOPY PROJECT

The Canopy housing project started in 1997, first in Chapeltown, then in Burley Lodge. The founders who lived in Hyde Park realised that these were areas with a lot of derelict buildings, coupled with an abundance of young people who were excluded from mainstream provision. Rather than leave them to kick their heels in limbo, Canopy offered young volunteers the chance to learn a range of useful skills, while bringing derelict properties back into use. The volunteers worked alongside the people who would ultimately benefit from the house that was being renovated, the homeless.

It was the kind of work that young people enjoyed, while the homeless person was playing a part in his or her own future. Everyone was a winner. Derelict houses became homes for those in need, and in the process Canopy helped regenerate the local community and improve the area.

If it had bought the houses it improved, Canopy would presumably be embarrassed by its assets now. But it didn't.

'We wish we could have,' says Lisa, who has been with Canopy since the beginning. 'We wouldn't have the funding issues we have now … houses that only cost £15,000 a few years ago are now worth £70,000. The whole project came out of nothing. It was very hard at first to get councils and housing associations to work with us. Now we have a management agreement with the Council and housing associations.'

Canopy has refurbished twenty properties in Hyde Park, along with ten in Beeston. They have leases on another twelve disused properties in Beeston that are due to be renovated. The Council undertakes major works like re-roofing or putting in new windows. Canopy does the rest of the work to bring the property up to scratch, and then it manages the properties for a peppercorn rent for a fixed period, anything from five to fifteen years. For all this input Canopy has achieved a mortgage on only one house in Beeston. It is not what you would call a significant landlord portfolio.

A mix of rental income and private trust money keeps Canopy afloat, even if it doesn't pay for the significant amount of extra work required to support the tenants and train the volunteers. The private trust money which Canopy raises itself was particularly important in the early years. Canopy also received money from SRB 4 funding, for which it was very grateful and which it would willingly accept again.

The headquarters of the Canopy housing scheme on Ladypit Lane are busy as usual. This is Beeston on a sunny day, two months after the national media had swarmed up the M1, looking for disaffected communities to put under the microscope. Beeston isn't glamorous but it isn't Dante's Inferno either. You can see worse in 'multi-ethnic', 'culturally vibrant', self-promoting London. One of the tenants from Canopy sits in the kitchen, flicking through the Australian *Women's Weekly Book of Curries*. She has borrowed it from one of the full-time staff on this project.

Jake and Laura, two volunteers from a local school, move around the kitchen. This is new to them and worth doing. They are about to start work on a nearby house that Canopy is helping to renovate. Helen, the tenant reading up on curries, moved into just such a house nearly two years ago. It says a lot about Canopy that Helen still drops round on an informal basis. Stand outside the Canopy headquarters on any given day and you see a steady flow of people dropping by for a coffee, or for help with form-filling. They vary from asylum seekers to local mums.

'Problem areas seem to be quite contained geographically, just look at Beeston Hill. People want to live above the park but no one wants to touch the other side of the park.'
Private developer cited in 'The Leeds Housing Market: Perceptions of Change' (CRESC), Sheffield Hallam University June 2003

Rosie, one of the full-time workers from Canopy, is to take me to a house they are doing up. She leads the way to Ingleton Street, with Jake and Laura bringing up the rear. Jake sucks on a cigarette while Laura's creole earrings, the size of small plates, sway gently. Crossing from row to row of redbrick houses, there's little evidence of vandalism, and there isn't much trash in the streets. The people aren't hostile. There are, however, lots of front doors and ground floor windows with lockable metal grilles for protection. Some of them even are quite decorative; but they're not there to make things look pretty.

The house on Ingleton Street is all floorboards and walls that need filling. The builders have finished the roof repairs and put in new windows; the new kitchen and bathroom are being fitted, and a small posse of volunteers is stripping off wallpaper, filling in cracks and sanding woodwork. There are an awful lot of walls and ceilings to skim. Jake and Laura disappear upstairs. Rosie discusses the state of the ceiling with a volunteer perched on a stepladder. Up another flight of steps is Sonia, Canopy's star volunteer, who is steaming off wallpaper under the watchful eye of another Canopy staffer, Gary.

Our next stop is a nearly completed house just over the road. Alex, a full-time Canopy worker, is chipping paintwork from an outside widow. Inside, a group of three volunteers from Cameroon - all asylum seekers - are working on the kitchen, while a young man is sealing woodwork on the stairs. The whole interior looks like something from a *Good Housekeeping* colour spread.

We return to the headquarters on Ladypit Lane and settle outside the door in the sunshine. Rosie is here to explain as much as she can about Canopy. She is a relative newcomer, but knows about the day-to-day experiences of the tenants and volunteers. While Canopy in Hyde Park dealt with general homelessness, the Beeston model specifically addresses the needs of refugees and asylum seekers.

Rosie explains that some of the properties are leased to them for as little as five years because of the threat of demolition. The possibility of a future compulsory purchase order - the 'Beverleys' in Beeston are an obvious example - creates uncertainty and makes it harder to regenerate an area of need. There are some areas of Beeston that have remained derelict since 1998 because of the threat of demolition. Neither private nor public sector

investors gain any benefit from improving the housing stock under these conditions. The residents are the inevitable losers. In this climate community roots are shallow.

Would Rosie be glad to see the old back-to-backs go, should the Council find a private partner for its Beeston Hill regeneration plans? She quite likes the back-to-backs, she declares. 'You can always knock them through to make them bigger, and even add gardens. In the end, back-to-backs are no different from a high-rise flat; same size, and no garden. Only with a back-to-back you get your own door and access to a street. You find a lot of back-to-backs in Hyde Park, Burley, Hare Hills and East End Park. Some of those areas are really nice now.' Both Rosie and Lisa can cite examples of 'new-build' that resulted in worse housing.

The largest group to get help from Canopy in Beeston are refugees - single or with families - aged sixteen and up. So it is those who have just arrived in the UK or who have just received their refugee status, that form the core of their tenants. Prospective tenants can spend as much as three months working with volunteers to get the house up to scratch, and then they move in.

Jake and Laura, who made an appearance earlier on, are part of a different training strand being developed by Canopy. They belong to a trial schools project. Local pupils who are not doing full-time GCSEs spend three months volunteering on a house renewal scheme. They are not in housing need, but they benefit from the training and support. In this way, local kids get to work with refugees, and people who would not normally mix together get to know each other better.

Helen comes to sit on the doorstep with the rest of us and explains how she came to live in Beeston. 'I was in a hostel with my kids and my supporting keyworker phoned up Canopy to see if there was any accommodation for me. They showed me two houses and I chose the biggest one!' Helen has four children.

Stand outside the Canopy headquarters on any given day and you see a steady flow of people dropping by for a coffee, or for help with form-filling. They vary from asylum seekers to local mums.

'Are you still decorating it, Helen?' asks Rosie.

'Yes,' says Helen. 'I've decorated it six times in two years. I did a lot of the painting and decorating before I moved in, as well as all the other stuff. I'd never plastered anything before, never done any woodwork. It was a good experience for me and I enjoyed sanding wood and doing the skirting boards.'

Helen's house had been a burnt-out shell before she moved in, a bare brick structure in need of new ceilings and walls. But the house is just one part of her new life. 'I know most of the tenants here - Sandra, Michelle, Joseph, Mike and Sasha and Sam - and half of the people with Canopy in Hyde Park, too.' Helen likes Beeston.

Canopy is making quite a difference to a considerable number of people. It's the quality of support that they provide that is so unusual. But the project is at a crossroads. It has been asked to abandon its version of tenant support for the more usual 'floating support' provided by other agencies.

Lisa explains: 'With us, housing is part of a package. The kind of help our people get from their support workers is intense. We see people a lot, and when they don't need our support any more, we help them move out.

'Floating support would mean we would have no drop-in office, and we would literally float in and out of people's lives. So for instance, I'd go round to Helen's house, see her maybe for one hour twice a week, and leave again. We'd also be visiting people who would be scattered around the city. We'd spend a lot of our time travelling - there would be no room for support workers to just pop round and check that everything was OK. There would be less sense of community.'

Canopy in Beeston provides an unusual service. Not only does the voluntary work benefit young people and isolated asylum seekers, but the improvement to housing stock brings up the area, and the drop-in centre provides a much needed sense of neighbourliness. People know each other and are inclined to lend a hand.

For instance, when Canopy made a video of its nascent schools project - the kind that Jake and Laura are involved in - it needed to play it back on a video recorder. Helen provided the facilities, and also laid on ham sandwiches, cakes and juice for five kids and one support worker. Rosie is very pleased with the mix of volunteers they have accumulated. There's a 16-year old asylum seeker from Cameroon called Alain who will hopefully be starting college next week. Without Canopy he would be stuck in his bed and breakfast accommodation, a French speaker cast adrift with few contacts and nowhere to go.

'We want to work more with Social Services,' says Rosie. 'There are a lot of unaccompanied minors like Alain who arrive in this country. We want to help get them skills and training. And then there are the young people who have just come out of care and have no roots. This kind of project is good for them too. We have one building in Sefton Flatts which is being converted into three self-contained living spaces, plus a communal area. It's ideal for that type of isolated young person.'

And in spite of the negative press surrounding asylum seekers, refugee status does not automatically confer on each newcomer the mindset of a street-wise survivor. Rosie can cite examples of people whose naivety is such, she wonders what might have become of them had they not found their way to the drop-in centre on Ladypit Lane. The hope is that more asylum seekers will be signposted to Canopy in the future; it offers them somewhere to go for advice and support. It also helps integration within the community.

Not everyone has a speedy decision. Rosie knows of one volunteer from Pakistan who has been waiting three years for a final answer. The project has helped him immensely. It has stopped him feeling isolated and helped his confidence. He finds the volunteer work therapeutic, given the levels of uncertainty in his life.

'In the end, back-to-backs are no different from a high-rise flat; same size, and no garden. Only with a back-to-back you get your own door and access to a street.'
Canopy housing volunteer

There are plans afoot to start up a social enterprise business, a profit making company that will mean an extra source of revenue to keep Canopy going. The idea is that when the Council puts roofing and related contracts out to tender on Canopy houses, Canopy should bid for this work itself.

Today everyone is thinking long and hard about ways of maintaining the level of support that Canopy provides this community. Part of Canopy's problem is that it doesn't fit neatly into a single defined area of activity. Canopy ticks boxes for regeneration, integration, housing needs, exclusion, unemployment, mental health and learning disabilities. What should be a shining example of 'joined-up thinking' becomes, in the world of bureaucrats and funding initiatives, a form-filling nightmare. It falls between too many stools.

Canopy's workers are cautiously optimistic. Perhaps they will stay the same, perhaps they will change beyond all recognition. But for Alain and Helen and Sonia and Sasha and a host of others, Canopy has already made a lasting difference.

Long may it continue.

BEESTON AND THE BOMBS

The Beeston that belongs to the poet Tony Harrison provided the backdrop for a bright working class boy who seized his educational chances and painfully destroyed his family context as a result. The playwright Mark Catley's Beeston produced a story of white moral squalor and disappointed hero worship. But it turns out there was another story: about a boy who once wanted to play for the English Cricket Team; who was perhaps implicated in the mob attack and murder of a 16 year-old in Beeston in April 2004; who became a loner and regular mosque attender, and who ended his life one morning by detonating a bomb in Aldgate Tube Station on 7 July 2005.

Two months later, as we drove into the area, the car radio revealed that BBC Radio 5 was broadcasting 'live from Beeston'. Even now, after acres of media coverage, the journalist struggled to find the influences that had made the London bombers do what they did. A significant part of her report actually came from Bradford, where the history of racial problems is more substantiated.

Beeston has however known a high level of racism. Max Farrar, a sociologist at Leeds Metropolitan University, remembers working here to protect Muslim homes against racist attacks in the early 80s. But revisiting

Craven politicians offering only better management demand nothing noble.

Polly Toynbee 2005

the area after the London bombing, Farrar concluded 'this was a neighbourhood where 'race' was not a major problem.' He is unusual. Most of the print media that came to Beeston found disaffected youths on street corners, who readily obliged them with racist remarks.

Meanwhile, the Reverend Neil Bishop and Hanif Malik were inevitably sucked into the feeding frenzy. Neil, who speaks Spanish, was especially impressed by a Spanish journalist and went out of his way to help him; but when he came across the newspaper several days later the opening line read: 'There is a hell, and it's called Beeston…'

The 'rationale' behind the bombings seemed to have no special relevance to either SRB 4 funding or 'Beeston' as an area. We did not want to be part of the ghoulish order of journalists that had descended on the village and written about a Beeston that was 'deprived and punctuated at every street corner with rotting mattresses and stinking skips,' or 'a fearful community divided by ignorance and racial tension.'

But of course, what happened to us was that everyone actually wanted to talk about the incident, for the quite legitimate reason that the news had impacted on their status. And this could almost be a good thing.

The Evaluation Document (produced in May 2005 by FWA Consulting) on the SRB projects in the Beeston Hilll and Holbeck programme refers to a 'danger gap' experienced in other parts of the country when the momentum inspired by SRB funding has been allowed to drop. The Document concludes: 'There is probably a cost-benefit argument in favour of retaining a strategic and suitably resourced commitment to support community engagement in Beeston Hill and Holbeck until such time as it reaches its own critical mass of strength, stability and independence.'

It is small compensation for the loss of life, but the bombers just might have given renewed importance to SRB 4 projects that might otherwise have run out of steam. Of course if this 'danger gap' had been allowed to happen or, even now, is not prevented it would be outrageous. But no-one should glibly assume that there is an easy 'pro-active' option. In Beeston the Council is engaged in a community nurturing project that is essentially a lure to attract private investment. It is gilding a costume jewellery ring in the hope that someone will help to replace the chipped glass with a precious gem.

At least one Beeston resident has asserted to us that the emphasis places on the area's 'fugitive' population is wrong. There are long-term residents, we are told, who are genuinely fond of the area. This is certainly true. But it needs to be stressed that we are essentially talking about Beeston Hill here. It has a higher than average crime rate, a higher than average collection of empty houses, and a higher than average Pakistani and Bangladeshi population.

There is a great deal to admire in Leeds City Council's new, collaborative model of area management that has evolved from the Community Action Team that was instigated as part of SRB 4 funding. There are, though, curious dangers in being too strongly led by a consultation approach. It is evident that a number of housing managers feel thwarted by having to direct sparse resources to 'superficial' concerns such as 'street tidiness'. It is however risky to pay too much attention to the concerns of the population when it is likely that more than half of them will be moving out of the area within a decade.

As part of its 'gilding' exercise the City Council invested over £1m in a 'facelift' of Tempest Road. Roofs have been smoothed, gutters have been plucked, and porches have been botoxed at a price of £4,500 per house. Everyone you talk to admires the results. However, when the Council asked the Tempest Road residents what they wanted done with their small front gardens, virtually all of them asked for their trees to be removed.

What should be a shining example of 'joined-up thinking' becomes – in the world of bureaucrats and funding initiatives – a form-filling nightmare. It falls between too many stools.

Short-stay residents don't want hassle. Should the Council have removed these trees? Would it have paid the same weight of attention to the wishes of the student population in Headingley?

This volatile population means that, for the moment at least, Beeston Hill can be pretty much anything you want to make it. And this puts the Council

- who recognise the need to regenerate the area - in the position of being committed to a profound piece of social manipulation. The instinct seems to be to follow the lead of the 1999-2000 Sheffield Hallam University survey, which advised encouraging the Asian community to put down roots.

This may well be right, but it needs to be done sensitively. The percentage of ethnic minorities in Leeds almost mirrors the UK average. The city does not need to have an area of undiluted ethnicity. For instance, Chapeltown - whatever the national press might think - is not exclusively Afro-Caribbean. In Sheffield Hallam University's 2003 report on Leeds Housing an estate agent - hardly a conventional arbiter of social justice - remarks how Leeds' Black and Asian populations buy houses in almost any area of the city without worrying about their potential neighbours. Do we want that to change?

As we climbed up Tar Pit Lane on the day of Radio 5's bold foray out of London, we passed through a throng of young Asian men who spotted us for journalists. 'That smile must mean you need a taxi!' laughed one, opportunistically pointing to his car.

'Sorry,' we responded. 'We're Yorkshire journalists, not London journalists.'

This time the whole group laughed. They liked that.

GRIMSBY

Karen Maitland

At the Grimsby Telegraph we are really proud of what has been achieved so far. Our hope is that the Community Press goes from strength to strength.

Nigel Lowther, Deputy Editor, *Grimsby Telegraph*

THE COMMUNITY PRESS

This project enabled communities to produce their own community letter as a tool to increase participation in community economic development and community life. Eight Priority 3 areas in North East Lincolnshire, were targeted in a response to a community demand for sustainable newspapers.

SRB Funding £199,682, 2002 to 2003

There probably aren't many offices where you can glance out of the window and see a huge cargo ship sailing majestically along on the road. Of course, it isn't actually sailing on the road. The offices of the Community Press are tucked in behind a fly-over which partially conceals the Grimsby docks behind it, and so at first glance the ships appear to be floating magically along the fly-over.

First impressions can be deceptive. Stepping into the offices of the Community Press you could easily be deceived into thinking this is a purpose built modern office, where quality magazines are produced by a large team of professional journalists, typesetters, photographers and editors. Even the people in the 34,000 households who receive the magazines often think that they are the work of paid professional journalists. They frequently phone the office asking to speak to one of the editors listed in the magazines, only to discover that the team of editors, like the writers and photographers, are volunteers largely working from home. Even the office is not what it seems; just six years ago it was a store room used by the *Grimsby Telegraph.*

Thanks to SRB funding, vision and thinking that went way beyond the box, the store room was refurbished into an open-plan, carpeted office with a separate glass-enclosed conference room for editorial meetings. It is plainly decorated but bright, airy and welcoming. It is also entirely user-friendly, including the automatic doors wide enough for wheelchairs and baby-buggies, and with an automatic voice to guide visually impaired users. Four computer workstations face each other around a wide segmented table, which allows both privacy for what is on the screen, but also invites conversation across the table so that those working on editing and lay-out can share ideas or offer advice. The waiting area is furnished with comfortable easy chairs and is within the office space itself, so that the visitor feels immediately included in the workspace and not shut out. Light, soothing, classical music plays on a nearby CD-player and the volunteers are encouraged to bring in what music they want to help them work.

The Community Press Office (CPO) has its own separate entrance and reception, but also has a discreet door at the back connecting it to the main *Grimsby Telegraph* building. This encapsulates the relationship between the newspaper and the Community Press. The Community Press has its own identity and financial independence but can call upon its big brother for help and advice when needed.

Unlike typical refurbishments under many grant schemes, here money has been spent on what really matters. Desks were second-hand, brought in from Scunthorpe. There are no elaborate displays of silk flowers or over-priced designer décor. The money has instead been spent on computers with good quality software, cameras, training, and getting exactly the right professional staff. Funders should hold this up as a shining example of how to spend a grant wisely and well.

COMMUNITY IDENTITY

Few things identify and define a town or village as strongly as its local newspaper, especially when that newspaper has a long and distinguished history. To lose a town newspaper is to lose the voice of the town, to gain one is to give the place a personality. With increasing industrial and urban spread, villages and individual communities are becoming absorbed into the sprawl of the larger towns, losing their distinctiveness and boundaries. Perversely, as globalisation grows, people search for localisation, identity based not on country or even county but on their local community. So it is particularly hard for towns such as Immingham trying to maintain their own identity to find that their 'local' newspaper is the *Grimsby Telegraph*. And, however hard the newspaper staff try to ensure that all villages and towns in their area are fairly represented,

The Community Press should be the communication tool for urban renaissance and neighbourhood renewal everywhere.
Local Government Officer

inevitably people outside the town feel that a Grimsby-based newspaper can never truly speak for them.

So even before the Community Press initiative, there were three or four local magazines or newsletters in existence, put together on a shoe-string by local people in an attempt to plug this gap. Odd bits of funding to print these newsletters came from Nick Triplow at Community Partnership, but in the end, Nick was forced to say, 'We can't keep giving you funding.' Overstretched and frantically busy, no-one would have blamed Nick for simply shutting the door and leaving the community magazines and newspapers to wither quietly away, but instead Nick went to the *Grimsby Telegraph* and together they put in a bid for £199,682 of SRB funding to publish eight community magazines in priority wards in the area - six in Grimsby, one in Cleethorpes North and another in Immingham. They also received £92,847 from the European Regional Development Fund and the *Grimsby Telegraph* contributed £50,000 of 'in kind' funding. Salaries, IT costs, refurbishment, rent, printing and distribution costs are paid for by public funding, while consultancy work and advertising is beginning to bring in much needed additional money. In April 2004, CPO received additional SRB funding of £180,000.

The eight community magazines funded under SRB are:

- *Clee View* (Cleethorpes North) circulation 5,000 copies
- *East Marsh Echo* (East Marsh) circulation 4,000 copies
- *The Voice* (Hainton & Henge) circulation 4,000 copies
- *Toot Hill and round about* (Yarborough) circulation 4,000 copies
- *Generations* (Grange, Laceby Acres, Westward Ho) circulation 5,000 copies
- *Livewire* (Nunsthorpe) circulation 3,000 copies
- *Riverside* (West Marsh) circulation 5,000 copies
- *IMMport* (All of Immingham Town) circulation 5,000 copies.

The *Grimsby Telegraph* provided office space and they initially put in a two-person team to recruit and work with the volunteers and help the local people to produce professional-quality magazines which would be the voice of their community. Clair Suddaby, appointed as CPO Manager, formerly sub-editor of the *Radio Times*, was a professional journalist but

Gillian Kapka had no journalistic experience at all when she was appointed as the Field Advisor. Gillian has since taken over as CPO Manager. They were joined in 2003 by the third member of the team, Fiona Oades, Team Co-ordinator, and in 2004 by Stephen Ryder, CPO Editorial Advisor, and finally in 2005 by Leah Hamilton, CPO Development Officer and Caroline Newbold, Sales Advisor.

Each magazine also has its own editorial board made up of volunteers, including residents with local knowledge, youth representatives, residents with specific skills such as typing, proof reading and lay-out, representatives from 'subjects of interest' such as history or sport, representatives from main facilities or groups in the magazine area, a community development worker and CPO volunteer reporters and photographers.

SPLITTING THE INFINITIVE

Some jobs can have no brief, because rather like early settlers opening up uncharted territory, you don't know exactly what skills you will need because you have no idea what lies beyond. All you do is hope for a pioneer, someone able 'to boldly go' as Trekkies would say or 'to go boldly' as the earth-bound grammarians insist, into the uncharted territories. Sometimes when you look at the CV of a pioneer you realise that although the job never existed before, it is as if that person's life has been the preparation for it.

Gillian Kapka, CPO Manager, is not a journalist and had no background in publishing when she joined the team as Field Advisor in 2002. She is a local girl, born and bred in Cleethorpes. After leaving school she took a degree in Sports Studies. Tall, bronzed and full of energy, this comes as no surprise; she looks every inch the athlete. She went on to join the police force working in Grimsby and Immingham in the key areas covered by several of the magazines, so she got to know the area, people and problems in a way that would be denied to even experienced journalists. After leaving the force she worked as a sports development officer trying to get people interested in sports and creating opportunities for people to take part. She was made redundant the week the Community Press post was advertised. It seems that the job was just waiting for her.

At first we had to coax the volunteers to come in, now they ask us to put them in the diary to make sure they can get on the PC.
Stephen Ryder, Editorial Advisor

When Gillian began, there was no guidebook or map, not even a list of people. How do you go into the most deprived areas and convince local people, who often have poor educational experience, low self-confidence and little training in IT, to write, edit and lay-out a professional quality community magazine?

Gillian started by approaching the community development officers and set up countless meetings in local areas to find out what people wanted to read about in their magazine. She had to balance the meetings so that no single interest group or age group could take control of the agenda and squeeze everyone else out. At first, predictably, the meetings fall into the usual pattern of complaints that arise whenever there is a public meeting on a local estate - vandalism, dog mess, crime, lack of facilities, not enough being done for *our* area by *them*. But gradually people began to talk themselves round. Things weren't all bad, lots of good things were happening on their estate, people were helping each other, taking care of elderly people, trying to organise activities for the kids. The trouble was that the press never reported the good news stories about their estate; they only reported the crime and vandalism which reinforced an estate's bad name and made the residents feel that they were being labelled as 'trouble' simply because they came from that area. So as Gillian said, 'The solution is to produce your own community magazine. Make it good enough to stand up against the newspaper, tell everyone about the good things that are happening and give a place some pride in itself. Inspire others to think, if they can do that so can I.' Now they have a database of 700 people willing to help with the magazines.

THE PEOPLE'S PAPARAZZI

'If it's happening *in* the community it should be reported *by* the community,' says Gillian, but community news doesn't mean those subjects once dreaded by cub reporters such as jumble sales and the vicar's sermon. Nor does community mean amateur. When the Duchess of Wessex recently paid a visit to local projects in the area, a volunteer CPO reporter and photographer were both issued with press passes in exactly the same way as the other newspaper journalists, which meant they were able to interview her and take good quality, close-up pictures to rival any taken by the newspapers' photographers.

Teaching new skills is very much part of the CPO objectives. Volunteers attend in-house editing courses and learn how to use computer software to word process, lay-out text and photos. There are short courses in writing articles and headlines, and photographers are taught how to use digital cameras. Currently two of the courses run by CPO for volunteers are accredited - the Sub-editing Course and the Digital Photography Course - but there are plans to seek accreditation for more. And media students from the local college are often provided with work experience by CPO so that they can build up their professional portfolio.

Literary skills are, as you would expect, low in all of the target areas. Many of the volunteers left school with a profound sense of failure and lack of confidence. Though most of them do not want to go into journalism, the skills they develop in communication, advanced IT and their new-found self-esteem through working on the magazines are eminently transferable, often giving people both the confidence and the references to be able to apply successfully for jobs in other areas of work.

Grimsby is an area of high unemployment where many of the major employers in the food industry have pulled out in recent years, but despite the problems of finding work, as Stephen Ryder says, 'alarm bells start to ring for most employers when they see blank time gaps in a CV. People now recognise that doing volunteer work helps fill in those gaps and we always insist that whenever anyone comes into the office to write a piece or lay-out a page they take a print of what they have done to build up their portfolio. And of course, the experience of talking to people to get stories develops communication skills that really show when it comes to job interviews.'

The Nunsthorpe and Bradley Park History Group got off the ground through their community magazine and it now feeds the magazine. Community magazines are a catalyst for community action.
Gillian Kapka, CPO Manager, Grimsby

Giving people time is something that is important to the professional staff and goes way beyond measurable outcomes. Take the Nigerian man, an experienced journalist in his own country, but unable to find work here. His wife, a qualified nurse, was recruited from Nigeria to come and help plug the shortage of nurses in Grimsby's busy hospital, but as the husband of a worker here, he is not eligible for the kinds of training courses or advice that would help him find work in this country. He works as a volunteer on the magazine and Stephen tries to squeeze in time whenever he can to work with him on in-depth articles such as top-up fees and ASBOs, helping him to learn the style of writing and reporting required by British newspapers.

The skills of the volunteers grow daily. When the magazines began, the CPO staff used to write 25 out of the 30 headlines in the magazines, now they rarely have to change one. As they sit round the table laying-out the pages, it often is the volunteers themselves who will explain to their colleagues how to do something on the computer. Sadly, of course, none of this is shown up in the figures which have to be filed to the grant awarding bodies. These outcomes can't be measured by cold statistics.

I'VE GOT A COMPLAINT TO MAKE

'I've got a complaint to make about Stagey.'
Stephen Ryder, Editorial Advisor, was somewhat startled when he heard the irate woman's voice on the phone. The whole professional team have to be extremely careful to make sure that none of the magazines stumble unwittingly into printing libellous pieces, and the team have undergone intensive training in libel and copyright law so that they can offer tactful guidance to the volunteers. They are always fearful that something will slip through the net, but surely the regular column Stagey couldn't have offended anyone.

Stagey, written by Tim Mickleburgh, is a delightful little ongoing fictional story intended for children, which appears in *Riverside,* about the adventures of a Stagecoach bus, Stagecoach being the local bus company in Grimsby. What could poor Stagey have done to upset the reader?
'Stagey didn't arrive yesterday and I was late for my hospital appointment. Everyone is so kind at the hospital, I hate to let them down.'

Stephen tried tactfully to explain that Stagey didn't actually exist, he was a fictional character. If she had a problem with the bus company she should phone them. 'I've already done that,' replied the caller. 'They wouldn't do anything, but you're the press so I thought you'd be able to sort it out for me.'

It is a tribute to the professional quality of *Riverside* that the unfortunate lady regarded the magazine as having the power of the press and that she chose to ring them rather than the local newspaper when she wanted the weight of the media behind her. It also is a testament to how much the magazine has been taken to the heart of the community. But Stephen is an expert in turning complaints into positives, finding a win-win in every situation. He pointed out that the woman obviously thought very highly of the hospital staff if she felt that being late was 'letting them down' and suggested she write a positive article about the hospital instead.

Of course, there are bad news stories. These are very deprived areas and no-one would be so rose-tinted in their view as to pretend otherwise, so complaints do get published but only when a solution can be offered by the editorial or community teams. Complaints that the Freshney River has seen a drastic rise in the rat population, due to the rubbish being dumped in it, are perfectly justified. Since the river flows close to houses, cafés and shops, this is a matter for concern. But alongside the complaint comes the solution. Through the magazine they set up a group called the Friends of Freshney to mount a big clean-up campaign. So the challenge to the community is, if you are concerned, as you have every right to be, then come and help to clean it up.

HOW MANY PEOPLE DOES IT TAKE?

Everyone knows the answer to the old light bulb jokes:
How many consultants does it take to change a light bulb?
Answer: We don't know. They never get past the feasibility study.
How many local government officers does it take to change a light bulb?
Answer: There are no light bulbs; the budget's been cut again.

But do you know how many volunteers it takes to produce a magazine? The short answer is up to 60 maybe, involved in the publication of just one issue from writing articles, editing, lay-out, photography, art work, gathering and passing on news and helping to organise meetings, with numerous skills being utilised along the way. The oldest volunteer is 87 and the youngest so far is 10 years old. Disability is no barrier either as they have volunteers who are blind and deaf as well as those who have mobility problems or have had strokes.

Learning a skill such as page design on the job is much better than trying to learn it on a course. It sinks in because you are doing it and you are much more motivated because you are providing something for real, not just doing an exercise.
Mandi Winterburn, CPO volunteer

Eight magazines are issued four times a year with full colour photos. Each team works independently of each other. So how is an issue produced? First an open meeting is held in a café or community centre in the magazine area where anyone who is interested can come along and offer their services or share their opinions about what ought to be covered. The contents of the last magazine are reviewed to find out what people liked and what they didn't, and organisations and individuals are asked if they know of any forthcoming events which should be covered. One of the professional team will attend the meeting as a neutral chair to ensure that no one interest group dominates the proceedings.

Volunteer reporters are given badges to identify themselves and are expected to work to a strict code of conduct, respecting confidentiality, making appointments, checking names and facts and ensuring accuracy. Copy is submitted by email, or reporters can come into the centre to type up their own articles, and Stephen Ryder, the CPO Editorial Advisor, is available for advice. Occasionally, if articles are too long or badly structured, he will suggest ways to change this, though he admits delightedly that as the volunteer reporters gain skill and experience, changes need to be made less and less frequently. Volunteer photographers can borrow one of the two digital cameras belonging to the group. But after they've been trained in digital photography, most get so fascinated by photography, they choose to buy their own camera. As digital cameras become ever cheaper, this is now a realistic option for many people.

A month before the publication deadline, the volunteers on the editorial board meet to discuss the articles and photos which have been submitted. The teams are so well trained that no professional staff now need to attend these meetings. Then just after the deadline for the articles the third and final meeting takes place between the smaller managerial team and Stephen Ryder. Stephen produces a blank flat plan and the team decide what articles should go on which page, making the sometimes difficult decision that some articles need to be shortened or held-over if there is too much to go in. Pages must be in multiples of four and most magazines are 16 pages, though Immingham's magazine, *IMMport,* runs to 24 pages.

Stephen then assigns each volunteer a page of the magazine to lay-out on the CPO computers, with those new to the skill getting the easier lay-outs, while the more experienced people get pages with several articles and photos to lay-out. Once the magazine is checked it goes to the newspaper printers, but it is delivered separately to 34,000 homes that receive it for free to make quite sure that it is seen as independent publication and not a newspaper supplement. They even take copies of one magazine to a church to be given out with the hymn sheets. The magazines are delivered commercially to households so that the valuable time of trained volunteers is not taken up by trudging door to door, another important signal that the magazines are treated with the same professionalism as the publication and distribution of any commercial newspaper. Interest in the magazines is so keen now that around publication date, the office takes frequent calls from residents demanding to know when their copy will be delivered. Volunteers also record the magazines onto Talking Book for visually impaired residents.

LAY IT ON ME

Today is lay-out day for the magazine *Toot Hill and round about*, so named because the area it covers lies between two roundabouts. Production and lay-out of the magazines is staggered throughout the year so that each magazine gets an equal amount of time and attention. Three volunteers have booked in to do the lay-out for the magazine. They book to come in whenever they have the time and often work on the lay-out of magazines belonging to other communities as well as their own. Some write for the magazines as well, but some just come in to do the lay-out. Following the management meeting, Editorial Advisor Stephen Ryder has marked up which stories and pictures should go on each page and has stored these on the computer.

To produce a professional magazine, you must take a professional approach to everything you do. Start and end meetings on time. Send apologies if you can't attend. A professional attitude soon filters through a group and people start to take a pride in what they are doing.
Gillian Kapka, CPO Manager, Grimsby

When each magazine was first set up, the editorial board were given a mix and match file from which they could design an overall style for their magazine. They had to select fonts, column widths, headline styles, decide whether photos should have a border or a shadow, and choose a palette of colours for the magazine, with Stephen on hand to advise. Each page is set up in advance with the correct column width and headline style, so all the volunteers have to do is drop the text and illustrations into it, think up some snappy headlines and a page is born. Did I say *all*? In fact it's not quite as easy as that.

First of all you have to get the material to fit. Invariably there is either too much for the page or too little. Colour photos must be cropped to achieve the best shot, and enlarged or reduced, with shadows put behind them or borders round them. Articles have to be shortened or re-laid so that they expand to fill the space. Illustrations must be correctly captioned and positioned so that they look balanced on the page. 'Widows' and 'orphans' must be ruthlessly exterminated. House style has to be checked, so that dates and numbers and many other details are written in the same way consistently throughout the magazine. Bear in mind that all this is carried out by people who in many cases have only just learnt to switch on a computer. The skills that the volunteers learn, just to be able to put one page together, are staggering - IT, editing, graphic design, page design and creative writing.

Stephen watches the volunteers from his desk ready to spring into action when the cries go up - 'I pressed something and it's all disappeared' - 'Help, I think I've just duplicated Janice' - 'Does this colour look right to you?' He is patience personified, as one volunteer says: 'It doesn't matter how many times I ask him to show me the same thing, he never gets annoyed. His favourite catch phrase is, 'Don't panic, Mr Mannering.'

As the volunteers edit, they talk. Julie downloads a photo, 'I know him,' she says, reminding us of the essence of a community magazine, it is about and for your own community. When she finishes, Stephen comes over, 'Right, Julie, criticise your own page. Anything not right about it?' She stands back and spots a couple of very minor things without prompting. He helps her put them right.

After the volunteers are gone, Stephen will check each page again making minute adjustments to lines and correcting details which no-one but an editor would notice. Every magazine that goes out has 'professional' stamped all over it.

TAKE THREE VOLUNTEERS

Julie is the first to arrive. She is worried; she lost her purse this morning and as a result had to cancel her hospital appointment, but she still came here because she didn't want to let the Community Press Office down. She has dyslexia, a fifteen year old son to raise by herself, and a year ago she couldn't switch on a PC. She is about to go into hospital for an operation on her foot. Both feet need surgery but she can't have them done together because with only her young son at home she has to be able to look after him. She says she can't expect him to carry her to the bathroom - one of the hidden problems of being a lone parent.

Julie became a volunteer through the lone parent scheme. Her confidence was shattered and she had no qualifications. She took courses in English and Maths, and through the STEPS course which takes learners out into the community, she discovered the CPO office. This was a chance to meet people, gain confidence and build up her portfolio for a future job. She started off wanting to work on the art side as she is a portrait painter, and found herself gradually learning lay-out skills.

'It's given me so much confidence. When you've had a knock in one area of your life, it pulls you down in every area, but working in CPO has built it back up again, because I've decided to do something with my life. You have to learn to help yourself and the only way you can do that is by trying something new.'

Mandi is a young student taking a degree in English. She drives herself to the office and then transfers to her wheelchair and rolls into the building. As she takes her place in front of the PC I suddenly realise how well designed the desks are with a concave curve to the front, allowing wheelchair users, pregnant mums and short people like me, to get comfortably close to the keyboard for once. Mandi is one of the more experienced volunteers and is assigned a complex two page lay-out involving pieces written by young school children, and their drawings. Her skill and concentration are mesmerising.

'Did you know how to use QuarkXPress before you started here?' I ask her.

In a community project you have to start with a few basic common sense principles. Every time you talk to someone, treat them the way you'd like to be treated. Treat everyone as equals. Look for the win-win in every situation.

Gillian Kapka, CPO Manager, Grimsby

'No, and I wouldn't say I know it now, but I'm getting there. I saw an appeal in the *East Marsh Echo* for writers for the magazine and thought, I fancy that. What attracted me was the writing; I never thought I'd end up doing lay out as well.'

Mandi balances her studies for a degree with the volunteer work she does with CPO. She can decide how much time she wants to spend depending on her workload at university for that week. 'The staff here are fantastic,' she says, 'very welcoming. I wouldn't keep coming back if they weren't.' She gets the kind of practical experience here she would never get on her degree course. 'The design skills I learned here have really helped when it comes to doing presentations at university.'

Last to arrive is Tim. I'd been curious to meet him. Pick up almost any of the CPO magazines and there is a piece in there by Tim - articles, fiction, children's stories, poetry and even photographs. His involvement began when he was a member of the Welholme Community Museum Group. Alison Hobbs, then a community development worker, suggested he might like to volunteer for *The Voice* magazine as a way of getting publicity for the Welholme Galleries. Having already written several local history books, Tim threw himself into CPO with the enthusiasm and drive with which he tackles everything. As well as writing, interviewing, photography and page lay-out, he is also on the editorial team for *The Voice*. Tim didn't get on well at school. 'It was a very restrictive environment with people always on your back telling you what do. But here people support you and give you space.'

Tim is currently looking for paid employment, but you could never describe him as 'unemployed'. The time and energy he pours into community projects must rival that of a junior hospital doctor. Whatever the state pays him in benefit, they get back ten times over in what he gives to the local community.

The session draws to a close and the volunteers prepare to leave.
'Are you coming in next week?' Stephen calls to Julie.
'Yes, but the week after I'm having the operation. I'll be off for a week, but they say I'll be able to get around on crutches after that so I'll be in the following week. Book a space for me.'

If it is community led, it should be community reported.
Stephen Ryder, Editorial Advisor

WHAT MAKES A GOOD VOLUNTEER?

'It's someone who really wants to be here,' says Stephen Ryder, Editorial Advisor. 'We don't ask them to commit to a certain number of hours; they can do as much or as little as they want. They usually come in with an interest in doing one thing - writing - or simply taking part in the meetings and we let them do what they want to do first. Then we might say to a writer, 'Do you fancy seeing what your piece is going to look like on the page?' I'll probably lay it in for them while they watch, then encourage them to play and before long they find themselves starting to edit or do the page lay-out. Most of the writers and board members do most things now. The only exception are the photographers, who for some reason only want to do photography.

'As an English teacher I was one of the generation who believed that a fountain pen was the only thing worth writing with, so I understand that people are timid about IT. I often start by saying, 'It would really help us if you could email that piece in.' With help they do and find it is not as difficult as they thought. We've had many volunteers who came in scared to touch a keyboard in case they blew the whole thing up and have become so hooked they ended up buying their own computer.'

WALKING THE COMMUNITY TIGHTROPE

The roles for the teams are evolving. Tim, one of the volunteers, says that the term 'editorial team' has now become a bit misleading, and their role is more of a contribution or support team. As their skills develop, the smaller management teams are gradually taking on more work for the magazine, such as organising meetings to free up the time of the professional staff. The volunteers have discovered that they need to limit the number of people who become involved in the final discussions about what should go into an issue and what should be held over. As Tim says, 'Twelve people around a table, though democratic, is unworkable and often people are trying to push pieces for their own interest at the lay-out stage and not for the good of the magazine. So while you need lots of people at the first stage of gathering material you need a small group to make the final decision about the contents.'

Producing community magazines often involves a difficult balancing act. As part of the code, all volunteers have to agree to 'keep their community magazine independent and representative of the community as a whole.' But in practice this is not always easy. There are three main dangers.

'The first danger is the magazine being hi-jacked by one particular interest group. This is not always easy to prevent, especially if the members of that interest group are the only ones to show up at meetings; hence the need to constantly try to contact and involve different community groups and leaders. This process has to be ongoing, not a one-off, otherwise one group can gradually take control and others start to drop out. Tensions can also arise between different groups in a community, and another role the team have to take on is to balance column inches for each group, so that one group doesn't feel that another is getting more magazine space than they, which can aggravate bad feeling.

'Danger number two is the dominant individual. They come in two guises. Firstly there is the person who sends in dozens of articles for each issue so that the magazine becomes their personal publishing channel. The second type is the person who is so good and so involved that no-one else gets a look-in or a chance to try out new skills. This can be a major problem if that person then leaves the area. With the magazine being virtually a one-man operation, the whole thing will fold. Again there is the constant need to skill people in several areas, regardless of what they came in to do, so that they have the skills and confidence to take over or at least help out. But it takes skill to gently coax technophobes, who only came to write, into taking on other areas. Of course, the people who write and produce the magazine will colour it with their own interests and personalities, and in many senses this is what a community magazine is about. The difficult balancing act is to maintain that personal voice without letting it become a personal rant.

Some residents just want to come to the meetings, find out what's going on and put their ideas in and that's fine.We don't push it, we say 'How do you want to do it? How do you want to progress?' With help and encouragement many end up turning their ideas into their first article.
Stephen Ryder, Editorial Advisor

'Finally there is the problem of the lack of volunteers in a particular community, so that all the work falls on one or two people who become increasingly overworked and resentful. This situation arose with *Parklife,* one of the magazines that existed in Cleethorpes before CPO. The magazine had started with a team of volunteers but by the time CPO came along, they had drifted away one by one until one poor lady found herself producing the magazine virtually single-handedly. With the support of CPO she took the decision to simply suspend the magazine. If local people wanted it back they had to volunteer to help write and produce it. They did, and the magazine was re-launched with a brand-new look by CPO under the new title *Clee View* and is now going from strength to strength.'

SELLING YOURSELF

The first rule of selling anything is to learn to sell yourself, but you can't do that if you don't have any confidence in yourself or your own abilities. Caroline was left as a lone parent to raise four children who are now aged 15, 12, 11 and 10 without any help from the children's father after her relationship of 17 years broke up. That really dints your confidence and self-esteem and she came into CPO initially as a volunteer through the Pathways 2 Lone Parents Scheme. She began working on page lay-out and helping out on the admin side, and she proudly shows me a neat row of files on the wall, part of the filing system she instituted.

When the person employed to sell advertising space for the magazines left after just six weeks, Caroline was asked if she thought she could have a go. She did, although she had never done anything like that before and soon found that she had a flair for it. She now works selling advertising on a commission basis and she loves it so much that she is doing an intensive marketing course at Immingham.

Her first job when she was taken on was to try and get advertising business for the magazines at the Job and Recruitment Fair. She says, 'I was so nervous and scared of approaching anyone, then I saw this man sitting by himself looking as nervous as me, so I plucked up the courage and approached him. He turned out to be from Sainsbury's and was really nice, my first success. I felt confident about going up to anybody after that.'

Caroline designs and sends out packs about advertising in the community magazines to local companies, organisations and leisure facilities, and makes follow-up calls to targeted companies. If businesses don't have their own in-house designers, she designs and words the adverts for them, doing the research for the slogans and finding colours for the design that reflect the product or organisation being advertised. With all adverts automatically being in full colour, at rates much cheaper than in the newspaper and with a circulation to every home in the businesses' area, local firms can readily be persuaded to place adverts with the magazines.

Caroline lives on the East Marsh, one of the areas covered by the magazines. 'It's good and bad, but then there are good and bad areas everywhere. The main thing is to make sure the kids don't get into trouble. So I coach football in the evenings for the Lincolnshire Soccer School, both boys and girls, up to the age of 16. Then I come home and do my college work from about 11 to 2pm when the kids are in bed and it's quiet.' She is also taking a coaching qualification and plays for a ladies soccer team, though these days she prefers to help on the sidelines rather than play because as a single working mum she can't risk having to have time off through injury.

No one would guess, looking at the bright, bubbly woman, smartly dressed in a suit, that this was someone who once felt so low she didn't know where to turn. She is taking her first ever holiday abroad this year and she wants to do it every year. 'I want to have a life, make this job work and make it bigger.'

With that positive attitude, how can she fail? Volunteer to career woman in just a few months with a little encouragement and a lot of determination, now that is the power of community press.

If you see your neighbour's face in the paper or recognise the picture of the woman who works in the local shop and they have done something positive for the community, you start to think I could do that too.
Gillian Kapka,
CPO Manager, Grimsby

CHAMPIONING THE COMMUNITY

Newspapers don't have mission statements, they have by-lines. The by-line for the Grimsby and Scunthorpe Newspapers is 'Champion of the Community'. And this simple title has a lot more weight behind the words than your average mission statement. Historically, the company of

Grimsby and Scunthorpe Newspapers has deep roots in the area. As Mark Webb, Managing Director, puts it, 'We don't tiptoe around the edge; we are knee-deep in the community, in its triumphs and its problems.' As such, Mark sees his newspaper's involvement with CPO not as an add-on, but as something that lies at the very heart of what they believe in.

When Nick Triplow came to him a few years ago he had a small team of dedicated volunteers who were trying desperately to empower their local community through the community newsletters, but doing it all on a shoestring with a photocopier, goodwill and very little else. What they were achieving then was remarkable, considering the resources they had, but what they lacked in resources they made up for in enthusiasm and that is something you can't buy. And so the CPO was created out of three essential elements: the enthusiasm of the volunteers, the vital injection of money from SRB and the skills and knowledge of the local newspaper. Like the legs on a three-legged stool, take one of those away and the whole thing would have collapsed.

Out of those three strands a wonderful ring was forged. The newspaper provides the skills and expertise to local people who want to create community magazines. But the magazines themselves reach into places that the newspaper can't reach and communicate with the kind of people who would never approach a newspaper reporter or even read a newspaper. The volunteers gather news items and opinions from the heart of the community at street-level; even, you might say, at house, pub and club level. And many of these stories and opinions are, in turn, picked up by the newspaper itself and given a much wider readership than the magazine, bringing the whole process full circle. What is so encouraging is that the newspaper does not simply appropriate the news stories from the magazines. Whenever they use an item from the magazine they make sure that it is fully credited to the magazine writers, photographers and reporters, treating them with the same professional respect as they would any other journalist. 'We never see each other as competition; instead we complement each other's work.'

Mark loves to see local people developing the skills of journalism, photography and publishing - that is community empowerment - but he is quick to add that it could not have been done without Gillian and her team. Having staff with their skill, dedication and enthusiasm is the cornerstone to the project, and people like that are not to be found on every street corner.

Mark Webb is immensely proud of CPO. Talking to him even for a few minutes, it is obvious that he does not regard the volunteers as amateurs producing a little local newssheet, but as full partners in the process of championing the community. What could be achieved if other local newspapers around the country had the same vision?

SUSTAINING THE WORD

SRB funding for this project runs out in March 2006, but the staff are not sitting around waiting for the money to run out. They are in the process of turning themselves into a limited company. Already they have put together an exciting business plan, not simply to sustain the existing magazines, but to roll out the project into new and challenging areas.

Schools magazines, even those produced by private schools, have been dying over the past few years, squeezed out by time pressure on overworked staff. CPO has already helped a number of schools to get their magazines up and running again. Mathew Humberston School won an award of £10,000 from Barclays Bank to produce six issues of a school magazine called the *The Grippin' Griffin*. Children from the school came into the CP office to be trained on QuarkXPress software, which the school then bought to allow them to continue work at school. The magazine was then sent back to CPO for tightening and printing.

Over the last year we have recruited around 25 of the programme participants from advertising with the Community Press Office.
Simon King, Project Development Officer, Communities Explored

Putting together a magazine involves many different skills for children including literacy, numeracy, IT skills, photography, art, design, creative writing and team work. To learn by producing a properly printed magazine, which he or she can then show to relatives, is far more rewarding for a child than some class-room exercise. It utilises the skills of children with a wide range of abilities from the brightest to the less academically gifted. CPO hope to extend their work in schools in partnership, by becoming accredited to work with young people, using the teacher down-time in classes to engage the children in producing magazines rather than simply doing a bit of craftwork or colouring to keep them occupied.

Both private and corporate sponsorship is being actively sought to fund the overall CPO project and to fund the printing of the individual magazines. After SRB funding comes to an end in March 2006, all areas in North Lincolnshire will get equal rights to use the CPO to set up and produce their own magazines, and this includes not just villages, such as Waltham, but also tenants' groups within other areas. They would apply for funding using the CPO as the umbrella organisation for support, resources, advice, skills and training.

The pioneering nature of the CPO project is shown by the increasing calls from all over the country from people who would like to do the same thing and want to know how to set about it. Groups in Bridlington, Doncaster, and even Greenwich in London have sought advice from the CPO in Grimsby. Recently eight volunteers from Barrow in Furness came to spend time with the CPO and learn how it was done. So CPO hope to both formalise and increase their consultancy work, enabling community magazines to be started in other parts of Grimsby, and in Scunthorpe, Crosby and all over Lincolnshire, as well as acting as a consultancy for villages, towns, communities, schools and groups all over the country who might want to do the same thing.

CPO in Grimsby have shown the value of the Community Press in giving communities a voice, empowering local people, changing negative attitudes into positive solutions and becoming a catalyst for a whole range of community projects from local history societies to clean-up campaigns. They have proved that the power of the press can be just as great at community level as it can on a national level. So prepare for change, Community Press could soon be coming to a town near you.

HULL

Brian Lewis

There are three kinds of people; one who watches things happen,
one who makes things happen and one who asks 'what happened?'
Anon

AN EVENING AT THE UNIVERSITIES

Hull Cityventure - Learning Youth and Using Our Abilities - is citywide, concentrating on learning youth, the 0 to 25 age group specifically, who are disadvantaged through learning disability or difficulty. It links 4 themes: parenting skills, raising educational aspiration and achievement, easing the difficult transition between school and the adult world, and encouraging youth participation on community life.

The Children's University *project will contribute to raising educational aspirations and achievement, encouraging progression to higher levels of learning. Its activities are designed to strengthen basic skills as the foundation for success in 20 primary schools in the City and therefore in later working life. The project is made up of two related elements, Basic Skills for Life: Stage 2 (age 11) in the 20 targeted schools and Children's University (CU). The purpose is to provide 'out of school' learning opportunities for primary school pupils, focused on literacy skills.*

Total Project Costs: Revenue: £1,618,551 Capital: £72,821 six year scheme, (1998/99 – 2003/4) £5,975,000

I counted ten people in the classroom of Hull University when the first meeting of a new batch of the Hull Children's University mentors began. They had 1980s names, Claire, Bridget, Laura; two with wholly different names were teachers from Ghana. They explained that they were there because they wanted to put something back into a society which had given them quite a lot. Many had been graduates of the university; one was a young mother, another was looking for a career change.

It is unusual these days to be sitting with a group of twenty year olds who are there because they want to help the development of community life. The best they could wish for, or so Andrew Holmes, a lecturer at the host university and a key player in the development of the Children's University, said 'was something to look forward to on a cold winter's evening in Hull.' We are in a normal university room, a bit cleaner than most, with sound-proof walls. Then it was, 'Over to John.'

196 SRB 4 & 5

John Buttrick, the Children's University Manager, is a natural storyteller who tells you that each anecdote is 'gospel true'. As you listen you realise that it is an account full of ornamental language and a good deal of passion. One of the Mentor-Packs, the tool kits of the Children's University, is about myths and legends. Listening I thought that this must have been the way Homer spoke the *Odyssey*. That old Greek would also speak a well rehearsed narrative honed by several tellings, in which every spear of information was enhanced with spontaneous flashes of lightning.

At one point John Buttrick tells of a trip to somewhere, probably London, for he has, or so he says, 'a great love of the place.' This story starts on Paragon Station when 35 top primary school children leave a district of Hull for the capital. They are on their way to a matinee performance of *Maskarade* at Covent Garden.

On the journey down these eleven year olds are quiet - they won't be like that on the way back - and this atmosphere of respectfulness and awe continues until John and two of the boys sit on an ornamental wall in the Royal Park and open their lunch packs. It is then that he realises that the boy on his right - let's call him Jason - has been sent on a day trip with a packet of Carr's Water Biscuits, 'the driest biscuits known to mankind', and the other has custard creams. Neither have water. John pools resources, and they go off together to see London.

Jason's dad is in prison and his mother is on the game. The lad is undernourished. He never gets to school on time, at least not until he receives a letter from Alan Johnson, MP for Hull West and Hessle and at that time a Minister in Tony Blair's third government. The letter is so important to him that at eight ten he is banging on John Buttrick's car window.

'Eh sir, eh sir. They do care sir, they do care.' The reason for his passion is a letter he has received that morning. Three months earlier John Buttrick had encouraged ten children who had met the MP to write back to him thanking him for receiving them, and including a note on something that worried them. Jason had said that he lived on the opposite side of a busy road from the park and that his parents were 'often out'. Between him and the football pitches was a dirty pedestrian underpass used by sniffers, druggies and alcopoppers. He was scared to go past them.

How can you win if you have predicted the outputs and outcomes before you set out on the journey?

'Sir, it says that this Friday they are going to paint all of the underpass in a new sort of paint and they are going to send round security guards and wardens.'

When a lad from Gypsyville, Hull, asked Kevin Keegan on a 'university' excursion to his Premier League soccer ground if he could have a ball that was going spare in the midfield, the manager replied, 'No, not unless you earn it. You have to work hard in this world.'

John's anecdotes and educational philosophy stay with you for a long time.

OUR GREATEST ASSETS COME CHEAP

When Michael Young, the educationist who coined the word 'meritocracy', set up the *University of the Third Age* he relied on the enthusiasm of volunteer tutors. Pay did not come into Young's equation. John Buttrick relies on the same source for his mentors; the committed are unpaid.

This source of mentors/tutors is as old as civilisation itself. Such women and men will come to teach because they are grabbed by a big idea or because they feel an obligation to improve society. Like the young women in the Mentors' Introduction Session, they see this as 'a way of giving back the things I was given.' Echoing through a sterile room just off the main entrance to Hull University were ideas that sent young Clement Attlee out from Toynbee Hall into the London slums, William Morris crusading all over England on behalf of the 'Commonweal' and John Ball to the gallows. In 1381 this hedge-row preaching friar taught that 'things cannot go well to pass in England and shall not until all men are created equal.' John Buttrick with his stories of deprivation and spiritually deprived children taps into the same ideas.

John Buttrick's pitch to proto-mentors on their introduction to the Children's University is interesting. When he speaks he assumes that they are dedicated to the project as he is but three times he throws in the observation, 'If you are here to have something to put on your CV, there's nothing wrong with that.'

John is an idealist with a strong realist streak. Many in the room are undergraduates or recent graduates and I suspect this is welcome news. When they apply for a job they are told that they lack experience. In an 'Alice in Wonderland' scenario they can only get initial experience if they already 'have experience'. It is the classic Catch 22. Mentoring for the Children's University gets them off that hook. CVs matter to a young person trying to establish credentials.

John is reassuring. 'The work will be hard but you will not be alone. You will be supported by a well thought through module pack, and a trained teacher will be with you at all times. Your work place will be safe. Apart from the occasions when you go out to factories that offer to help with the development of our models or to London you will work from a primary school between 3.30 pm and 5.00pm.'

The focus on mentors must not diminish the importance of the class teachers or the headteacher in the delivery of the Children's University. Primary school teachers - members of an under-rated profession if ever there was one - often rise to the occasion when a new idea is offered. Although they could be paid, many of them neglect to ask for the money and help at the Children's University as if it was a voluntary after-school club. This is a valuable extra-curricular activity and they know it. The 2002-2003 evaluation of the Children's University said that 'teachers were possibly the strongest advocate of the Children's University as an agent of a child's development.'

ORIGINS

Too long have we lost sight of the fact that education is fun and that cleverness is a virtue. 'Chilling out' and 'being smashed' are seen as pleasurable experience, systematic learning is not.

John Buttrick went to a seminar given by Tim Brighouse, Director of Education, Chief Education Officer for Birmingham, in Autumn 1996. He asked if he could come to Birmingham and talk at length about 'aspirational' education and the impact of deprivation in general. A few weeks later, while shadowing Tim and listening to the plans to establish a University of the First Age in the Midlands city, he started thinking very seriously about a children's university for Hull.

Although it is possible to tell John Buttrick's story as the story of a man who has a mission that comes to him as a flash, things rarely work out that way. Usually there is no 'blinding light' experience. Ideas gestate over a long period though there are defining moments. The Tim Brighouse seminar was such a moment. On the visit to Birmingham John fleshed out ideas which had been in his mind for some time.

John had started his teaching career up on the Bransholme Estate in Hull in 1971 at Kinloss Junior High and was well aware of all the problems that living on an over-large council estate brought with it. He knew from experience how the atmosphere of an estate which had been thrown up with little regard to community development affected the aspirations of primary and young secondary school children and their parents.

Five miles from Hull City Centre, with bus prices rising yearly in line, or so it seemed, with unemployment, Bransholme was not the place to be if you had ambitions for your children. There were few shops and no bookshops. The library looked from the outside one of the ugliest, uninviting libraries I have ever seen. In every way the estate was over-big. In the 1990s Hull people would say, not without pride, that their estate was the 'biggest council housing estate in Europe.' In an age where the statement 'small is beautiful' was taken for granted at the dining tables of every leafy suburb home between Cottingham and Beverley, in Bransholme it was 'the bigger the better' that mattered.

In areas like this, or in Orchard Park or Gypsyville, areas where John Buttrick subsequently worked as a teacher, the local heroes were the best fighter on the block or the street's best drinker. In such areas you had trouble in encouraging children and their parents to think beyond their immediate horizons. Education, never high on the list of priorities, had hardly mattered just after the War when the fishing fleet was gargantuan and the sea-faring destinies of boys were mapped out at birth. Then there were 120 locomotives working in the inward yard from 30 sidings across six turntables on the docks. Coal came in and fish went out - why worry about education when your job was mapped out for you?

This level and type of economic activity had gone long ago but in the 1980s people seemed to act as if the cod would return. In Welsh mining villages and in Scottish crofts, a continuous tradition of sending a boy to university stretched back into the early nineteenth century at least. This culture of prioritising education had almost passed Hull by. In the early 1990s schooling beyond sixteen was low on parents' agendas. It is hard to get a measure of this indifference; in the absence of more sophisticated data the statistic that only 10% of parents attended school open evenings in areas like Gypsyville will have to do.

In an attempt to combat this indifference, and recognising that some small impact might take place if schools had home-school liaison officers, the local authority started to encourage teachers to apply for these new posts. John Buttrick, the Deputy Head at Driffield Junior School, did; and in 1991 he started work at Orchard Park.

Two things that you notice on first meeting John Buttrick are his enthusiasm for his own experience and his understanding of what used to be called 'working class culture'. Thank goodness. In districts where you can come across families where no-one has worked for three generations you need energy and a feeling of self-worth. John Buttrick has both. Like a fish that understands the sea it swims through, he understands the communities he works in.

At Orchard Park his vision was clear-sighted. He sought to encourage high aspirations in the children, and more particularly amongst the parents. He knew that before he could do anything he had to get those parents on his side. His priorities could not be too direct. It was no use preaching 'aspiration'. His first seeding priority was to get the parents into the school. If that meant Bingo and American Line Dancing, then that was what he would provide. His introduction to many of the parents was as a 'bingo caller'. He was shouting 'two fat ladies eighty-eight', 'rubber ducks twenty-two' and 'legs eleven' before he was shouting the odds about the need to come to parenting sessions.

It takes a village to educate a child.
University of the First Age Report.
Birmingham 1995

John Buttrick: 'From there we graduated to something more advanced and mind-stretching. This was after I had circulated information which was carried home by the children. I had also gone round door-stepping, telling people about the courses we would run in the following term. The first one I introduced was an afternoon class on Psychology - later we also had one on Philosophy. I argued that everyone is interested in how their minds worked and that interest would hold their attention.

'In one memory forming event I was approached by two mothers who told me how enthusiastic they were about the new classes but said - as if in some way they expected this to disqualify them - that they could not read. I explained that while reading was important, not having this skill could be countered. I said that it was listening and taking part in the debate that mattered.' He still says that.

SRB AND ITS USES

It was at Francis Askew Primary School, Gypsyville Primary School, West Hull that John Buttrick had his first encounter with SRB budgets. The school had failed an OFSTED inspection and the headteacher decided to think constructively about working closer with the parents. He gave John the job and managed to squeeze out of a SRB 2 budget enough money to release John from his teaching duties and let him become a key worker delivering the child/parent agenda. When Hull received money from SRB 4 in 1998 to support an extensive programme called *Youth and Using Your Abilities 1998 - 2004* John was prepared. He had a pilot-scheme working in one school even before the money was on tap.

The citywide *Youth and Using Your Abilities* programme originally had a seven year life span but following negotiations with Yorkshire Forward this has been re-profiled to six years. Every effort was made to ensure that the projects were, where applicable, sustainable when the SRB 4 funding finished. Although many of them are now history, the Children's University shows that some degree of sustainability was considered from the beginning.

Like most SRB 4 programmes they focused on forming partnerships with the local authority and on recognising their agendas. Like the Children's University the *Youth and Using Your Abilities* schemes focused on the

Learning Chapter in the *Kingston upon Hull City Regeneration Strategy*. All projects sought to meet one or more of the four identified themes within the programme. The target group was broad and the themes were:

- Enhancing Parenting Skills
- Raising Educational Aspiration and Achievement
- Youth Participation and Empowerment
- Facilitating the Transition Between Youth and the Adult World.

With a budget of £5.9 million, the programme particularly aimed to influence life-long learning, from pre-school through to post-16 education, and was committed to raising aspirations and achievements within the City. It not only focused on delivery within the twenty lowest achieving districts, it also focused on providing learning opportunities communitywide. The plan was to deliver programmes that were complementary to school provision. The origins and the delivery methods of the Children's University stemmed from that primary ambition. It entered a partnership with the schools but was freer in its programming.

The first students of Hull Children's University were 60 Francis Askew Primary School pupils in Spring 1997. They worked with volunteers from the community on improving literacy skills. By December 2000, 22 more schools had joined the scheme, and the number of mentors had risen to 400. Currently they have 2,185 mentors on their database.

We would do well to reflect that the combined paid-up active membership of the Hull Labour, Conservative and Lib-Dem parties will not exceed the mentors the Children's University has recruited in the City over the last few years.

Mentors are asked to give about 20 hours of their time each year on helping primary school children, aged from seven to eleven, out of normal school hours usually between 3.30 pm and 5.00 pm. These were popular with the schools - from the first the children were enthusiastic, responsive and eager to learn. Quickly headteachers recognised that the pupils' all-round performance improved with the arrival of the Children's University. The after-school meetings not only offered 'education as recreation' but also presented a more structured opportunity for parents and other adults to be involved in the development of literacy and numeracy skills.

However, the history of the Children's University goes back further than Spring 1997.

THE UNIVERSITY OF THE FIRST AGE

Birmingham had the idea of a University of the First Age but Hull was first with the idea for a university to improve young people's motivation through module-based mentoring on a significantly different, and ultimately more sustainable, scale. Birmingham relied on the development of a costly model, Hull on a much cheaper one.

The Birmingham modules were expensive to develop. On the 'costings' page of the preliminary report of *First Age - The Vision* (1995) it was estimated that the cost per module was £13,600, and forty-four modules plus two would cost £625,600. The Children's University modules by contrast have been created for less than 5% of this price. Many have been written by John Buttrick himself and others by colleagues for next to nothing. Recognising that his mentor volunteers enjoy the challenge of writing to a formula with a clear lay-out structure, he has exploited the opportunity and got them to do the development work for the fun of doing it. Their name is on the cover of the module, that is all. Presumably some write into their CVs that they have been responsible for writing a mentoring module. On the whole, they work for job satisfaction.

Ten years after its inception it is reported that Birmingham's University of the First Age is in trouble but the Hull organisation is holding its own. It is striving to be sustainable, and although it needs grant aid, it is not wholly dependent upon it. It is part of a general educational culture. Both schemes emphasise commitment to raising achievement in urban areas and preparing young people for the 'challenges of adult life', and extending choice through an out-of-school curriculum.

In Hull they concentrate on working closely with young people who have low self-esteem and come from areas were aspiration and ambition are under-developed.

When it was functioning to full capacity the Birmingham University of

the First Age capitalised on the 'improved' teaching and learning opportunities presented by developments including the information super-highway. The Children's University was much more 'people led' rather than 'technology led'. They have focused on activities, like for example a visit to the Humber BBC and use of its resources, but IT is not pivotal.

Originally, the University of the First Age's headquarters were located at the heart of the Digbeth Millennium Campus. Three minutes' walk from the Bull Ring - the city's ancient market place - and close to all of the big stores, the centre was at the hub of the 'new' Birmingham. Preliminary estimates indicated in 1995 that the central buildings and IT infrastructure would cost £30 million. By contrast, the Children's University has its administration located in a 'regenerated' secondary school at the centre of a council estate, a £6.50 taxi drive from the central railway station.

In retrospect, now that the University of the First Age seems to be toppling into the 'history of interesting educational ideas', it is easy to see that its roots were shallow. For a variety of reasons, though impoverished, the Hull Children's University is still on its feet wondering quite what happened to its parent.

WHO SHOULD BE PAID

There is a tendency these days to assume that people who give their services for nothing are 'nutters' or 'do-gooders'. I have always felt that a 'do-gooder' was preferable to a 'do-badder'. I doubt 'do-gooders' ever existed in quantity and if they did, today they will be rare birds indeed. When the law requires modern volunteers to be trained and police-vetted there are few that volunteer without a great deal of thought.

The modules are examples of free learning within a framework. They offer a compromise between excessive restriction and excessive freedom.

Generally, the mentors come from a much more varied cross section of the population than are represented at the Hull University meeting. Originally, when there was an annual SRB 4 budget of £1.6m over five years, there were a number of classroom assistants. They have gone with the money. The notion that parents would play a significant part in the development of the Children's University has not materialised. There are a handful of parents who have trained to be mentors. To some extent this is because the recruitment of parents has been left to the school, and schools do not have the resources to implement a recruitment policy.

Today if a teacher works on the two more expensive modules, then she or he can be paid. At the beginning Classroom Supervisory Assistants (CSA) also received payment. This practice ended with the cuts. Now only the classroom teacher gets support if a school pays for the Children's University Silver and Platinum 'packages'. This seems a pity - CSAs were receiving supervised training under the old regime, a fact that could easily go unrecognised.

WHAT THE CHILDREN SAID

Sixteen ten and eleven year old children of mixed ability dressed in the vermilion tops and badges of their school sat on gym apparatus in the school hall of St Nicholas School, Cottingham Road. The headteacher sat on the floor and I had a low chair.

Beryl Turner, the headteacher and a joint author of one of the mentoring programmes, started us all off by asking the group to tell me about the 'Tsunami Module'. This produced a good deal of knowledge. Even a very young girl illustrated how the movement of the 'tectonic plates' related to the wave by demonstrating their movement with her hands and explaining very simply how the upwards thrust of the earth's crust produced the giant wave.

This was a subject that interested me. My daughter had been caught up in a town on the tip of Shri Lanka and had managed to escape into the jungle only a mile away from where 800 people were drowned as they travelled south in a train. She remembered a child - the age of the children here at the school - running screaming into the hotel and crashing into a glass door.

What she also remembered was a block of water, its vertical edge carrying on its surface the deck chairs and sunbathing gear associated with a winter holiday on the sun-drenched beach racing towards them. I told them that the real wave was probably not like the one depicted on the cover of their tsunami folder. Someone in the Children's University design team had used the internet in a very intelligent way and had created his powerful image but it was not accurate. I said what they were looking at was a simplified representation of Hokusai's *In the Hollow of a Wave off the Coast at Kanagawa* (1801), a very powerful image of a wave but not like the one that hit the Shri Lankan coast on Boxing Day last year. I explained the real thing was different, though the representation of threat and power conveyed was appropriate.

Hokusai, the Japanese artist, has always fascinated me. He was always changing the name with which he signed his work. The one he used towards the end of his life meant *Old Man Mad About Drawing*. I mentioned this. On hearing this nugget of information the Head asked me to spell the printmaker's name. I did and Ben - a 1990s name if ever there was one - said he would look it up on the internet when he got back into the classroom.

This use of group discussion, individual research and new technology was fascinating and direct, and as they talked I realised how important direct contact with an individual mentor was. George, 'a mister who had been a headteacher' was especially singled out for praise. Clearly not all of the mentors were in their twenties. The children agreed that the mentors made the Hull Children's University. One of the strengths, according to a boy called Chris, was that the mentors learnt with the children. They shared information just as we had shared. Moves from discussion to computer and back again were common but talking with a computer was not enough.

My Uncle Eric, a maintenance foreman at Avery's, a man given to the reading of cowboy novels, sleeping by the fire and pronouncing on the merits of West Bromwich Albion, awoke in my presence - this would be about 1953 - having fallen asleep during a programme call Ballet For Beginners *- to say, That there was a lot to be said for ballet.' I have thought a lot about this as the years have passed and programme makers have tried to make programmes to interest working class audiences.*

I told them the full story and realised that I was behaving a bit like a mentor myself. Although our ratio was 1:16 rather than 1:3 I was bringing into their world my family's experiences, and for a minute or two I was talking with them rather than at them. I was digesting, listening and learning. Their information about 'tectonic plates' was a more than reasonable barter exchange for my information about a Japanese printmaker. After all, the tsunami knowledge of an eleven year old English school girl had saved a beach of people in December 2004.

I was also impressed by the speed with which the tsunami module had entered the educational food chain. The villages were destroyed on 26 December and by the following summer St Nicholas was twinned with a school in Batticalo - technology again.

THE MODULES

Since two of the children at St Nicholas had recently worked on 'Opera', we briefly discussed that module. It interested me because it seemed a little out of the ordinary.

The boys who had been chosen to speak were bright and totally unselfconscious. It is difficult to know, but given the catchment area - their primary school is very close to Hull University - I suspect that they were the children of professional parents. Led into the subject by the headteacher they were quickly giving us the low-down on demi-monde relationships in mid-nineteenth century France. Little girls looked gob-smacked as the taller of the two boys told us the story.

Use Google to go to *La Traviata* and there you will find the plot summary: 'Violetta, a consumptive courtesan, falls in love with Alfredo. Alfredo's father convinces Violetta that she must leave him for the honour of the family. Alfredo publicly insults Violetta at a party. The guests are shocked. Violetta dies.' At St Nicholas it was not told in that pithy way. As Ben drove the narrative relentlessly forward, Alex volunteered that the heroine needed to drink a lot of milk. On this the headmistress volunteered that this was because Violetta had consumption.

The range of modules the school could buy into in the 2005 Winter term included: *Behaviour at the Game, Old Faithful, Prison - Me No Way, A Better Me, Brain Gym, BAE Systems, BBC Module, Dance Me a Picture, The Deep, Popstars, Opera* and *Read It.* There is a mixture of modules devised in co-operation with 'partners' from the business and public service industries. Some make up for deficiencies in somewhat prescriptive syllabuses and others seek to protect the young child against ignorance and crime.

The *Learning To Learn Mentor Module Planning Guide* uses a printer's font called 'Comic Sans'. Many people in the 'communities' like this font because it comes with Windows. 'Helvetica' and 'Arial' have a touch of the fascist about them, 'Garamond' and 'Times New Roman' a sniff of the Victorian era but, 'Comic' suggests fun. It is just the right face for introducing mentors and children to the joys of learning.

The *Planning Guide* is a slim document, nothing more than a cover and three sheets of paper. Written by module tutors Andrew Holmes and Beryl Turner, it is an exemplar of good practice. I asked Andrew Holmes, a tutor at Hull University who devised the module, about this. I point out that I usually associate lecturers with over-writing rather than simplicity. He agrees that this is an occupational hazard but a repetitive strain injury and his dedication to KISS - Keep It Short and Simple - have determined the document's form.

It must have cost no more than 20p to produce, the bulk of the money being spent on the spine and the see-through protective cover. I see this as important when it comes to spending SRB - or indeed any government money. Too many organisations have been seduced into creating full-colour, designer delivered documents in which content is sacrificed to design just because the general culture - all spin and gloss - seems to demand it. There is a mid-position between stapled A4 sheets and high gloss publications. The mentoring packs demonstrate this.

Learning to Learn does not give 'Objectives' but 'Overall Aims' of the course, including:

- to provide pupils with a better and deeper understanding of the learning process
- to help pupils identify their own motivational factors and reasons for wanting to learn
- to provide pupils with an appreciation of multiple intelligence theory.

In Yorkshire you sometimes hear the phrase 'He's 'clever' used in a pejorative way. 'He's a clever sod', 'He's too clever by half ' are common in the North. This is odd because people should attempt to be clever.

All of these took me by surprise. What had caused me to seek out this module was the enthusiasm expressed for it by the St Nicholas children. This module was taking the children into the education process itself and explaining why and how they learn.

All of the information which came lower down in this three page module planning guide, such as skills covered, teaching activities to be used and the five week work programme, fascinated me, but nothing fascinated me as much as the third bullet point. In the Mentor's Manual, mentors were asked to include in the topics which they discussed with the two or three children assigned to them *Multiple Intelligences - Howard Gardener's Theory of Recognising, and Rewarding Diversity*.

I knew nothing about Harvard professor Howard Gardener's theory and therefore I did what any bright ten year old would do, I went and looked him up on Google:

'Howard Gardener's book *Frames Of Mind* has been about since 1983 and answers many of the questions asked by experienced teachers. We all have had students who didn't fit the mould; we knew the students were bright, but they didn't excel in tests. Gardener's claim that there are several different kinds of intelligence, gave us and others involved with teaching and learning a way of beginning to understand those students. We should look at what they could do well instead of what they could not do.'

As I read, my mind went back to John Maybury - if he's still living he would be well into his fifties by now - a boy who could copy anything but found reading very difficult. He once did me a drawing of Dürer's 'Praying Hands' in great detail, every wrinkle was there. I also thought of David Newton, a boy who I struggled to teach. He could not read, write or spell. Each day I tried on a one to one basis as far as the timetable allowed to teach him these skills as he languished in the eighth stream of a streamed secondary modern school.

Eventually I realised that I was too narrow in my appreciation of his intelligence. His ability was in listening and analysing what he had heard. I once watched him listen to a student teacher who started reading from a short story in which the opening line was, 'Everything in this room had a purpose.' He stopped her in her tracks about five hundred words on. His hand went up and he shouted, 'Miss, Miss, if everything in the room had purpose how could the bulb hang aimlessly? Miss, you've just said 'the bulb hung aimlessly.' Both boys had intelligence which was different from that usually appreciated in schools.

John Maybury had spatial intelligence, the ability 'to think in pictures; to perceive the visual world accurately and recreate it in the mind or on paper'. David Newton had a 'linguistic intelligence' but not in written form. He could listen intelligently and analytically like a literary critic but not write down an expression of that intelligence. Had he been in Iraq before the invention of cuneiform, he could have been Chancellor of the Exchequer; in the 1960s he was assigned to the dung heap were teachers often send those who cannot read or write.

'Logical/mathematical' and 'musical' intelligence are often given a superiority not given to those with 'spatial', 'bodily - kinaesthetic', 'interpersonal', 'intrapersonal' intelligence.

In Week One the mentors meet for two hours to discuss the module and raise questions with each other. The following and subsequent weeks, the mentors meet their young students and start to work their way through the Guide. Every paragraph is straightforward. 'What motivates you?' is followed by the instruction that mentors 'share ideas' and outline 'motivation in discussion and share goals with the pupils.'

One of the attractive things about the module pack is its simplicity, one of the St Nicholas school children said the 'mentors learn with us' but then the good teachers, the watching and listening teachers, always did from Socrates onwards. They cannot help it.

DAWN WHITTAKER'S CLASSROOM

Francis Askew School is situated in Gypsyville on one of the older Hull council estates to the west of the city. It has recently been 'regenerated' and some of the houses have been culled with green areas opening up in their place. When I arrive, the twenty children in the Children's University group are receiving small cartons of pure orange juice and a couple of biscuits from their teacher, Dawn Whittaker. It is 3.25 pm and John Buttrick is about to begin. I glance at my surroundings. As well as

Why should the devil have all the best tunes?
General Booth,
founder of the Salvation Army

having sections dedicated to science, history, art and prime numbers, the walls of the Year Six classroom also have a space dedicated to various 'writing genres'. In this classroom the introduction to new words and concepts is to the fore.

As I read I see that the wall displays show a respect for language and good manners. Under the header 'PSHE' is written 'The Golden Rule': 'Treat others as you would like to be treated, put yourself in someone's shoes. If you would be unhappy in their situation then they are probably unhappy too.'

The project writer as well as teacher on this occasion is John Buttrick himself. There are also five mentors plus the teacher; this makes a ratio of 4:1 children to mentors. I am here to watch an opening session of a module on popular music. In the course of discussion, the music of groups like *Westlife* and *Pussycat Dolls* will feature, but even when we talk about the up-to-date music of today, old-fashioned values of thanking and applauding success echo around.

John has not had a good day. This session relies on equipment, the school's projector is out of action and the Children's University do not own the right kind. He has anticipated this eventuality and arranged for a local businessman to bring in an up-to-date projector. Three hours previously John had gone to the Grand Hotel as arranged to pick it up but had found that the man who had promised the equipment was ill.

This led to him change his tack. Instead of embarking immediately on the module he entered into an animated conversation with the groups and the mentors about 'The Case of the Missing Boss'. John was angry and animated but did not for a moment show the extent of his emotion.

He told the story up to the point where he had no projector and then turned to the children in the class: 'I had this gentleman's home phone number and his mobile number. I phoned both, no answer. If the gentleman was dead, ill or in hospital I will apologise next week. In the meantime I would like you to discuss for two minutes the story and then share with us the reason why I was unable to get in touch with him.'

The children began discussing with the mentor and after two minutes John used an old teacher's trick that I always find impressive. He did not say, 'Please stop,' he simply raised his hand in the air and the children in a rehearsed signal all raised theirs. There was no bellowing above the hubbub of discussion, no shouting. All was silent. Everyone's arm was in the air. 'Now,' he said as his and everyone else's hand went down, 'I would like you to share your responses with us.' He pointed to a girl.

'We think he is twagging,' she said.

John said, 'Who else agrees with that?' All hands went up and then came down.

He then asked a second question, 'How do you think I felt?' A little boy's hand went up immediately: 'Gutted.'

John's ability to ensure that shared politeness underpins every response is quite remarkable. The module I was about to see was about the music of today, a subject where brutality of language is to the forefront but I began to see that the current government 'respect agenda' was central to the lesson plan. The way we talk to each other was what was being learnt, not information about the pop charts.

We were now into the subject. Pop was the menu from here onwards. He clicked a switch and the names of three bands came up on an interactive whiteboard. He clicked on the first and we watched a performance of *Pussycat Dolls*. Unfortunately it was a silent performance - the school amplifying system, brought in at a rush when he failed to get the up-to-date equipment, was incompatible with the interactive whiteboard. Despite this John pressed ever onward. He had a new resource and tried to use it only to discover that someone had trodden on the compilation CD he had prepared at home.

In Hull, 'ginnels' common in the West Riding, are called 'ten footers'. 'Twagging' is a dialect word only found in the city and its hinterland. Hull is different.

Dawn Whittaker and the mentors then gave out the work sheets and the children began to discuss them. They discussed hair-dos, shoes and makeup but also lifestyle presentation and musical 'genre'. This went on for the next ten minutes and then John asked us to share our thoughts in a general discussion. To this they brought their own experience of popular music and discussed it using what they had seen but also what they knew of the bands from other sources. Going round the tables I heard one girl say, 'This is urban pop with a rap background,' another indicated distastefully that it was 'commercial': 'They are there to sell a product.' A third added, 'In many ways this is about image. She needs to appeal to a variety of fans and so the lead singer is always changing her gear.' When we shared in a wider discussion one boy added that 'the lead singer's personality is too much in your face.'

The discussion was informed, and because John asked some of them to write out their opinions in full sentences this became an exercise in well taught written English. With twenty minutes to go and with no visual or aural aide on offer, John picked up an old blackboard ruler which was one and a half meters long and pretended it was a microphone. He then gave his rendition of *You Raised Me Up* by *Westlife*. The children then discussed John's presentation and performance.

At 4.50 pm John talked about how the project would proceed and how by Week Four they could be singing solo, in a pair, or as a group. He promised them that they would feel confident and that there may be a possibility that they could be starting their own 'groups' and writing their own music.

He told the story of Jason Etherington who had turned up at a class five years previously. When asked what he was good at, he had replied, 'I'm not good at owt, Sir.' Twelve weeks later Jason fronted a performance at a local hotel. This occasion was the Children's University Annual Conference. The five hundred guests included business representatives, parents, pupils and guest speaker Kevin Keegan. They listened as Jason was declared the winner of the rap-writing competition. 'I still keep in touch with him. He is now at North Lindsay Tech doing a music course leading to a degree. The writing is important but it is his self-confidence that really matters. Thank you for your time.'

He then thanked the mentors, the teachers and me but in particular 'the stars of the evening', the twenty children of Year Six. In a surprise thank-you at the very end he also thanked his twelve-year-old daughter 'and her mates', because they had spent their time helping him put together a compilation of up-to-date pop music.

A BUSINESS PARTNER

Ricky Alfred, Children's University Board member and full-time worker with the charity 'Business in the Community', is quite clear why Hull businesses like to work with the Children's University: 'They see it as something different that is delivering an agenda which appeals to them. They are fed up with bureaucracy. They find it in the schools and they find it in government, you cannot get anywhere without at least one meeting at which no decisions are made.

'It also addresses certain shortcomings in the education system that they consider need addressing. They are not satisfied with the literacy and numeracy standards that are being passed into the workplace. The Children's University involves them in the task of improving both of these key subjects through active involvement with children. Although the University takes children to the opera in London and on visits to Premier League Football clubs we should always remember that it is still totally committed to literacy. Businesses understand that agenda. They also know that the help they give switches children back on in these essential subjects. This is especially the case with boys who lack role models and who need to work with men.

'Businesses welcome the chance to be involved in the work of the University. In the early days, major companies like Reckitt Benckiser put in cash and Smith & Nephew offered volunteers. Now the agenda is such that more and more companies are happy to give help in kind. Involvement is easy and their employees love it. Workers from every department, and from every level in the hierarchy come together to perform a joint piece of work. It encourages co-operation. An earlier generation went into the hills and built rafts and lived in make-shift shelters to achieve this. Those 'away weekends' were costly and only touched the chosen few. CU mentoring is cheap and has the added advantage that it can be offered by anyone in a company. Contrary to

The units associated with vocational training such as NVQs have a part to play in the educational process, people like to parade qualifications, but they must not be allowed to entrap the spirit. There has to be a time for dreaming and one for sharpening pencils. Visions have to be underpinned with pragmatism though in the end it is the visions that matter and it is those that change people.

popular imagination many companies have a wish to be involved in community ventures. Reckitts, the predecessors of Reckitt Benckiser, have a history of social involvement in East Hull. They built a model village with a community centre, a library and improved houses for their workers over a hundred years ago. Some modern companies are driven by the same ambitions. Like Reckitts they prefer quality involvement to donating trifling amounts to support an annual gala or buy shirts for the school football team. They applaud the broad-based agenda which has its feet on the ground but is capable of looking above the horizon at subjects like Citizenship. If there were children's universities in other towns where they have subsidiaries, some of the bigger Hull companies would welcome the chance to work with them elsewhere.

'Companies also consider that educationists have been slow listening to the industrial sector. The Children's University listen and, what is more, involve them directly in the learning process. In an earlier period they took school parties around the works. Most of us will have been on factory visits at some time in our school careers, the Children's University goes one step further. It allows a contributing company to be involved in the production of a mentoring pack. It also gives employees a chance to be mentors and to even write the mentoring packs. Strengthening of the employee/employer relationship is always popular with a company and the Children's University encourages this.

'When I was first appointed to work within the Hull office of 'Business in the Community' three years ago I discovered that we originally worked closely with the Children's University but over time the relationship had become more distant. Our agenda is focused on getting businesses involved within their local communities with programmes that involve their employees. After learning about the work John was doing I arranged a meeting to discuss how we could once again work together. At this stage the Children's University were looking for more funding, we were able to help by providing £100 per-head in payment for every registered mentor. The businesses we both worked with saw the sense in us working together and the relationship prospered.

'Several of the modules, especially the 'Asda Experience', in which children take an in-depth look at how this food retailer manages its business, and the 'Marr Food Experience', a similar module but in this case devoted to food processing, have gained favour with the industrial and commercial sector.'

ACTION RESEARCH AT ITS BEST

To some extent the success of the Children's University depends on the entrepreneurial qualities of its pioneers. This is 'action research' at its best. People rise to their own level not overburdened by meetings, away days and attendance at conferences. When John Buttrick goes to one it is to speak. He chooses his colleagues with care so they offer something to the organisation.

Yet this is not a one-man band. Helen Miller, another senior teacher in a local school, is the backbone of the London programme. Andrew Holmes from Hull University provides key academic support as one of the people who will develop the Children's University as it moves onwards and ever upwards. There is no lack of succession planning.

There are two evaluation reports, both well structured and informative. Writing of one of the devisers of a module, one report says that 'the Deputy Head of a local school is well connected and able to bring in a whole range of speakers.'

The outcomes and outputs of a policy are not predetermined but arise from practice. The building blocks are small. No new initiative is so big that it can easily get out of hand. Every small increment is welcomed and then tested. When the team meet someone, they trust them and make them into a decisionmaker. In every situation a topic is less important than the treatment and organisation that surrounds it.

The Children's University supports school teaching but is separate from it. The modules are delivered in different ways to the set curriculum though they may complement it. That is where its strength lies.

The Children's University has a loyal, informed staff and that is a real bonus. There were seven administrators in the office when it was receiving money from SRB 4, now there are three. One has been there for seven years, one for six and the third, for a year. All are Hull women and work closely together. They are committed to the process and the vision and they will turn to any work that needs doing, including mentoring. They have clear written job descriptions but they all admit to being situation led. 'If Vicky is under pressure we will all muck in.'

Vicky Risenham is the Learning Co-ordinator. She oversees the creation of the modules and deals with the schools that have 'bought in' that term. Catherine Wright develops the website and sees to the publicity. Liza Coulman is the Finance Officer. The Children's University is lucky to have this sort of staff because keeping the organisation moving forward is not easy now that the financial future is unclear.

Most people in salaried work do not quite understand the isolation of someone who is carving out their own destiny or a new vision. They invariably work too hard. In situations where next year's money is not guaranteed you need someone who is on your side. When SRB funding was in place for six years John Buttrick could buy in the time of a colleague to help him think through where the Children's University went next. Today he cannot. The grind is constant. At the very point when you require money to buy in a teacher colleague to talk about the way ahead you cannot afford one. The educational entrepreneur is forever devising a whole brave new world but whether angels or demons will inhabit it, is anyone's guess. Too often, without someone to convince him otherwise, the community activist believes that demons are in the ascendancy.

Some might argue that the model is so driven by John Buttrick's enthusiasm that it could not be replicated without it. That is not the case. If there was the money this model could be sent out into the world and thrive. Its strength comes from the looseness of the organisation, the ability to control its size so that it does not need to be over-big to survive, and an attitude to the motivation of staff that allows the initiated to take on decisionmaking roles quickly. Little specialised training is required because people enter with the 'life skills' they need. Action takes them forward.

In Evaluation 2002-2003, the authors suggest that there may be a need for specialised training to give mentors who are not trained teachers more information about the teaching of reading. I do not see that. This is a skill that should be learnt elsewhere. It would be a mistake to distract the Children's University from its main task of creating mentors. The delivery and creation of five-week modules is what it is good at, specialised teacher training ought to be offered by other institutions.

It is normal for academic consultants to comment on the absence of data, and since the SRB concentrates on 'outcome' and 'output' reporting you expect it. This often tells us more about the thinking of the evaluator than the organisation that is being evaluated. In a pioneering organisation the entrepreneur has little time to be interested in paper work and statistics.

THE END OF THE SRB 4 MONEY

The seven years of grant passed quickly but when it came to an end John Buttrick and the team found that although most of the other schemes that had started out with them had ceased trading, often sinking without trace, they were hanging on.

The Single Regeneration Budget SRB 4 grant came to an end in March 2003. £1.6m of SRB funding had provided a free service to schools but in the future they would have to buy into the scheme. £20,000 additional SRB funding and financial support from the City Council helped fill the gap but that was not enough. Quickly the number of schools involved dropped by a half. This is hardly surprising - after all, the service started free.

Support from Hull City Council, City Venture, local businesses and the schools themselves ensured that the Children's University continued. Learning modules that had been developed with Hull City AFC, Hull Truck, The Deep and the BBC went forward although the paid administrative strength was three rather than seven people. Ice-skating at Hull Arena, football skills days at Manchester City and trips to theatres in London and Manchester continued to support children's interest in learning.

Sometimes the teachers work too hard. Every minute is accounted for. The pace has always been pretty frantic. Too little time is left for dreaming. 'Education - Education - Education' has too often been misinterpreted as 'Syllabus - Syllabus - Syllabus' and this is sad.

With the end of SRB funding John Buttrick the team looked around for other financial sources. Hull City Council continued to fund the administration and retained John Buttrick on a salary which recognised headteacher status. They had done well. Outputs had been met and City Vision - the accountable body - was happy. On the other hand, European money was drifting out of reach and additional Yorkshire Forward money was not forthcoming. Although the business community was becoming more aware of the Children's University and giving support there was no way that the CU could be sustainable on that money alone in the short run. Schools were strapped for cash, and as one of the CU administrators said, 'If it was a leaking roof or us, the roof won every time.'

By 2005 there are 30 schools on board and the number is growing. Schools are offered three plans: 'Bronze' (£800), 'Silver' (£1,800) and 'Platinum' (3,000). Of these schemes, 'Silver' is the most popular. For this a school gets three modules. Each module consists of six ninety minute sessions. One of the modules takes the children out of the area; London is the favoured destination. John Buttrick: 'It is important to us to encourage children to have wider perspectives. There are ten year olds in this city who have never moved off their housing estates, there are West Hullers who have never been to the city centre, let alone to East Hull or York. Trips to London are vital and so are the visits to see local firms and the support that we get from the business community.'

If the Children's University is to be sustainable, more administrative aid is needed. The Evaluation 2002-2003 said so, and everything I saw when I visited their headquarters in the Education Centre, Coronation Road North, confirmed that opinion. The organisation is particularly vulnerable in that area. It does not lack ideas but if it is to endure and grow then it must be able to phone schools, contact mentors, arrange train tickets, reproduce modules and do any one of a hundred and one things that the headquarters staff do now.

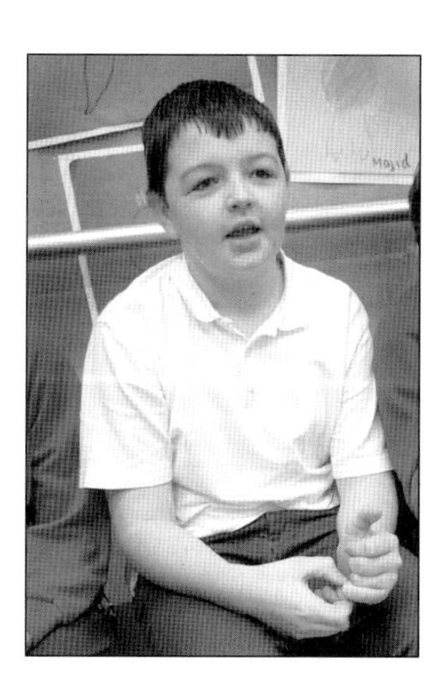

They are well into Phase II, the phase in which you search for stability and consolidate. You are at a crossroads and you know it.

To someone who has not seen the Children's University in action, some of the ideas must seem homespun, quaint even, but that is not how they seem up close. It is impressive and unusual. It succeeds by breaking rules.

STOCKSBRIDGE

Adèle Jagger

It's not the way it's got to be - People before Property –
We want a meeting place And not a traffic jam.

Folksong

WHERE THE LITTLE DON FLOWS

SHEFFIELD - STOCKSBRIDGE'S FUTURE *is a six year scheme targeting Stocksbridge and surrounding area, a single industry, steel dependent town. Priorities have been identified through extensive consultation focusing on measures to improve skills, literacy and numeracy, childcare provision and a job search programme. Job creation and the development of a local business culture will be encouraged through business start-ups, managed workspace and a project to reclaim contaminated sites. The scheme also addresses capacity building through community development workers and through the provision of a resource centre. Transport links are to be improved alongside projects to regenerate the town centre.*

Funding: SRB Total, £2m Scheme Total: £6m

Sheffield sits at the confluence of five rivers: Porter, Loxley, Sheaf, Rivelin and the Don. Many rivers rise from the lower southern slopes of the Pennines and these have gouged out well-wooded valleys which provide Sheffield with its seven hills - as many as Rome - splendid views and the accolade 'the greenest city in England'. Each valley in the past was a hive of industry, each river once supported hundreds of mills, tilts, wheels, forges, works and hammers. Now grown silent, each valley stretches long green fingers into the city. The Don or Dun as it was once called - grey brown but not at all mouse-like - is fed by the Little Don and it is this river which flows through Stocksbridge.

Today if you want to go to Stocksbridge you travel by car on the A616 from the M1 and look left. This part of the A616 is the Stocksbridge By-pass and there have been too many deaths already. That stretch sports speed cameras, travel faster than sixty miles per hour and you will hear about it! The by-pass has been squeezed into high land which has been carved through by the Little Don and the steel works. This is the southern boundary of Barnsley. Lack of room and this municipal boundary are the reasons why the Stocksbridge settlement has grown on the southern side of the valley. Over 13,000 people live on that valley side.

222 SRB 4 & 5

Anyone thinking of urban development and fitting Stocksbridge into an urban pattern might think, as they approach from the east by car along the older, twisting Manchester Road and coming into Stocksbridge after passing through a woodland, that they are in the sort of ribbon development that reaches into an agricultural area. They would be wrong. Stocksbridge was until recently an industrial town. This 'fair country' had been raped at the time of the nineteenth century industrial revolution as surely as were the valley towns of South Wales.

Stocksbridge lacks an obvious centre. This is not, nor has ever been, a market town. It is not like Penistone - Penis to rhyme with Dennis - ten minutes away. There are no obvious parking places. Looked at superficially it is hard to see much that suggests great age. Here the Clock Tower, built as a memorial to the one hundred and seven men and women who lost their lives in the Great War, seems old. There are some other buildings that date from the beginning of the last century: the Friendship Hotel (1903), the Stocksbridge Works Institute and the Town Hall (1928). There was a cinema (1921) but it lost its way and developed into shops and a depressing mall. A piece of not very original graffiti - 'Kick Tories Out' - fades on its high, east facing side façade close to St Matthias' Church (1890), built as a memorial to Samuel Fox. There is the Library cum Advice Centre (1968) with a forlorn space at its front.

In Stocksbridge there are all the shops that you could possibly want apart from a department store. That is one of its great attractions. You can drink in the pubs, dine in the Chinese and Thai restaurants, draw your cash from the banks and put it straight into the building societies or the betting shop. You can improve your looks in the hair salons or the beauty shop, buy flowers, look after your pets, visit the electrical and hardware stores and feed your family from the baker's, butcher's and the greengrocer's but there is little sophistication though there are one or two interesting shops.

After a book is finished
don't you wish you knew
everything that happened
AFTER it was through?
Aileen Fisher – 'After the End'

Crawshaw's, the butcher's, is famous. They have won awards for their sausages and it's hard to move in the store on Saturday mornings and at lunchtime. There is a Co-op, and has been for over a hundred years, but don't ask for dried porcini mushrooms! It moved into a new building in

2002 leaving the old one to the 'Factory Shop', the only place to purchase clothes here unless you can fit into the clothes sold at 'The Big Man Shop'. Further along are the fire station - no parking or turning here - the offices of *Look Local*, a free, weekly newspaper, the United Reform Church and the Rugby Union Club. Dotted along the main road are a handful of single storey wooden shops, some now re-clad but all surviving from the Victorian era. I hope they are the subjects of a preservation order but suspect they won't be. Other brick and stone shops line both sides of the road between stone clad houses whose doors open straight onto the road. These were not so much of a problem when you were walking out into a horse-drawn world but it's very different now and much noisier too. A sense of town planning or urban sensitivities? There is none.

On leaving the town, on the left hand side is a pub called 'The Silver Fox'. The painted board shows a wistful creature staring at a harvest moon. A literal and artistic interpretation this might be but not an accurate one. 'Silver Fox' was a form of stainless steel with many different qualities and applications. There was even a 'Silver Fox' stainless steel lawn tennis racquet! Forget four legs and a bushy tail when you see the name 'Fox' in this valley. Samuel Fox, iron-master and entrepreneur, made this valley and the industry he brought here was the steel industry

FOX'S STEEL WORKS

These days we have been told that 'putting all our eggs in one basket' is a mistake. In the past Stocksbridge and the surrounding area had brick and tile works, pipe works and glassworks but it was the presence of a combination of water, coal and ganister that shaped Stocksbridge, that and the vision and driving ambition of one man. His industry accounts for growth but as he was sowing the seeds of success he was also sowing those of decline. They became well rooted thirty years ago following one hundred years of prosperity.

Samuel (Sammy) Fox started his wire-drawing firm in 1842 on the banks of the river. He began modestly but was soon successfully producing light-weight 'Paragon' frames for umbrellas and crinoline frames for dresses. He was a 'hands on' master, living in a cottage at the works

entrance and an entrepreneur who, with his wife, would be on the shop floor at six in the morning.

Their diligence and tenacity of purpose paid off. After installing a Bessemer Converter and a 400HP beam engine they switched from the production of light-weight retail goods and began to produce tracks, tyres and springs for the railways. This was the Age of the Railway, which was fast becoming the favourite way to transport goods. A rail link with the Manchester, Sheffield and Lincolnshire Railway was installed in 1877 enabling Sammy Fox to avoid road tolls at Deepcar. In this period of prosperity the company diversified. His wire-drawing shops provided wire ropes for the mines of Yorkshire, Derbyshire, Nottingham, Lancashire and farther afield, and telegraph wire for that cutting edge communications industry.

His was a philanthropic and benevolent reign. Houses were built for the workforce and a school for their children. Churches were endowed and a benevolent fund begun. If he saw idle men in the street he would send for them and try to give them work. Many workers from Bradwell, Derbyshire - his home village - were employed in Stocksbridge. Some made enough money to return home and buy land; others studied to improve themselves and all thanked Samuel Fox for their start in life. He also helped develop the strong entrepreneurial spirit which made the north prosperous. Many leading regional steel manufacturers owed their success to the training they had received in Stocksbridge.

Stocksbridge's dependency on this one industry was significant and constant.

- ❒ 1891 - population of Stocksbridge 5,677
- ❒ 1893 - employed by S Fox 6,021

- ❒ 1951 - population of Stocksbridge 10,220
- ❒ 1946 - employed by S Fox 9,795

In my new clothing
I feel so different I must
Look like someone else.
Basho, Japanese poet

Dependency cannot be understood merely by looking at statistics. *The Spring* of 1946, a works magazine, price three pence, contains articles about steelmaking, electricity and production systems alongside those detailing numerous societies and clubs run for the workers. You could be a member of the Sports and Social Club for five shillings a year deducted at the rate of one penny a week from wages. Once you were a member you had access to physical culture, swimming, golf, cricket, archery, hockey, football, tennis, badminton and bowls. There was an orchestra, a drama society and a photography club. There were the annual vegetable and flower shows, orchestral concerts, outings to the seaside and to London, dances, potato weight lifting competitions, reunions and sports galas. The magazine featured poems, sketches, cartoons, photographs, union news, departmental news, letters, advice on books to read, obituaries and news of appalling accidents on the shop floor.

Anyone reading this magazine will be impressed by the total osmosis between life and work. Working at Sammy Fox's was a life, the question was: What happens to the dependent community when the firm disappears?

YESTERDAY AND TODAY

- 1991 - population of Stocksbridge 13,619
- 1991 - employed by S Fox 1,400

The loss of jobs since 1946 is striking, and the writing is on the wall - CORUS intends to remove all steel-melting processes to Rotherham. Although there will be some specialised steel making on the old Fox site it will be much reduced and it is proposed that the majority of the land will be developed for housing. The idea of becoming a dormitory town and a suburb of Sheffield is not popular with the people of Stocksbridge. The Stocksbridge community profile which is presented in one of the grant bids in 1996 comments:

'There still exists a strong sense of community, especially among those who have lived and worked in the area all their lives. The feeling of loss as opportunities for local employment and services of all kinds are withdrawn is grievous. In this former company town and its environs, the ghost of Samuel Fox, the philanthropic founder, has not been laid completely to rest,

circumstances seem to cry out urgently for a more forward looking attitude in the community to current problems and their possible solution.'

Local people have watched the principal industry of the town all but disappear, shops close, their college being demolished and their population suffer work related illnesses, yet they continued to fight on. The SRB award has to be seen in that context.

Stocksbridge College, opened with great ceremony in 1966 by Prime Minister Harold Wilson, was an early casualty of the Sheffield colleges funding crisis. It closed in 1998. The site was cleared and in 2002 a new Co-operative food store opened on the site. The College transferred into a much smaller space and adapted a former Co-operative building to cater for basic skills training and WEA classes. There was also a small crèche.

A treadmill-cycle of no work, no training and no job opportunities was difficult to stop and even more difficult to step off. In general terms the people of Stocksbridge were no worse and no better off than anyone else in South Yorkshire. Everywhere the future seemed grim.

In the 1980s and early 1990s people were talking and grumbling as people do but most realised that positive action was called for. The great steel moguls hadn't sat around moaning. They'd rolled their sleeves up and 'mucked in'. That is what a small group did.

Experts are needed if you are going to engage with government in any way; the town had several. One of the leaders was the late Terry Hardisty. Terry had worked at the College and had contacts with Sheffield TEC and local council officers. Another was Chris Prescott. His law degree and commitment to local politics had already furnished him with the necessary skills and the social conscience to take a lead. These two like-minded people saw what was happening in other parts of the city and decided to try for Single Regeneration Budget monies. 'If they can get it, why can't Stocksbridge?' Chris succinctly summed up, 'We had no funds to do bugger all and we needed some.' He was adamant that it was Stocksbridge's turn and that once the community was engaged, their need was such that they would inevitably get something.

I could be
shovelling stars into black holes
or digging the tunnels
for government moles
or the first nuclear scientist on the dole.
Dave Calder – Jokes

They had a strong sense of community cohesion. Public meetings were well attended and soon twenty people formed the nucleus of what was to become Stocksbridge Training and Enterprise Partnership (STEP). Andy Clarke, currently its Chief Executive says, 'Chris was the right man, in the right place, at the right time. Eventually we received £2 million SRB money and used this to lever in another £6 million!'

To illustrate, Chris Prescott produced box files, document folders, plastic shopping bags et al; a fraction, I am assured, of what he keeps at home. Every relevant piece of paper, every newspaper cutting, every photograph, even a rolled-up and rather tatty sheet of planning from a flip chart, he has kept. This attention to detail and the ability to find exactly the piece of paper he is referring to still impresses me and must have played a large part in ensuring that the bid was a success. Today, although no longer directly associated with STEP, he remains its unofficial archivist and can trace its development and offshoots in great detail. He acknowledges that once a project has legs it's bound to develop in different ways and that's as it should be.

He is worth listening to, especially about leadership. He contends that no individual should own a project. If someone does then it doesn't grow. There must be collective responsibility because as things develop modification to the original parameters will occur. Whilst not all of the plans submitted in 1999 have come to fruition many have, and he is - rightly - very proud of the difference STEP has made to Stocksbridge since it opened in 2001. Stocksbridge in its turn is proud of his diligence, vision and tenacity.

STOCKSBRIDGE TRAINING AND ENTERPRISE CENTRE

The STEP building is situated opposite Lidl, another food store, and sandwiched between a Nat West Bank and Britannia Building Society. On the outside it has the appearance of a red-brick nineteenth century parish hall or an old village school. It has been cleaned up, it was blacker in more prosperous times. Opened as 'The Stocksbridge Works Institute' in 1902, and still known by some as the 'Miners' Welfare' it once housed reading rooms, billiard tables, baths for the men and living accommodation for the caretaker. All-round care for the body and the mind was catered for here. On becoming redundant, the building had fallen into silence. If it had gone to auction, who knows how the site would have developed? A shop perhaps, a private dwelling, or more likely it would have been razed to the ground and become the site of a block of flats or a care home or a parking lot. This lovely and elegant building was spared these nightmares. It eventually opened as the main office and training centre for STEP.

Over 1,000 learners passed through its doors last year. They come to take advantage of:

- the JobNet Project - a community service that matches people skills to quality jobs
- ICT Education offering at least seven different kinds of courses
- community education - family learning, healthy living, personal and social development, leisure, craft and recreation, gender work and work with people with disabilities
- nursery/childcare - from six months to seven years
- summer holiday activities for children
- Employment and Education Guidance Service
- recreational courses - first aid, genealogy, food hygiene, wildlife and gardening

Andy Clarke continues to praise the original organisation: 'When I came it was already highly innovative, highly responsive and highly motivated. I came here in a roundabout way, via Stocksbridge College. It was an absolute crime to close that excellent community facility. It usually catered for people of sixteen to ninety but once we had to overstep our normal age group to accept a centenarian.'

How many miles to Babylon?
Four score miles and ten.
Shall I get there by candle-light?
Yes and back again.
Seventeenth century nursery rhyme

After a spell at Parson's Cross College Andy found himself out of work and deciding to upgrade his CV, he popped into the STEP building to use their computers. He is a talker and raconteur. He stopped to talk to an acquaintance and, as a result, found himself working one day a week as a volunteer. When this increased to three days he thought that it would be a good idea if they paid him. They did, he stayed and he is now Chief

Executive of STEP. 'And a very good one,' says Joan Banks, one of the Trustees. 'Working here bites you on t' bum,' says Andy, 'it's totally addictive.' Like every one else these days he recognises the importance of forward thinking. Now the SRB money has ended, there are ambitious plans for expansion, all with the community in mind.

The community is happy with STEP and says so in notes given by students in the computer courses to their tutor: 'Excellent tutor support and teaching. Nothing is too much trouble and explanations are never too much trouble.' - 'If all tutors gave the support to students like those at STEP, learning would be much more enjoyable.' - 'It was a nice friendly atmosphere. We are allowed to learn at a steady pace.'- 'The challenge to learn to study again became a reality.'

Beside comments that show gratitude for the chance to study, you hear the voice of people who wish to catch up on themselves and skill for different work patterns. Throughout you hear people explaining how the skilling they received at STEP helped businesses to survive and the voluntary sector to be strengthened. If SRB money had not been there these talents would have been lost to the community. Sheffield is a long way and they would not have travelled there easily.

Margaret Freestone, the ICT Manager, is totally committed to STEP and her enthusiasm is tangible and infectious. She started her working life as a music teacher but after taking a Personal Assistants Diploma came to Stocksbridge and volunteered to run computer courses for people wanting to start their own business. She now feels very much part of the community and says that she cannot walk down the road without bumping into all ages of people she has helped. Her mission is to increase the confidence of every single person who walks through STEP's door. This happens.

In many ways the aspirations of the students I met echoed the aspirations of their tutors. Anne Dawson is there because she wants to keep up with her granddaughter. Maggie Cain, had trained at drama college and had been a hospital social worker. Now she wanted to write 'but you're not a writer 'til you do it, so that is why I am here.' Word processing drew her to STEP. A remark by Enid Thornton, an ex-teacher, resonated with me. She said the world was dividing into PC and non-PC people and she knew on which side she wanted to be! And she didn't mean 'politically correct'.

A SUSTAINING STAFF

Access to the nursery and the children's centre is at the back of the building or down a front staircase that is painted with vibrant 'hungry caterpillar' designs. Here they cater for children from six months to seven years. Kelly Campbell says that the facility was originally for thirteen children and was free of charge. After a week in the job she had to present a paper to the Board of Trustees about ways to make it sustainable. It was seen that sustainability was possible and the demand for places grew as local working parents heard about it. Chris Prescott dug up details and found comparisons with other areas. The research paid off. Today this area of the STEP initiative is growing. They now have an after school club called 'Bright Sparks'.

The present government wants a children's centre, ideally attached to a school, in every area. Each will cater for children nought to sixteen years. It is its ambition to have under one roof health services, midwives, crèche facilities, nurseries, breakfast clubs and after school clubs; anything to do with children's well being. The government will provide £1 million for each centre but this will just about pay for the building. Stocksbridge goes into the exercise with the experience of Kelly Campbell and her colleagues to hand. Sustainability to that level is not easy. Exciting times are ahead.

Education, Education, Education!
Tony Blair
Revenue, Revenue, Revenue!
Glenys Campbell,
Community strategist

Helen Murphy, Education and Employment Guidance Manager, remembers the sticky times of the 1980s as a period of high unemployment, poor job prospects and loss of hope. Like others she experienced them and so was well placed to empathise with people coming in off the street and taking their first steps towards a new life. Jobnet is at the front of the building and well placed for those taking that first big step. It has a window onto the main road and passers-by can easily see what jobs and opportunities for training are currently available.

Helen knows too well that lack of qualification and/or skills disempowers. She set about obtaining her own long after leaving school. Since the 1990s she has been involved in community work of one form or another. She is very appreciative of Chris Prescott's vision to set up Joblink in 2002, and Jobnet in 2004. Over that period the numbers registered doubled to more than two hundred. These are tracked every four weeks. This system follows men and women in their efforts as they seek employment and retraining. She and her colleagues keep a watchful eye to see people do not fall into unemployment too easily. They were particularly helpful immediately after Corus announced that they were closing the rolling mill and melting shop. They could point older men to lighter part-time work and younger ones to HGV driving, fork lift work, gas fitting and electrical work; to show them that they had transferable skills not easily recognised in a steel works.

Like Andy Clarke, Margaret Freestone, Helen Murphy and Kelly Campbell, everyone I met at STEP has to plan ahead; no-one really knows about future funding. They do, however, make plans and try to balance what the community needs and what funders require. They certainly have the will and acumen to carry this off. But these are difficult times and when the chips are down, power often rests with the big battalions. All the staff I met at STEP display such enthusiasm and ability and joy in their work that I leave this building a couple of centimetres above the pavement. The spirit of SRB initiatives allowed a small group of enthusiasts to set up very interesting capacity building enterprises in a town which is on the edge of things but there is a danger that they could get lost, as an educational juggernaut moved forward with a tendency towards economies of scale and decisions based on cautiously monitored market-force criteria rather than community development.

IN THE FOX TRADITION

The STEP Business Centre, Deepcar, lies a few miles nearer Sheffield than the STEP headquarters and close to the By-pass. This new rectangular building houses offices, conference rooms and workshops. The foyer proudly displays a plaque which reads: 'For outstanding contribution to Community Regeneration - 2002.'

Centre Manager Frank Houghton talks me through the range of businesses using the site: financial advisers, electronics firms, metal traders, ecologists, sports equipment suppliers, civil engineers, suppliers of weighing machines for business, internet service providers, business advisers, fire alarm suppliers, plumbing and heating engineers, and the Steel Valley Project itself. Out of thirty-two spaces, four are vacant at the moment but they have already been taken. The workshops are totally flexible, internal walls can be moved to accommodate most people's needs. The Centre provides core secretarial services, photocopying and accommodation addresses. As companies become successful they move out when they need more space. This hundred percent record is impressive.

John Brierley, the Chair of the Business Centre, takes me round. By background he is a Fox's man. He fell into his role after attending meetings of the STEP Board. His history made for a suitable appointment: both his parents had worked at Sammy Fox's, his mum in the umbrella department and his dad as a labourer in the steel works. At the age of twelve John was accepted as a likely candidate for training along with many other boys from the area. After leaving school he spent six months at Belmont Training centre - once the Manager's House - then three months as a messenger boy. This was a totally necessary experience as the factory was three miles long and a quarter of a mile wide and everyone had to learn the geography. Then came three months training whilst his skills were assessed. John went into the Chemistry Laboratory. Towards the end of training and fully expecting to sit HNCs the boys were told they were trained enough to work at Sammy Fox's and didn't need external qualifications! The expectation that they had a job for life with the company was still going strong in the sixties. They didn't need to be flexible with qualifications that other employers would recognise as they would not be working anywhere else. So John stayed in the labs on £5 per week. If he had opted for the rolling mills he could have earned £17 per week over three shifts - a career option which many ex-grammar school boys chose - the secondary modern boys wanted the lab work.

1. If the game is rigged so you can't win, find another game or invent your own. 2. If you're not winning because you don't know the rules, learn the rules. 3. If you know the rules but aren't willing to follow them, there's either something wrong with the game or you need to change something in yourself. 4. Don't play the game in a half-baked way. Either get all the way in or all the way out. 5. It shouldn't be necessary for others to lose in order for you to win. If others have to lose, re-evaluate the game's goals.
'Game Rules' website,
Garry Hamilton

John ended his working life as a full time organiser for the GMB. His life experiences make him a strong Chair and one who is full of praise for the initiators of STEP. He acknowledges that the people of Stocksbridge were highly motivated and full of innovation, and he is full of praise for the way Chris Prescott pursued the SRB funding stream with tenacity.

The centre was mostly funded from SRB monies and very important to the overall growth strategy. At its inception Chris Prescott saw it as a sustainable element especially if it could be made to grow. Getting more land to do this has proved to be difficult so Phase 2 is marking time. The ideal land, just adjacent to the Business Centre, seems to have several owners and is not available for development.

THE SVCP LAUNDRY AND BUS

STEP was involved with the Steel Valley Community Partnership from its inception and provided support and funding. Its office is situated at the western end of the town in a small, crowded, but immaculately tidy room underneath the Leisure Centre. Dave Cooper is the company secretary.

He is another man with strong links to the local steel works. His father worked at Sammy Fox's for thirty-five years. After a lifetime in retailing Dave took himself off to Northern College in Barnsley, a community college that offers courses to second chance learners, on a course which gave training in management of groups of all kinds. Dave took to this like a duck to water and was so good that he was recently awarded the title of 'adult learner of the year'. The award came from NIACE, the National Institute of Adult Continuing Education. His name was submitted by his tutor and he led a field of several hundred people. This year Dave has been invited to speak on 'Voluntary Work Leading to Employment' at NIACE's annual conference.

Like John Brierley Dave Cooper is fanatically committed to helping people to help themselves. Being well supported by his directors, and especially Ruth Lewis, Chair of SVCP, he has managed to initiate a number of innovative schemes, in particular the Stocksbridge Community Laundry and the the Stocksbridge Flyer Community Transport Scheme.

Linen washed in public here.
We let out of the bag who we are.

Liz Lockhead – Laundrette

The Stocksbridge Flyer, driven by Tristran on the morning I was one of the passengers, is funded by South Yorkshire Passenger Transport Executive. They were concerned that the uptake for this service would be very limited but eventually SVCP was given the go-ahead to promote the Flyer. This was after Dave had laid out excellent plans for advertising and had met with upwards of fifty local groups to assess their needs.

Local papers and posters backed up presentations to local groups and to individuals. Groups were identified which could benefit from this service and one group, 'Lifestyle Matters', acknowledged that it would not have been able to run at all without the assistance of the service.

Basically this is a door to door taxi service for forty pence a trip in a bus seating about twelve people. Tristran, a round peg in a round hole if there ever was one, had always wanted to work with the elderly and had learned a new skill in driving this mini-van. All the passengers were delighted to see him, and he them. He escorted, he carried, he chatted, he made everyone comfortable and, as much as anything, he helped make this day special.

The benefits it brings to those who use the service are immeasurable. The commuters have problems ranging from walking disabilities to learning difficulties, others have sight and hearing problems. The buses can be used for visiting family and friends, lunch clubs, supermarkets, hairdressers, library, medical centres and anywhere between Langsett, Midhopestones, Stocksbridge and Deepcar.

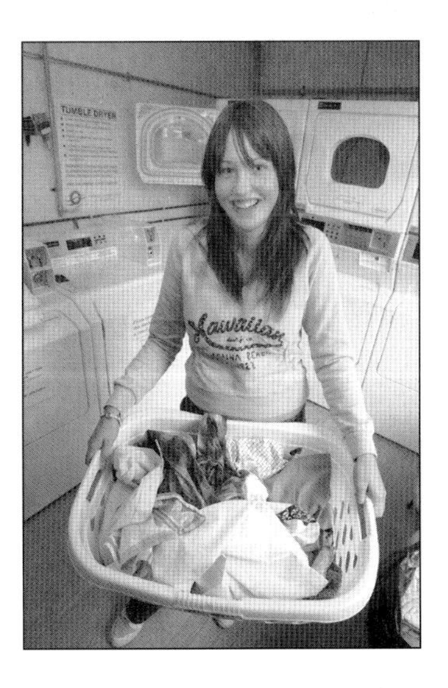

I met the bus as it was picking up passengers in Deepcar. Tristran was to take eight ladies to St John's Church for lunch. They were the nucleus of 'Lifestyle Matters', a pioneering course focusing on preventive health measures for older people. They had been meeting at the church for the last nine months and were overflowing with confidence and functioning well as a cohesive group. This had not been the case when Dave had first met them. He said it was positive proof that the course had worked wonders. He had been invited to their last meeting and the award ceremony where everyone had been given a certificate for finishing the course and this had moved him. He had written to Claire Craig, Senior

Lecturer and Researcher at Hallam University and instigator of this programme: 'All too often in community development we use words like capacity building, increased self esteem, empowerment, inclusion and aspirations without reflecting on the true meaning of such words. Well, I saw all those things yesterday. Well done you lot, and never give up on changing people's lives in such a profound way.'

The Stocksbridge Community Laundry is a 'not for profit' organisation that occupies a spare room in Newton Grange Residential Home. In some ways it has to manage itself so the notices which adorn the walls of are explicit. Along with the odd socks, de-rigueur for any laundry, there are very clear instructions on how to use the five washing machines and three dryers supplied by Maytag, a company that, or so a label assures me, 'complies with Australian gas ratings'!

The decision to use SRB money to open this utility came because the laundrette in Stocksbridge had closed down. Residents said that this was a loss to the community. Following consultation this led to SVCP finding premises, helping with the organisation and funding. One person is employed eleven hours per week for service washes. She tackles football and rugby kits, pub and hairdressers' towels and a delivery and collection service. It breaks even, all that a non-profit organisation needs to do.

A great deal of thought has gone into providing comfort for this laundry's users. There's a box of toys, newspapers, a radio and J cloths kept wet in two zipped plastic bags 'for spills'. There's even a pad of 'post-its' with pens. One customer has written: 'It's a great local service. Many thanks.' This has been stuck on the notice board itemising the portable goods which have been pilfered - a clock and laundry baskets - with an invitation to the thieves to 'seek help and ring this number.'

Women and men are wise in proportion, not to their experience, but to their capacity for experience.
The Revolutionists' Handbook,
George Bernard Shaw (1903)

Sitting in a laundry enables one to read the paper or a book, listen to the radio or chat to a complete stranger. I couldn't do this as there were no other customers during the one and a half hours I spent there. This was a pity because I had hoped to meet the husband of the lady who, I was told, hates washing and spends £40 per week on the family's wash distancing herself completely by sending him with the clothes!

One of the notices informs me that, along with washing powder and laundry bags, I can buy Comfort' and 'Bounce Sheets'. They sound fun. The service washes happen on Tuesday, Wednesday and Thursday. A lady is employed just to iron. This friendly and intimate place deserves to prosper. It sounds like Paradise.

There are, of course, other organisations in Stocks Bridge, which have benefited from SRB monies. If they have produced the same calibre of people that I have met, then all is not lost for the future.

Sammy Fox came into this valley one hundred and sixty years ago intent on making a living for himself and his family. In doing so he created thousands of jobs and, incidentally, contributed to the growth of Stocksbridge in an unprecedented way. He made a huge personal fortune, being, as they say, the right man in the right place at the right time. As we have learned to our cost, however, single industries bring spectacular collapse to communities when their time is over.

The SRB monies have provided strong, community minded, men and women with the wherewithal to begin to retrieve what has been lost. Opportunities to retrain, to improve skills, gain confidence, find new jobs, and diversify are there for everyone who wants them.

We should all be extremely proud that we have such able, caring and committed men and women working in our communities. The glass isn't half empty; it's more than half full.

RYEDALE

Alison Seabrooke and Brian Lewis

The thing that you should remember about a file and a saw is that they only cut on the push stroke, that is the way that the teeth point. In life that is worth at least a moment's thought.

TALKING OF FILES AND VERTICAL MACHINING CENTRES

The Social and Economic Regeneration of Ryedale (SRB 5) scheme was established to improve the confidence, employability and opportunities of Ryedale's young people in order to enable them to continue both to live, and work, in their home communities. There are currently more social and economic opportunities for young people outside the Ryedale district than within and the overall aim was to help stem the current trend for outward migration of young people from Ryedale. Most projects are based in and around centres of population, such as the key market towns of Malton, Norton, Kirkbymoorside, Helmsley and Pickering.

The Social and Economic Regeneration of Ryedale (SRB 5) was a five year SRB scheme started in 2003/04 - SRB contribution £2.3m.

When we reached the central workshop of the Derwent Training Association, David Sanderson and I started talking in basic English about files and ended up standing by the Bridgeport Vertical Machining Centre (VMC) that 'understood the language of Heidenhain'. These days a good metal file costs in the region of £10, the VMC cost something in the region of £30,000.

The engineering workshop was a mass of machines that I understood - lathes, milling machines, vertical power drills, shapers and grinders - and also machines close to the cutting edge of technology, 'computer assisted design' machines. Yet in all, because of my schooling fifty years before, I understood the tradition which was being worked through in this North Yorkshire workshop and knew this to be an exciting thing to see; as I stood looking at a pile of files which lay on an old workshop bench close to a vice and a marking-off table I began to see why this SRB funded project was so important.

There is a story about the eighteenth century tool maker Henry Maudsley. After his death one of his 'school' of machine-tool inventors, Richard Roberts, Joseph Whitworth or the greatest of them all James Nasmyth, was asked where his skills lay. The tale teller paused and considered, carefully weighing the question, balancing one invention and one skill against another before replying: 'Maudsley had a brilliantly inventive mind and could use any tool but he was truly a magnificent artist when it came to using the six inch file.'

One of the things it is easy to miss is that the Derwent Training Association is there to serve an engineering community which still has workshops needing files, lathes and milling machines as well as machinery every bit as complicated as the VMC. The pile of files took me back into my personal history and brought me bang up to the here and now.

TECHNOLOGY AND ASPIRATION

'Never run after an interesting woman, or a bus or a new educational idea; there will be another one along soon,' was a principle instilled into me by my first employer. With a few adjustments this useful advice still holds in the twenty-first century. Never running after a new idea is particularly pertinent here. Specialised schools of excellence in engineering training had been around before; I went to one back in the 1940s.

In 1948 I was not sent to the grammar school because I was said to be good with my hands and I lived in a town where things were made, rather than thought about. High praise in the Black Country was, 'He is a good mekker, he can mek anything.' If your parents were from what was in those days called 'the working class' there was a tendency for them to think jobs first and education second; a child got educated so that she or he could get a job and earn. Long-term goals like being a doctor or lawyer never got mentioned, and in our community the university was so remote it was meaningless.

In the Butler Education Act of 1944 government had decided that for convenience's sake the nation's young people would be sent to different types of schools according to the three 'A's: age, aptitude and ability. My profile suggested that I was not an intellectual sheep destined for the professions, nor a scapegoat ready to be sent into menial trades but an 'in-between'; someone capable of being anything between a captain of industry and a skilled craftsman.

Engineering is underrated in Britain, a country that became 'Great' because of its engineers.

Of course progress onward and upward wasn't as simple as that but at least there was a progressive pathway. There are lessons from that period that should be remembered as we gear up for educational reforms involving youth employment and skilling.

In the early 1950s it was not the curriculum that determined where a boy or girl ended up. It was family background, parental vision and knowledge of higher education but also where you lived and your personal determination. The boys who went to the grammar school in working class areas did not end up doctors, dentists, lawyers and judges but bank tellers, teachers and office clerks. In the year I started at the Tech hardly anyone in my town went on to the university from any of the local schools. From the James Watt one lad went to do Chemistry at Leeds. It was the same at the local grammar school although my cousin went from his council house to Birmingham University to do Physics but that was very much the exception given his background. Perhaps, if we had lived in a Welsh valley or a Scottish glen with a strong non-conformist tradition and a longstanding respect for education, things might have been different but we were in an industrial wasteland which was on the move and traditions were collapsing all around us. Few became entrepreneurs but those who did often went off and set up their own little engineering works.

University education was remote but there was a parallel ladder which you could climb. The General Certificate of Education (GCE) was not the only qualification you could take. Night school classes offered a whole array of step by step qualifications such as City and Guilds. There were also classes run by the Workers Education Association (WEA) and others run by trade unions at local universities. These were for those people who lived in working class districts and were interested in community development and politics. Today the WEA is usually involved in recreational education but in the days when the Labour Party had a high proportion of ex-manual workers these two educational routes, trade union education courses and the WEA, ensured that community leaders got that theoretical training in economics, labour law and history that allowed them to stand their corner in what was called the 'class struggle'.

The main technical qualification for those who entered industry was not the GCE but the 'National' and the 'Higher National' qualification. The latter was the equivalent of GCE 'A' Level' and could also be used as a university entry qualification. A worker who wanted to rise through the factory ranks used it to get onto an external degree course at a city college. To manage that he - it was usually a 'he' in those days - went to night school three nights a week for three years minimum and attended classes on a Saturday morning. After qualifying he was able to put letters after his name, and he had earned them.

If he wanted to have more letters he usually became a member of one of the prestigious science or technology institutes whose origins lay in the consolidation of the Industrial Revolution in the early nineteenth century. They still exist, their names evoking the smell of furniture polish on leather armchairs and their London addresses having the ring of true worth and quality: the Engineering Council WC2 3ER, the Institute of Gas Engineers, W1N 3AF, the Institute of Material Studies SW1Y 5DB. There is a parallel educational universe that runs alongside the tradition of GCSE and university qualifications. When SRB 5 funded Derwent Training Association they put their toe into this educational universe. It was funded by the Learning and Skills Council but seemed closer to the old traditions of the Royal Society of Arts (RSA) which in my youth offered a wide range of vocational qualifications and credit accumulation. Candidates could take a single unit or complete a qualification.

The residue of this system just about hangs on but it is being replaced by something new and very twenty-first century.

A CENTRE OF VOCATIONAL EXCELLENCE

We have to sell engineering as a quality product in a totally different way to the way that it has been sold in the recent past.

Derwent Training Association is a 'social enterprise' which is risk-taking, innovative and has close links with the local community through training young people. It is a main player in the North Yorkshire engineering tradition. Their Centre of Vocational Excellence status is keenly sought-after by the more traditional education establishments and not given to many. Dave Sanderson enjoys the accolade. They had managed to pip much bigger colleges to the post: 'We presented our proposal to the

Learning and Skills Council using a traffic light chart format. This presentation was clear and innovative. The parts of the proposal not yet started were coloured red, those that were ongoing, orange, and the areas that we had completed, green. This appealed to the panel. Panel members could home in on the area of interest to them, immediately see its progress status and ask specific questions, rather than trawl through over-wordy text. That is how we managed to become a Centre of Vocational Excellence in the North Yorkshire Advanced Engineering Technology Training Partnership.'

Presentation matters. Derwent Training Association are keen on communication. They have their own *Acronym Survival Guide*. This lists all those annoying capital letters that create a secret language for only those 'in the know'. This was produced for the board of directors to try and help guide them through the complex list of government initiatives, inspection hierarchies, accreditation bodies and course titles.

As the lead partner - the one responsible for making the application, taking the glory or carrying the can for its failure - Derwent Training Association has been a victim of its own success. The original contract value had been £300,000, but Derwent Training Association has managed to recruit almost 50% more trainees than they had predicted. As a result the Learning and Skills Council would only agree to funding the additional trainees at 50% of the unit cost. So, for example, Derwent Training Association might receive £10,000 per person for the anticipated trainees but only £5,000 per person for the extra trainees.

They have attracted 28 trainees instead of the profiled 20 and have been penalised for over-achieving. This seems as unfair as it is stupid. Although bids have to be based on track record and market knowledge, it is impossible to always accurately predict the numbers. If there was no sector skills shortage then the logic might be understandable. But this is not the case and it is a bitter pill to swallow. Derwent Training Association had to fund their commitments to the students from other resources.

Smaller, more innovative and responsive training providers who know the lie of the land, speak the engineering sector language and produce

brilliant results receive well-deserved plaudits but inadequate funding. Colleges have a lot of room for manoeuvre, small social enterprises do not. Funding delivery is flawed. Accessing mainstream funds, like those funds received by colleges, for day-to-day training activities, is pretty impossible and assessment difficult. Mainstream funds get passed from central government to its agencies at regional and local level to deliver public services. The Learning and Skills Council, a government agency, argues that central government does not provide sufficient resources for them to be able to manage lots of small mainstream contracts, so training providers such as Derwent Training Association suffer because of their size.

CREAMING OFF AND MAINSTREAM PROVIDERS

I shared Dave Sanderson's frustration. My own social enterprise, also in North Yorkshire, built up a reputation for being responsive, flexible and innovative, but hit a stone wall when it came to receiving mainstream funds to deliver one of the Government's main priorities, a Skills for Life programme offered to help people needing enhanced reading, writing, maths and computer skills. Riccall Regen 2000 has developed successful drop-in Skills for Life sessions every Friday in its community centre. Those who want Skills for Life assistance are usually very sensitive about the issue and want to take courses in relative secrecy. The community environment meant that the student could attend at the time when any one of a number of other activities was going on at the centre. They could hide the reason why they were there. It could be to drink in the bar or to play in a badminton match. In addition, if they worked shifts, or had family commitments, they could change the time of their session on a weekly basis. They could also receive one-to-one tuition for as long as they needed it; this could be a year or more. Our size and degree of flexibility mattered.

I still remembered the name of the biggest file, the one with the greatest number of teeth per inch. But then every school boy who did engineering as a school subject in the 1950s does. This was the Bastard File.That information is now stored in my 'pub-quiz' memory along with other pieces of useless information. The study of engineering has moved on.

Riccall Regen 2000 began to talk to a local employer, a salad grower, about delivering Skills for Life tuition to some of their 600 strong workforce. This employer has a high proportion of young people who have left school at 16 with little or no qualifications - you don't need a GCSE to pick a tomato. The employer is attracting significant numbers of migrant workers, for whom our minimum wage for a monotonous job is more attractive than it is to our native adult workforce. These EU visitors are sometimes well-qualified in their own country, but struggle to communicate in English. We were located in a rural community and this made us an ideal venue.

The company had already tried to provide Skills for Life support by sending workers to the local college at a set time each week. They travelled by minibus, only to find the tertiary college environment of mainly sixteen to nineteen year-olds unwelcoming. The lessons, which require a certain number of students to run, were set at the same time every week, regardless of the students' changing shift patterns. As a consequence attendance was erratic, drop-out was high, tutors were regularly changed. A key requirement of Skills for Life tuition is that the tutor builds a close and strong relationship with the student in order to understand the wider problems and barriers to learning the student faces. As a result no-one attends the college course any longer.

By contrast Riccall Regen 2000 suggested that they brought a tutor onto the company's premises and branded the tuition in a way that would make it more attractive, less stigmatic. They asked the training manager what time the shifts began and ended and offered to run a weekly course that would capture those coming off a day shift, or starting a night shift. That way, as the individual's shift changed, they could attend the lesson at a different time each week. The training manager was astounded that this was an option - she was only used to being presented with off-the-peg, rather than bespoke, solutions. To Riccall Regen 2000 it was nothing complicated, just common sense.

As a charity and company limited by guarantee Riccall Regen 2000, like Derwent Training Association, is used to juggling the funding. The course was resourced in the short-term from an existing project budget. With continuity and longevity absolutely essential to Skills for Life success, they approached the Learning and Skills Council for longer-term funding. The stock reply was, 'We (mainstream) fund the college to deliver Skills for Life in your area, you need to work with them.'

The plot thickens. The only way that a smaller organisation can access the mainstream funding is through a franchise agreement. But with a franchise the college will cream off a percentage of the mainstream funding it receives from the Learning and Skills Council for each learner for administration, and pass on the remainder to the franchisee. In this case it means that Riccall Regen 2000 will only receive 70% of any delivery costs, even though there is also administration to do at their end, too. The other unpalatable fact is that, although the smaller community organisation is delivering excellent results, the franchise arrangement means that all the paperwork that the student receives is college branded. So the community organisation, Derwent or Riccall - can't even take credit for its innovative, flexible and responsive approach.

Colleges are often a 'Jack of all trades, but master of none'. It is clear that Derwent Training Association is a master of engineering trades as well as being well-informed on latest training practices and principles. Dave Sanderson is a director of KADTAL, (Keighley and District Training Association Ltd), a work-based learning providers' consortium which extends into the Craven area of North Yorkshire. Their influence is not restricted to the Ryedale area but extends as far as the foot hills of the Pennines.

We have benefited greatly from Derwent Training Association's flexible and adaptable approach' and ' Derwent Training Association's reliability and professionalism have helped us to improve performance and profitability throughout the company.' Derwent Training Association's clients speak highly of the service they receive, comments about professionalism, flexibility and appreciation of what has been learned pepper a promotional pack which is devoid of worthy or woolly charity-speak.

Alison Seabrooke

Derwent Training Association has also worked with York College to produce a foundation degree course in engineering. During its development Dave didn't feel all of the modules were quite right for the contemporary engineering market. Derwent Training Association's directors are all managers of small engineering businesses and therefore he handed a module to each of them for their comment. This rigorous and instant expert assessment is clearly something that would not easily be available to a large college.

Dave is forthright in his criticism: 'Many of the courses delivered in colleges just don't meet employers' needs. For example, the building trades departments still teach very specific skills such as dove-tail joints, whereas in reality a house builder will use a nail-gun for most of the job. A normal house has to be up in sixteen weeks. I am not arguing that the more traditional skills aren't necessary, but it would be more useful to get people into jobs with the basic requirements and get them to learn the more specific skills while they are at work through day release. This is the whole principle of work-based learning. The employer gets what he needs and the trainee gets a realistic view of the work environment.'

The Leeds Metropolitan University report cited Derwent Training Association as a star project in its post SRB review and recommended investment and development. You can see why.

Such is their success, that Derwent Training Association has welcomed numerous visits, ranging from the Department for Education and Skills to Baroness Lockwood and John Greenway MP. They are able to boast an impressive 95% retention rate and 96% achievement rate. Even so, a request to the Learning and Skills Council for £165,000 to expand their premises fell on deaf ears, whereas Yorkshire Coast College and York College received £28 million and £70 million respectively for their capital expansion plans, without ado.

These large investments assumingly provide a cost effective alternative to Derwent Training Association. The colleges have the ability to place relatively good students onto an educational conveyor belt. At their best they will deliver young people with a good education who can access higher education, or more easily enter a particular jobs market. What a college doesn't easily do - and what Derwent Training Association does - is to produce a young person whose education and training precisely meets the needs of the employer. This essential requirement of vocational education should be shouted about loud and clear by central government. It is what Derwent Training Association delivers by default against heavy odds and for relatively little money. SRB was a godsend, for it showed what was possible. The follow-up has been hard.

Dave: 'We have to jump through all the same quality assurance hoops as the local college providers - Adult Learning Inspectorate, Customer First, Investors in People, BSI 9001, Learning and Skills Council audit, as well as all our examining body accreditations - but we still can't access the funds that they can. The Learning and Skills Council audit team staff agree that our results are consistent and robust. Even so, we can't get support for expansion. I sometimes feel that, had we been less successful, we would have been more respected and supported.'

The half a million pound building was part-funded by SRB to the tune of £200,000. This includes the building and contents. Half of the mortgage has already been paid off and Dave and his board of directors have begun to have discussions about how they can meet expansion plans.

The value of locally owned organisations delivering activity which meets very local needs has, on paper at least, been recognised by central government. As the voluntary and community sectors are expected to move from grant dependency to sustainability, Government has also recognised that grants to fund capital projects such as buildings can hinder the development of organisations. In effect, the funder usually 'owns' a percentage of the building they have funded for a given length of time - usually 20 years or so, depending on the size of the award. The funders also have a right to claw back their proportion of the building if they feel that the grant is not being used for the original intended purpose. Initially they failed to recognise that local needs change and organisations 'grow up'.

The Treasury plans to relax these rules. This will enable organisations to sell an asset or raise further money against it, in order to expand or develop the organisation, provided there is continuing evidence of community benefit. As a social enterprise – that is, as an organisation which is run on business principles but for social benefit - this sort of route might be one Derwent Training Association could consider. It would certainly increase their independence and support their plans to develop their training packages.

The mode of operation, the way that information is given and received, matters. The teaching of respect for learning alongside respect for each other is essential in schools, colleges and in society at large .

Another hurdle they have encountered is non-recoverable VAT on their new building. Whereas the local authority does not have to bear the burden of 17.5% VAT during capital development programmes, not-for-profit organisations often do. There don't seem to be very clear guidelines for new-build projects. The decision seems to depend on the view of the particular tax inspector who assesses the project. Either way, as recommended by the Leeds Metropolitan University report, investment and development are essential for the future security of Derwent Training Association.

Dave is clear about at least one route to sustainability - more co-operation with the local schools: 'We support four secondary schools in the area, but we have insufficient space to meet their vocational demands, as well as the needs of our apprentices. We are in the process of licensing the schools to deliver engineering courses, too. The students attend an induction here and then carry on with the rest of the course at school. We have a second cohort of Year Eleven students here on Friday. We send one of our tutors out to the school to support the 'A' level students and also their teacher who needs to be aware of contemporary engineering practices. These students are tested at the beginning of their two-year course for literacy, numeracy, spatial and verbal skills. This means that two years before they leave we can be very focused on the skills gaps they might have, and on where they need to be when they finish the course. Our tutor assesses their progress at school and when they are ready the students are brought back here to take their test. All of our testing now takes place online. This is a fairly fluid process which matches the student's progress and is not dictated by exam dates as it was in the past. This is the only way we manage to access mainstream funds.

'The work with schools, and delivering adult engineering courses, either through day-release or evening courses, are the areas we want to expand. We are finding that the colleges are significantly increasing the costs of their engineering courses. Previously they costed about £54 for a course and now it is around £300. We need to be aware of what is being charged if we want to develop our own commercial arm. All of this activity is additional to our Centre of Vocational Excellence work. This is about work with school, not with apprenticeships.'

The Derwent Training Association booklet provides a hefty list of courses: electrical training, engineering - CAD, welding, fork lift truck, slings and slinging, as well as health and safety and other business management skills - project management, human resources, and finance.

Dave Sanderson felt assured that they would continue to attract apprentices: 'We have really good relationships with the small engineering businesses and act as their 'critical friend' in all sorts of ways. We are able to produce a prototype of a potential product from a drawing. A company will bring us a drawing and we will put it onto our CAD (Computer Aided Design) system and run off the product. We will then work with the company to make sure they can put it into production. They might need to adapt machinery or work out cost efficient manufacture programmes. We can help them with this. Another way in which we help is advising the company on the correct machinery to purchase. For example, one small business was three years into operations but failing to make a profit because they had to sub-contract out manufacture. We advised them to invest in a specific piece of equipment for £23,000. Now they are in profit. These small companies are very hands-on and don't spend enough time on research, design and development. We encourage the company to send their apprentices in to work with us on a model, which we can help them develop. As is often the case, the SRB money brought in added values that could not be guessed at when the award was made.'

I was shown an intriguing-looking figure which had been turned from paper into plastic. I asked Dave how they charged for these services. He admitted that they generally didn't charge anything. To an outsider this doesn't seem a sustainable way to run a business but that misses the concept of the social enterprise model. As Dave explained: 'When we make the first prototype, the companies provide us with materials and the apprentices can work on what is left over. This way they get to work on a wide variety of current materials and we don't have to put in orders for quantities that we couldn't hope to use. By staying in constant contact with these businesses our staff competencies are very high and current. Our social model develops a virtuous circle; we are continuously able to offer courses that reflect the latest engineering innovation and developments - funded through mainstream school arrangements, contracts and commercial fees - that the other training providers would find hard to deliver. Of course we charge the bigger companies such as Nestlé.

Physical regeneration is not enough to ensure sustainability of neighbourhoods and communities. We need to protect our investment in the area through innovation and flexibility, using a toolbox of different solutions.

'We don't only work in the Malton area. Our clients come from Stokesley in the north of North Yorkshire to Selby in the south. We also work throughout the UK and abroad. One of our staff is in China at the moment. He will be there for three weeks teaching welding skills to staff working for the Chan Chung railway. We recently had six Chinese visitors here who took photos of everything in sight. The problem with the Chinese engineering sector is that it is very good at copying but not at developing products.

'Our overall aim is to keep in front of technology and show small local businesses how to be flexible and entrepreneurial. For example, we have had to educate them not to shut shop at lunchtime on Friday, but to organise their staff rotas and communication systems so that they retain customers and expand business. We have developed a booklet for employers. This states the roles and responsibilities of the employer and employee. We provide employment law advice and are constantly thinking about ways in which we can help them improve their businesses. Because we are members of the Institute of Incorporated Engineers via the EEF, the Employers' Engineering Federation, we are in the process of establishing an associate membership scheme for apprentices. This will give them more credibility as they enter into the work environment.'

The energy and vision of the staff at the Derwent Training Association is tangible. How they have applied this to the needs of the local community is evident. A week or so earlier, they had hosted an event for all their local partners and customers. The hog roast attracted 110 guests, which included sixty representatives from local employers. I have experience of mounting this sort of local promotion event and know the difficulties of attracting this quality audience. Colleges and local authorities struggle to attract company bosses to get involved in local activity. Business leaders quite simply are too busy running their business to attend. This, it seems, does not happen where Derwent Training Association is concerned.

This sort of commitment extends to all ten members of staff. The office administrators had spent time organising the hog roast but instead of leaving the clearing up to the next day, they had stayed behind to sort it out. They hadn't been asked to. Their action represented a business culture that was tied closely to the success of Derwent Training Association. Nobody has had a day off sick in eight years.

YOUTH AND THE ENGINEERING AGENDA

The strength of the Derwent Training Association lies in its size, vision, independence, strategy and partnership with local factories. When it first began operations in 1988 using Manpower Service money, it worked out of premises close to the centre of Malton. At that stage Derwent Training Association took a building next to the council recycling plant in Showfield Lane. Empty wine bottles spilled towards the entrance and there were piles of paper everywhere but this old building, given for a peppercorn rent, and a portacabin both gave it a start. Without these wilderness years it is doubtful if Derwent Training Association would have received any SRB money.

North Yorkshire is an agricultural county. Therefore you might expect that what engineering there was here twenty years ago when the original college opened stemmed from the blacksmith's shop and the tractor repair workshop. This is not the case. There are companies that have those sorts of origins but of the original seven companies that came together because they wanted to pool resources into a training scheme to train new workers, most came from a wider variety of sectors of engineering.

During the Second World War a number of light engineering factories had located in Ryedale. Some were very specialised makers of precision products, others came from a much more rough and ready tradition of popular engineering, companies that made metal staircases and garden furniture. What they had in common was young people who needed training and who for a variety of reasons were not being catered for at the local college. They were prepared to offer their young workers day release but needed somewhere to send them. In the short term the Showfield Road site fitted the bill.

Malton is a market town of two parts, Old Malton, with its stone houses and St Mary's Priory, and the town that grew originally around a Norman Castle, the modern day Malton. Over the river you can find Norton on Derwent, a centre for racehorse training, but it is all one town. There are plenty of shops and a market. Its major industries were farming and brewing, but only one brewery remains today. It is the nearest town to Castle Howard.
Google

Andrew Leeming, one of Ryedale District Council's officers responsible for delivering the SRB programme, said that the Derwent Training Association engineering centre fitted into the plans of the council strategists but went further. It recognised that at the point when the national focus was predominantly on urban decline, it was important to ensure that rural experiments continued and that the movement of enriching ideas could still move both ways.

Andrew had joined Ryedale District Council shortly after the SRB bid had been won and was there for its duration. As we talked he explained how, alongside other rural councils, Ryedale had become increasingly concerned in recent years about how the movement out from the local area was creating a serious population imbalance. Quite simply, young people were leaving the area to seek their fortunes elsewhere. Small-town nightlife in Malton, Norton, Pickering, Kirkbymoorside or Helmsley could hardly match the lights of Leeds. Therefore any strategies which aimed to halt the rural to urban drift were welcome.

Although local training and education providers had tried to get young people to look at local jobs, the offer was narrow. In particular they had not noticed that there was a developing and growing engineering sector with a good track record that could be presented as an exciting alternative to agricultural and service industry work. Young people and their parents hadn't considered that the many engineering companies weren't just looking for grease monkeys, but required high level skills such as 'computer aided design' (CAD). On the other hand, companies who might need engineering skills were unaware that they existed in Ryedale. Leeds Metropolitan University carried out some research for the Council, and as a result they saw there were youth issues which included employment problems. It was clear that they had to do something to promote engineering training in a new way. The trainers needed to devise programmes that would both keep new school-leavers in the area and entice back home those who had already gone further afield looking for work. The Council needed to forge strong links with the employers, some of whom were experiencing recruitment problems, to make sure that the newly learnt skills led to jobs. In all ways the profile of that local economy sector had to be enhanced.

In its success the awareness-raising North Yorkshire Education Partnership (NYBEP) acted as a broker and, working with both the growing engineering sector and Derwent College, forged a key partnership. A number of factors made this possible:

- an active local authority that saw the benefits of NYBEP for education and business
- a local NYBEP group that included business people

- an excellent local NYBEP officer with good connections to schools, businesses and colleges
- a recognition of new opportunities in the Ryedale economy that would benefit young people in the future.

Together they staged information events for young people. They also brought in York University and companies from Science City York to drive home the message that high-level skill centres existed in Ryedale. They were successful. Now, in 2005, Derwent Training Association needs to expand into new premises.

CURRICULUM AND STAFF

What seems to attract students to Derwent Training Association is the degree of flexibility. The centre does not solely focus on the September to September model of course-delivery, though it prefers students to follow this pattern. Size means that they can afford to be less rigid. The numbers are growing. In 1996/97 they had eight students, today that figure has risen by a factor of ten. This has largely been due to support from SRB 5.

The majority of the students sign up for a one day a week day release course for four years. Year One is devoted to workshop practice and includes welding, electrical, casting, machining and assembly. There are also classes on computer aided design. In Year Two they take the EAL Advanced Diploma in Engineering and Technology. In Years Three and Four the teaching team's ability to deliver bespoke courses which are directly linked to a company's requirements remain attractive. Assessment is on site. That is partly because no two students have the same needs. A student working at Perry Slingsby in Kirkbymoorside doing precision work on submersibles, one at Thomas the Bakers, Helmsley, working on factory maintenance, and another with McKehies, working on specialised automobile repairs, do not have the same requirements. The scale of the Derwent Training Association operation makes this versatile education regime possible.

You can lead a horse to water
but a pencil must be lead
Stan Laurel

This is a slim organisation. David Sanderson no longer teaches. As chief executive of a developing charity he does not have time. Currently they have two full-time and three part-time tutors and a two person administrative base. The other member of the senior management team is Valerie Richards.

Her job has changed since she entered Derwent Training Association through a kaleidoscope of jobs which included working for nineteen years in a Derbyshire manufacturing company, and also IT Training and business centre experience. As her last employer prepared her for redundancy and they moved towards receivership she saw a two-liner in the *Malton Gazette*: 'Fancy a new challenge in Training?' She did. That was three years ago, a year after the organisation had settled down on the York Road Industrial Estate.

There is an elegance in the manner of the advert which fits the organisation. The wording is challenging but not flash. Had David Sanderson advertised in the *Guardian* or the *Yorkshire Post* then an advertisement which set out the parameters of the job would have cost upwards of £700 and the job pack photocopying, plus the labour cost, would have topped £1,000. It probably cost no more than fish and chips for two. The formal approach would have been pointless, for when she eventually got the job it was in the process of expanding, and things have gone further that way ever since.

When she arrived she thought that she would spend the bulk of her time chasing funding, looking after the payroll and managing reception. She does, but also arranges and minutes board meetings, sources and negotiates new pieces of equipment, negotiates with partners, organises parents' evenings, prepares for quality assessment evaluation, develops a marketing strategy, prepares the budget and, when David Sanderson is unavailable, deputises for him.

Over the last two years she has helped develop relationships with the local high schools in Malton, Norton, Pickering and Kirkbymoorside. In 2005, sixteen girls from Year Eleven came for a week's taster course. Girls have always been targeted. Karen Hurworth, an apprentice from Clanalvex in the early years of Derwent Training Association, was a star pupil and since then they have been keen to attract young women students. She and her partner opened a local company.

This is an exception. The entrepreneurial spirit is no more evident here than it is anywhere else but Derwent Training Association is helping the economy in a number of ways. It occasionally runs two day courses and delegates come into the area from other parts of the UK and stay in the area. One came from Plymouth but usually the catchment area is the region with an outer circle which extends to Lancaster, Northumberland and the industrial Midlands.

At the moment these are small elements in the company's sustainability strategy, for their main revenue stream consists of the contracts with the Learning and Skills Council to deliver the annual programme. Currently they are developing partnerships with the community college and they would seem to be well placed - if small - to also offer consultancy advice. They are more experienced than most other organisations in the region, and their size and independence suggest a model which might be explored elsewhere.

THE APPRENTICESHIP AGENDA

Derwent Training Asociation received SRB 5 support at an appropriate time when government was beginning to be aware that they were close to a crisis as far as the training of young people was concerned. In 2005 only 28 per cent of the UK's working age population have skills at apprenticeship, technical or craft level, compared with 51 per cent in France and 65 per cent in Germany, according to a statistical report on global competitiveness. The Government's *Skills Strategy White Paper* reports that up to 20 per cent of young people still left school with no qualifications, and the number of young people starting an Advanced Apprenticeship has halved since 1997, according to the *Tomlinson Report on 14-19 reform.* The difficulty occurred within the very time frame which Derwent Training Association was focusing on. Young people at fourteen years of age were already forming choices about what they want to do with their lives. The challenge is now to increase the choices available and to include a notion of apprenticeships in the agenda.

In the nineteenth century apprentice contracts were written twice on the same piece of paper and when the agreement was made and signed, cut apart with scissors so that the edges were irregular and unique. By this simple device both the 'master' and 'man' could guarantee the contract. The contract could be shown to be original if the jagged edges fitted together.

Evidence of the need for a new approach was set out in a whole array of papers and reports such as: *Modern apprenticeships: the way to work* (the

Cassels Report 2001), *Twenty-first century apprenticeships: end to end review of the delivery of Modern Apprenticeships* (2002), *Twenty-first Century Skills: Realising our potential* (2003), Edexcel's *Apprenticeship reforms* (2004), *Five year strategy for children and learners* (2004) and Mike Tomlinson's proposals for a fundamental reform of the new diploma framework, of which apprenticeships would be a part. At 16 years of age 84 % of young people remain in formal education or work-based learning. This seems a favourable reflection for an industrial civilisation until you realise that at 17 this falls to 75%. By age 18, just 52% of young people remain in learning. High on Tomlimson's list of priorities was the development of partnerships with employers in order to strengthen vocational routes in learning. Derwent Training Association had been doing this since 1988 and therefore they were well ahead of the game.

GETTING THERE AND STAYING

Some of the students arrive by car - those from Selby do - and more come on the York to Scarborough train. A 'wheels-to-work' scheme helps to supplement public transport. It is no use creating a training centre and encouraging young people to stay in the district, if they cannot rely on the buses to get them to a new job or to a new training centre from their home in one of the outlying villages. Bus services are sporadic - it is difficult to argue a business case for a regular service without subsidy, when the bus may only pick up one or two people from a number of outlying areas.

It is likely, too, that a young person will not be able to afford their own reliable transport and insurance when they start their first job. If a family car is available then they also need to be of a legal age to drive, so this misses out the first year of work after leaving school. The wheels-to-work scheme, run by Ryedale Voluntary Action, filled this gap. Scooters were purchased by the organisation and loaned to the young person who needed transport to get to work. This provided a cheap and efficient form of transport and the scooters could be bought by the young rider once the wages started to roll in.

Jobs alone would not keep young people in their home town. The Ryedale Regeneration Partnership had to consider many more pieces in a complicated jigsaw. The local council did not have sole responsibility for dealing with young people's issues, as they were part of a two-tier system. Ryedale District Council's plans and budgets were partly determined in the North Yorkshire County Hall in Northallerton. Situated right at the top of England's largest county, this small market town would go almost unnoticed elsewhere in Yorkshire. Effective rail links are underdeveloped and there is no direct motorway link. The A1(M) is not directly connected by a spur to this county town. It seems remote from its administrative hinterland and this in itself has created challenges for the partnership, whose key partners were representatives from education, business, social housing associations, landowners and community.

THE RYEDALE AREA

Ryedale has 48,800 residents and covers 575 square miles. The students come from all over the local area but especially from companies in Helmsley, Kirkbymoorside and Pickering. In recent years companies outside the area have also sent students into Malton. There is a regular train to York and Scarborough and the road routes from those places are fast. Students from Sherburn in Elmet can be at the centre in 40 minutes by car, and from Selby, in about the same time.

The towns of Malton and Norton are joined at the hip. In the world of SRB the naming of one town in a sentence automatically implies that the other will be involved in some way. Like Siamese twins these towns are inseparable but with their own, slightly different characteristics. The main difference is that Malton is the more historic market town with a square and shops, and Norton, the residential area with a small commercial centre along one street. They are divided by the river Derwent. Prior to the 1974 boundary changes Malton was in the North Riding and Norton in the East. So they may be spoken about in one breath, but they have their own town council identity.

I met an old man who'd a frog in his throat for years. He retched it out - and started to jump.
Joe Warrington, Poet
The Urbane Gorilla 1970

The people who live in them have the same needs - entertainment, advice and information services, housing and transport, yet they are separate because the range of services can be slightly different. Andrew Leeming pointed this out when he described the range of other projects offered through SRB 4.

Some were small projects, such as the skatepark North Yorkshire Police developed in Norton. High quality equipment was installed between the two towns and young people were encouraged to self-police it, with the help of the North Yorkshire Constabulary and community safety partnership. This may have affected the general economy; I later drove down Malton High Street and noticed the trendy skateboarders'/bladers'/bikers' shop, a shop my teenage children would have died for - and liked to imagine that this business had sprung up as a result of the park. I asked Andrew why Norton had been chosen over Malton. He explained that this wasn't how it worked - a site had become available at the same time as the SRB opportunity had arisen. There was a general acceptance that Norton had more youth issues but on the whole facilities went where the opportunities were.

Pickering and Malton already had some accommodation for young people but the SRB programme increased the types of accommodation and tenure available. Ryedale Housing had plans to open ten units of housing each year for five years, but when they went out looking for refurbishment of suitable properties on the open market they found the strategy was fraught with difficulties. Slippage occurred. The main problem was that by the time properties had been located by the association, and in the time it took to ratify the decision, the property had been snapped up by someone else. In a volatile market they missed out to private developers or to homeowners who, in a period of relative prosperity, were seeking to move up the property ladder.

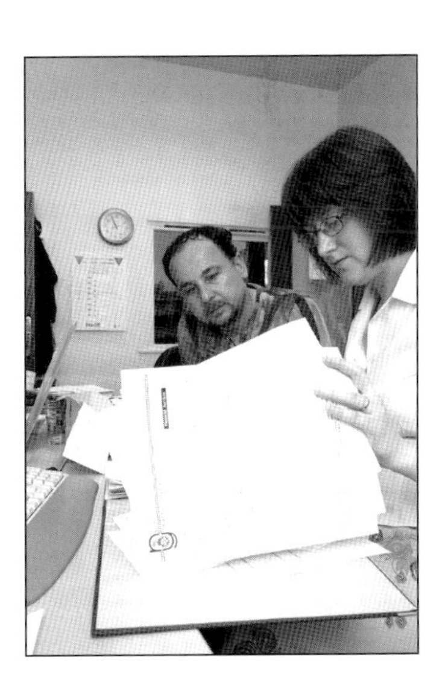

When a solution was found it came from an unusual local source. In the course of the initial briefing Andrew Leeming said it was 'a partnership struck with the Fitzwilliam Estate.' When he said it to me, a long time serving community development worker, I must admit that I was seriously taken aback. Had I been in South Yorkshire where there was Manor, Parsons Cross and Kendray, or in West Yorkshire with a knowledge of Royds, everything would have seemed possible. A housing estate with millions floating about might well support a new-build initiative. But in North Yorkshire?

It was then that I realised that this was not a local reference to a council estate, but he was talking about *Lord* Fitzwilliam's properties! The Fitzwilliam Estate looked at their housing stock in Malton and picked out those houses most suitable for young people. In the spirit of enlightened paternalism the notion of community service and local responsibility lingered, and they wanted to help by supporting a programme to restrict tenure and thereby ensure that young people wanting to live and work locally got first choice.

With this support the partners began to retain more control of the programme. It was not without problems, though. There were tensions over who was officially 'young' and who was officially 'local'. Some of the new occupants were young enough, but had moved from outside the area for employment at the Malton bacon factory, now owned by Grampian Country Foods.

The YMCA provided housing in Malton and Ryedale before SRB 4 came along. Local branches are set up by the YMCA England, a national organisation which buys the land and buildings so that homeless young people can have accommodation. A committee of local people, the Ryedale YMCA Foyer, manages these local 'branches', with a national representative attending local board meetings. They have their budget set nationally, are given management guidelines and are left to get on with it. For example, the Malton Foyer, which opened in 1996, charges a client rent - £93.28 per week, plus £2.07 water rates - for a flat. The Foyer in turn pays rent for the land and building. This is paid back to the national YMCA but the local branch retains responsibility for the programme. On the back of this type of management committee, Malton YMCA undertook an interesting SRB project, the Ryedale YMCA Cyber Café.

A young man, about 20 years old, entered the office where Karlie and I were speaking to ask for tokens for the washing and drying machines. There was an air of mutual respect and trust as Karlie rang them through the cash register. His polite manner and presentable appearance were at odds with the image associated with young people with chaotic lives.
Foyer visitor

Kevin Cooke, now a general worker with the Foyer Project, was employed by Ryedale YMCA Foyer as an outreach support worker from 2001 to 2003 on this project. He was brought in to run the Cyber Café, a venue created in old shop premises in Malton town centre for use mainly by young people. The café had closed after three years of SRB funding when the general award ran out. They had hoped it would be sustainable, but Kevin described what had happened and why it wasn't:

'I have twenty years of youth work background and I am a senior youth worker for the area. I wasn't involved in designing the Cyber Café - if I had been, things would have looked a lot different. My role was to get activities up and running for young people and to make connections with local organisations. That wasn't difficult as I knew most people already.

'The building was on two floors, off the beaten track up a Malton back street. It was very popular with young people. We had had a youth zone upstairs for eleven year olds and upwards. On the ground floor there was a café on one side of the room and computers on the other side. And to some extent that was where the trouble lay.

'The location and mixed use just spelt trouble. The doors opened onto a road and the kids would leave their bikes outside; it was also next to a pub. Access was poor as there were only stairs up to the first floor. Then there was the usual problem of young people being loud, and the visitors to the café and computer training coming in for a bit of peace and quiet clashing with the younger, boisterous end. Some of the language would be choice, too, which doesn't go down well with the elderly or young mums coming in with toddlers. There was never any violence, but then that was down to putting the right type of youth workers in there.'

I felt a great empathy with Kevin. My own community project - also in a rural area - had experienced similar problems. Most teenage kids are pussycats on their own, but you just can't stop them appearing threatening if they are in large groups. What they really want in a mixed-use venue is a discrete, preferably sound-proofed, room of their own away from other customers. Or, even better - or so I think when I am at my most pessimistic - is a darkened building of their own down the end of a lane, far away from civilisation, until that time when they decide to re-emerge, blinking and civilised, approximately ten years later. Single-use buildings are hard to fund and sustain, particularly in a rural area, so we go for mixed use and fail.

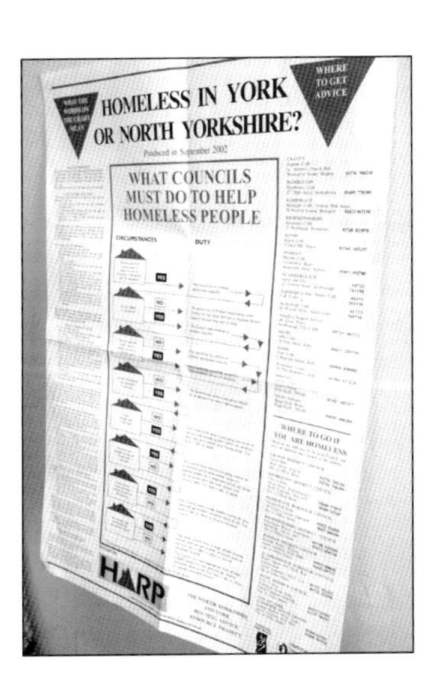

Kevin commented: 'We also let out rooms on the first floor to the Primary Care Trust and a counselling service. Again there were the problems with noise from the young people which created a barrier. While our paying customers tried to hold a business meeting they banged about.

'When I got there I quickly recognised that we were not operating with the correct ratio of adults to young people, either. The centre was not clear about either strategy or operation. I started to change things and the situation started to improve. But still we didn't overcome the identity problem. Nobody was quite sure what the café was supposed to be.'

From the point of view of the young people the operation was very successful and not the failure that closure might suggest. Kevin stressed that young people need boundaries and organised activities: 'They came to the building from Malton, Norton and Pickering, our catchment area, during usual café daytime opening hours and we also opened for them until 9pm on Tuesdays and Thursdays. Howard Lewis, another youth worker, would pick them up from central and north Ryedale, a distance of sixteen miles maximum, and bring them into the café. This was part of the role of the Community Education Detached Youth Workers Programme. We regularly had around 30 to 35 young people coming in through the day and evening. At the café they could access all types of information - sexual health, drugs, alcohol and careers advice - in an informal atmosphere.

'We also hooked the kids in through the types of activities we arranged. Detached careers workers would drop in, talk to them and create other activities they could become involved with. Rural Arts North Yorkshire facilitated an inter-generational project with older people from the Hawthorns Centre in Norton. This was a six week programme. Professional artists got the kids to interview residents about the games they had played and songs they had sung in the 1920s and 1930s. We ended up with a production performance to the older people which was a mixture of modern rap and songs from their era.

'Although there were problems with the mixed use of the centre, particularly during the school holidays, in time we did manage to make some links with our 'partners'. We ran some 'mentoring' projects where the young people showed the older people how to use the computers downstairs. We also involved them in other parts of the building. For example, several of them carried out their work placements in the café.

It is the dead who govern. Look how they work their will upon us! Who have made the laws? The dead! Who have made the customs that we obey and that form and shape our lives? The dead! All the writers, when they would give weight and authority to their opinions, quote the dead. Our lives follow grooves that the dead have run out with their thumbnails!
Melville Davisson Post *Uncle Abner, Master of Mysteries.(d 1930)*

'There wasn't anything formal such as a youth council but we fully involved them from the start. We sat around the table whenever they wanted to democratically decide on matters affecting them. This could be anything from the choice of colour on the walls to agreeing the set of ground rules and the programme of activities that would take place.'

The evidence suggests that there was a real sense of regret that the Cyber Café closed. This was at the same time as Norton Youth Centre shut. Norton later opened a dry bar in a local pub. Like the Cyber Café this had been set up by well-meaning people without much experience of youth work One of the youth workers thought that both suffered due to a lack of strategic foresight. This strategy might have worked in time as they might have found a structure in which the young people would have learned to accept 'empowerment with boundaries'. In Norton the dry bar soon closed down due to a lack of structure and later re-opened with a stronger youthwork framework in place. The youth agenda is under-resourced by its nature and location as it only provides limited choice to young people from across a wide rural area.

THE FOYER

Driving up to the Foyer the approach is picturesque, but as with many rural settings the attractive countryside - in this case a floodplain meadow in early summer - masks the underbelly of rural living. The road runs alongside one bank of the River Derwent. Across the stretch of water, an expanse of fields, leafy trees and large, slightly worn character buildings in the Georgian or Regency style rests in the middle distance. This is the sort of setting you read of in *Country Living*, a place to which city types from Leeds beat a rural retreat drawn by an enticing, yet often deceptive, picture of rural life. They do not think of rural poverty, unemployment and the fact that, if they have teenage children, they will spend the bulk of their active years operating an unpaid taxi service to their kids' friends, leisure activities and employment.

As I approached the new-build Foyer the street was quiet, the children's playground empty and no-one was walking their dog on the newly-shaped mound of the flood bank, a reminder of the devastating floods of

2000. Fortunately the Foyer had not been affected then, but at least it now had some assurance against the future combined threats of global warming, spring tides and heavy rains or melting snow running down from the Yorkshire Wolds.

Until recently the Foyer had a bad reputation with local residents. It was the place for 'druggies and drop-outs', a noisy place to which uninvited guests turned up at any time of day or night, a place where local people felt very threatened. A change had come about with the arrival of Karlie Peters, its energetic manager.

When Karlie started, all of the clients had been on benefits. She had quickly stamped her authority on the 'business'. Not only were their neighbours' perceptions changed, but speedily also those of the police. Karlie had joined the Foyer at a time when it had been without a manager for six months and was in financial difficulties. Some of this had been due to losses from the closure of the Cyber Café. Staff had had to cover several roles, but without any particular assignment of duties. It highlighted the need for voluntarily led organisations to take succession planning seriously. Fortunately, under Karlie's management the Foyer's fortunes had been turned around; they were now allowed to submit accounts to the national body on a monthly basis, rather than weekly.

The Foyer houses fourteen self-contained flats which accommodate 'young people aged 16 - 25 who are homeless or in need of accommodation.'

Karlie: 'Our clients come in on referral from other agencies, and on self-referral. There isn't a first come, first served option. They are interviewed to assess needs and risks. We cater for low to medium risk young people. They may have criminal records but we assess whether they pose a significant threat to the staff, other hostel residents and those living nearby. If they are accepted they have to sign up to a licence agreement, which means that they agree with the house rules. They also have to accept the personal support package that runs alongside the licence, which means that they have to meet with a support worker once a week. They can stay here for up to two years, provided they stick to the agreement. If they don't we can issue a 28-day eviction notice.

For all the huge social advances of the last fifty years, it is clear that some things can go awry. We have become a less integrated society: more divided by class, income and geography. Inequalities persist, our lives are more fractured. The social fabic has been stretched, bruised and damaged. We prosper economically, but we suffer too from a quiet crisis of unhappiness.
Alessandra Buonfino, 2006

'The aim is to move them on to education, employment and training or, if they are already in it, to keep them there. We are quite strict. If they miss three support worker meetings they get a warning, if they get two warnings then we can issue an eviction notice. We try to talk it through first but the threat is there. If they are caught with drugs, or are dealing, trashing their room, or commit assault, eviction is immediate. We involve Ryedale District Council housing team, Safe Moves (outreach housing support), the police, Connexions, Community Education and Social Services to a greater or lesser extent, depending on whether they are either current tenants, or have been evicted.

'Currently we are trying to bring a range of these organisations under one roof. Kevin did that at the Cyber Café and it is a good model. This is preventative activity and helps build relationships between our residents and the agencies, and to develop better cross-agency networks. We have a project called 'Facing Barriers Together'. This brings under one roof adult basic skills tuition, a Youth Offending Team, drugs workers, Connexions, youth service and Safe Moves.'

Karlie had set up Safe Moves before joining the Foyer. 'It was a Foyer Federation Initiative, and started off as a pilot project to look at introducing preventative measures to reduce homelessness. The project started in Ryedale in May 2003 and the aim was to use three key interventions - mediation, life skills and peer mentoring in a bid to help keep young people in the home or assist them with a planned move. The project has gone beyond the pilot stage and is still operational in Ryedale and is now part of Ryedale YMCA Foyer.'

Karlie has stamped her authority on the Foyer with a list of do's and don'ts: 'No letting keys out, no booze in communal areas, no banned guests in the building, advance notice of guests, no incorrect use of fire equipment, attendance of weekly support meetings.' As we chatted residents popped in and out of the office for tokens for the washers (80p) and driers (40p). None of them looked down at heel. There seemed to be a good adult-to-adult rapport, which often signifies a relationship of mutual (and self) respect.

I asked her why people came to the Foyer. She described the range of problems, which often meant that they brought with them some heavy emotional baggage. 'Often they have been kicked out either through lack of space or relationship breakdown. Some parents move and the kids don't want to go, or they are leaving care. Others live in the sticks and can't get to employment in the town. We have one girl here whose mother asked for her to be housed. She was concerned that her daughter was spending the week kipping on friends' floors so that she could get to work in the morning. Sometimes real rural issues come into play. We have another young man who was close to an ASBO and we have to monitor his behaviour closely. Elements of the ASBO are contained within his licence.

'There is a real need to help them build some self-respect, and their living environment is very important. When I joined the Foyer the rooms were very 70s. It wasn't somewhere you would want to live yourself. There isn't enough in our budget to undertake big capital works, and so extra income for improvements has to be met by bids to the National Housing Corporation. We redecorated the flats. Now they have contemporary furniture, laminate floors, cream walls. Today the residents feel a certain pride in living here.' This pride, like with any locally managed project, extended to the management board: 'The Chairman and his wife were here every day for ten weeks helping to paint the rooms.'

It was also with pride that Karlie told me that they now had only 50% residents on benefits and 50% were earning a wage. It really did seem that success with young people was very much down to the personal support which helped develop self-esteem and empowerment through providing structure to their lives, where it had previously been lacking or absent.

Let Andrew Leeming sum up: 'The programme started in 1999 but didn't really get going until 2000. The outcomes were difficult to measure as they were not physical developments. When visitors came to Ryedale they were shown the Derwent Training Association Centre as this was the most significant capital project to come from SRB. The Foyer and the Cyber Café though were also interesting, partly for the difficulties involved. It will always be difficult to promote activity which is linked to rural youth culture.'

Whether I shall turn out to be the hero of my own life, or whether that station will be held by anybody else, these pages must show.
Charles Dickens' *David Copperfield.*

The SRB programme had not been without its problems but nonetheless there was a strong legacy from SRB. 'The Regeneration Partnership came to a natural end with the formation of the Local Strategic Partnerships. But more significantly, youth priorities and partnership working became a key agenda for the Local Strategic Partnership (LSP), which was evident in the Connecting Ryedale strategy. There is a huge amount of activity which continues to take place on the ground. I don't think that this would have happened, or have been as effective, without the impetus of the SRB bid.'

TO BOLDLY GO WHERE NO MAN HAS GONE BEFORE

Don Stewart

Mankind stands tall, proud and undefeated. God bless the human race.

Prime Minister Harriet Jones (Dr Who) after defeating aliens, 2005

ENTER YORKSHIRE FORWARD

With the arrival in 1997 of a New Labour administration, the devolution agenda took on a whole new energy. The Labour manifesto for the 1997 General Election promised that 'a sovereign Westminster Parliament will devolve power to Scotland and Wales.' So national devolution was firmly on the menu and the story goes that John Prescott as Deputy Prime Minister and a keen advocate of the devolution of power was determined that the English regions should also be included in the first Queen's speech of the new administration. All-out regional assemblies were not likely to be acceptable or achievable in a first term, but backed by the Millan economic arguments, and using Scottish Enterprise and the Welsh Development Agency as models, the creation of economic development agencies in each of the English regions was possible. This too had been foreshadowed in both the Millan Report and in the manifesto.

Yorkshire Forward started life on 1 April 1999. It would be an understatement to say that the new Board were surprised to discover the extent to which the budget was already committed. How, they asked, could they be expected to change anything if all their spending decisions for years ahead had already been made for them? After all, change was the reason that Yorkshire Forward along with the other regional development agencies had been created. The Annual Report for the 1999-2000 financial year showed that 84% of the Agency's grant expenditure was committed to the Single Regeneration Budget. The Board were also faced with a done deal with Round Five of the Single Regeneration Budget. It had started out prior to their inception, and in July 1999 they were required to rubber stamp fourteen more schemes with a lifetime value of another £100 million. Add to that the fact that Round Six was also underway, and it is not hard to see that in preparing the first Regional Economic Strategy, the Board were already starting to think hard about how a change in direction could be brought about.

Some key decisions were taken. Major among them was the decision to work towards a 'single pot' of funding for regional development agencies, a first step in 'joining up' at the regional level the numerous funding streams from central government. Round Six of SRB would be the last one in Yorkshire and the Humber. And they would renegotiate with existing SRB partners to seek more economic outputs from schemes already up and running.

To understand the thinking, we need to go back to the rationale for the invention of regional development agencies. Again, in simple terms, the story starts with the Millan report, which looked at England's comparative performance in Europe since joining the European Community. In essence it concluded that the English regions had lost out in economic terms to the other regions of Europe. This table taken from the report shows the basis of the argument. It compares the economic performance of the English regions with the average for the 15 EU member countries in 1993:

Table 1 Regional GDP per head as a percentage of EU15 Average (1993):
Source: Statistiques en Bref: Regions, Eurostat 27.2.96

	GDP
❐ North	89
❐ North West	90
❐ Yorkshire and Humberside	91
❐ East Midlands	93
❐ West Midlands	91
❐ East Anglia	101
❐ South West	94
❐ South East	116
❐ Scotland	97
❐ Wales	84
❐ Northern Ireland	79
❐ UK	99

Res - matter (Latin, as in res publica - public matter) Note: republic
RES - Regional Economic Strategy

This was a bold step. These new bodies were to be Quangos (Quasi Autonomous Non Governmental Organisations). That in itself presented ideological issues. Not all locally elected politicians liked the idea of this huge new cuckoo in the regional economic nest. In some cases, the Single

Regeneration Budget itself was still seen as money 'taken away' from local government. Now worse, its control was being given to a Quango. Had we not campaigned against Quangos, they asked themselves. To add to their misery, the democratic oversight of these bodies which would ideally have been at the regional level would, in the immediate absence of regional elected assemblies, have to be left to national government in the interim. Seven years later as we now know, the ideal of regional government remains some way off following the decision of the North East electorate in November 2004 not to vote in favour of directly elected regional government.

So the arrival of nine new powerful, unelected agencies, with boards deliberately appointed to be independent and private-sector led, was bound to signal a shake-up in the economic development agenda.

The task they were given was simple enough to describe: develop a strategy to boost the economy of your region to a point near to the European average; simply put but much more difficult to achieve. And the instructions were clear. Bold, innovative thinking was to be the order of the day. A simple continuation of old policies was out of the question. A sharper, more focused approach to public sector investment in economic development was to be driven forward. Skills, both vocational and higher level, were to be in the spotlight, businesses support needed an overhaul, the property needs of towns and cities required a new approach, inward investment needed improving, as did the marketing of the region.

The Yorkshire Forward Board quickly realised that the balance of its inherited spending was heavily skewed towards the community regeneration agenda. That did not reflect the key needs of the regional economy agreed with a wide range of partners by the middle of the first year of operation. The Regional Economic Strategy (RES) signed off by Government pointed firmly to the need for significant investment in business and the environment as well as for the need for an inclusive approach. So how to turn the ship around?

One obvious answer was to squeeze existing spend to achieve more economic outputs. That initially looked like a tough call. But in reality partners, by now pretty experienced at delivery, were quickly able to deliver 15% more economic outputs without damage to the original vision of the schemes. Calling a halt to the rather scatter gun approach to Single Regeneration Budget investment was the next stage. Round Six was already underway, but a more focused approach in which Yorkshire Forward was able to lead the national work on developing the guidelines, ensured that the investments made were directly in line with the Regional Economic Strategy. For example, coming on top of £15 million provided in Round Five, the award of £80 million to the South Yorkshire Coalfield Partnership, the biggest ever award, enabled the community to gear up to matchfund the community elements of Objective One funding from Europe. Similar clinical targeting of Bradford, Hull and the largest ever investment in North Yorkshire showed that the Board were determined to make difficult choices based on the priorities agreed with partners through the Regional Economic Strategy.

But the bigger goal was to better balance the investment portfolio to develop new investments in business and the environment. The only way to find the money for that was to radically overhaul the existing spending streams from Government and that meant persuading Government that regional development agencies should have greater control of their own funds and not just administrate historic government programmes.

Initially that argument looked unlikely to succeed. But by the end of the third year, 2001-2002, Sir Graham Hall, Chair of Yorkshire Forward, was able to report that the year 'has been marked by preparations for the Single Pot method of funding economic development.' He added that Yorkshire Forward had managed to develop a war chest in preparation for this, by holding back £3 million to spearhead its new era of investment in the forthcoming year. It is worth bearing in mind that at the end of the third year of operation, the Single Regeneration Budget still accounted for half of the agency's total expenditure.

If you want to build a ship, don't herd people together to collect wood and don't assign them tasks and work; but rather, teach them to long for the endless immensity of the sea.
Anon

But the tide had turned. And was the tide now about to wash away the very rock on which so much community regeneration had been based? Was the edge of the cliff being eroded and edging ever closer to the foundations?

NEW STRATEGY, NEW APPROACH

The Regional Economic Strategy set out clearly the need for action on the inclusion front. It also agreed who should take the actions required, and in the main this was not Yorkshire Forward but its partners. Local government, the voluntary sector, chambers of commerce, the CBI, the TUC, schools, universities, the private sector businesses themselves, the Training and Enterprise Councils (soon to become Learning and Skills Councils). It was agreed with partners that most of the necessary actions in relation to social inclusion were for partners other than the development agency to take forward. That led Yorkshire Forward to consider what its approach should be in relation to economic inclusion.

Whilst this separation of social inclusion from economic inclusion might seem to the casual reader to be a semantic difference, it points to an important aspect of the success of the region since 1997. The strength of partnership evident in Yorkshire and the Humber has been a major success. This is built on sound strategic foundations. The relationship between the unelected and voluntary Regional Assembly for Yorkshire and the Humber (RAYH) and Yorkshire Forward has always been good. The key players realised quickly that there was everything to gain from working together. Under the legislation creating development agencies the RAYH would have the job of approving the Regional Economic Strategy and of scrutinising the policies for its delivery. It was crucial this should be a constructive relationship. And so it has proved to be, not just in itself, but in setting the tone for others to follow.

That in turn has led to a much greater clarity in understanding and acceptance of roles and responsibilities. On the skills front for example, the advent of the Learning and Skills Council (LSC), could have led to a tension about the respective roles of the LSC and the development agency. But the LSC immediately recognised the maturity of the regional infrastructure and accepted the economic strategy and Yorkshire Forward's strategic lead. Similarly the development of strong partnerships in areas like culture has led to a clear focus of roles without the descent into turf wars that has characterised some other regions.

The Yorkshire Forward approach to its role in economic inclusion was to be inclusive in itself. We determined at an early stage that this would not simply be the job of the People Directorate. If we were ultimately to be successful, then it had to be a whole organisation approach. The most obvious area to start in was education, learning and skills. In the long run - and we always viewed it as a long-term game - improving the region's ability to learn and develop throughout life was going to be crucial. As the 1998 State of the Region report had shown, the region had a clear issue with basic educational attainment. That fed through into poor primary school results and so on into GCSE and 'A' level results. The report noted that 'in 1996 the Region ranked 36 out of 38 when compared to other European Union regions regarding the percentage of 16-18 year olds that were in some form of education and training.'

Clearly, the mainstream policy decisions and the funding of education were not our territory. Even now the contribution to the Yorkshire Forward Single Pot from the Department for Education and Skills (DfES) is no more than 2% or roughly £6 million a year; a drop in the ocean in terms of education and skills funding. But we could make links between education and emerging business areas. So for example, in response to the focus on business cluster development - a key plank of the Regional Economic Strategy - we determined that a focus on the key education and skills needs in those clusters was essential. Science, Technology, Engineering and Mathematics, or as our American cousins have it 'the math', would be crucial.

It was up to us to be innovative. So we linked Batley and Dewsbury Girl Guides to the Russian Cosmonaut programme. We linked science based museums, such as Eureka in Halifax or the National Museum of Photography Film and Television in Bradford, to schools. And helping to save and then using such icons as the Flying Scotsman now based at the National Railway Museum at York for educational purposes is a direct attempt to stimulate an interest in science and engineering among young people who might not otherwise make the connection between a Maths lesson and an exciting career and life. In these ways our Science Technology Engineering and Maths (STEM) activity has linked business clusters to young children.

Man in Base Ball Cap: *I have grown up in this area and know most of my neighbours. I love my home.*
Woman in Suit: *We want to get rid of all those old terraces and build a bright new town.*
Man in Old School Tie: *It's the North, nobody wants to live in the North.*
Reebok Regeneration Conference Cabaret, 2005

In similar ways we have looked outside the mainstream areas of education and skills for the older and perhaps disaffected age groups. The mainstream is rightly the working area for the LSC. We will of course still seek to influence them, but the circa £750 million which the LSC spend in the Region each year is the main funding stream.

There are many third sector organisations working in and around the non-mainstream education and skills area. We saw it as our task to work to secure the future of these organisations, to try to build a network of provision that would be sustainable in a way that moved from public grant dependency to a more business-like - dare I say - social enterprise footing. So supporting the Community Construction Training Company in Grimsby directly linked disaffected young people with the world of construction where we have a skills shortage.

Tommy Noble (20) of Wellowgate, Grimsby, was given the Young Builder of the Year Award at the annual Youth Building UK Conference at the National Museum of Photography, Film and Television in Bradford. Things did not always look so rosy for Tommy. Just three years earlier he was constantly getting into trouble with the police. His fortunes changed, however, when he became a member of the very successful Community Construction Training Company (CCTC), a project supported by Yorkshire Forward which helps unemployed young people learn practical skills.

Tommy said: 'I was having problems at home and was always in trouble with the police. I was at Grimsby College when I heard about the training programme. I came and joined this team because I wanted a trade behind me. If I hadn't I would probably be working in a job with no prospects and I would still be getting into trouble.'

Tommy is now in full-time employment with the company as a bricklayer and surveyor. He was put forward for the award by his employers at CCTC. To qualify he wrote a log book detailing his time there and how it changed his life. As well as the recognition, he was also given £1,500 towards further training, which he has already invested in tools.

Culture change and education will be the start point for encouraging more people to go into business and self-employment. Action will cover know-how about starting a business, positive role models and the experience of enterprise. It will focus on ways of promoting self-belief and instil confidence to take risks, aspiration and enterprising behaviour.

Regional Economic Strategy for Yorkshire and Humber 2006-2015.

Supporting the Prince's Trust in the region and particularly their XL programme pushed the boundaries of vocational learning for those who find the academic route unsuited to their personal learning styles.

As a result of Yorkshire Forward support - £3 million over three years - the Prince's Trust in Yorkshire and Humber are supporting young people who are experiencing disadvantage to enter education, training or employment. The Trust also supports young people in starting their own businesses.

Since April 2002 the project has helped create 331 new businesses and helped 2,024 young people enter education, training or employment.

The achievements of young people and volunteers involved with the Prince's Trust throughout the UK were recently celebrated by the Trust at a high profile awards ceremony in London. Out of a total of eight awards two people from Yorkshire and Humber won and two young people were runners up.

The winner of the Special Achievement Award was Kenny Ross (26) from Hull, who has overcome drug addiction and homelessness to turn his life around and become a youth worker and team leader for the Prince's Trust. Through the support of The Prince's Trust's Sound Live programme development awards and the Trust's Personal Development Team Programme, Kenny moved from being a young person with debilitating problems and low self-esteem to someone who could see a future for himself. The Prince's Trust helped Kenny with the advice and support he needed to apply to the University of Hull for a youth work degree.

'In just sixteen months from having the leaflet placed in my hand, I have been on numerous courses and work placements. I've done voluntary work at a youth club and became a qualified mentor for the Prince's Trust. I have even played live to Prince Charles as part of the scheme. It has been incredible.'

We encouraged long time community regeneration groups like Royds Community Association in Bradford and the Manor and Castle

Development Trust in Sheffield to move away from a culture in which so much of their time was spent chasing the next grant scheme towards a future based on community owned assets and a trading approach to life. We encouraged the Churches Regional Commission to develop the role that faith and faith groups can have in bringing people together in communities, as well as in using the physical assets of the Church for linking the world of exclusion to the world of economic inclusion. And we encouraged the use of the arts and culture and, much more recently sport, to link people to the economy through leisure, recreation, health and well being; in short, a lateral approach that used all avenues to get to our goal of a truly inclusive society.

If we believed in economic inclusion then it was logical that social enterprise should be supported from a business perspective rather than a social one. Our basic approach was set out in a Framework for Social Enterprise published in October 2002. We were convinced from an early stage that our support for social enterprise should be on the same footing as support for any other form of enterprise. We deliberately did not differentiate the sectors. As we move to a 'no wrong doors, single point of contact for all business in the region', under the banner of *Better Deal for Business* (BD4B), social enterprise will continue to be seen as an integral part of the business life of the region.

But what of the individual groups and organisations at the local level? How were they to survive? How could they access support from the single pot? As often happens with policy changes some of the immediate effects are unforeseen. The Single Regeneration Budget had always been designed as an arms-length programme. At Yorkshire Forward we had pushed back the boundaries further than many: leaving the local bodies accountable for their own actions as far as possible; encouraging local authorities to let go of the strings and pioneering individual community groups as accountable bodies in their own right; where possible increasing delegated powers to the maximum to enable local control and decisionmaking to be really effective. In many cases this had resulted in people forgetting that the Single Regeneration Budget came from the development agency at all. Often our involvement in projects was never mentioned. With the decision to end the programme however, we were

We are constantly faced by great opportunities brilliantly disguised as insoluble problems.
Anon

immediately back in the frontline again. I came to wonder whether in fact we were International Rescue and I was Scott Tracey! Despite all the assurances given in bidding documents and delivery plans about exit strategies or sustainability plans, the calls for rescue packages started to come in.

In their scrutiny of the impact of the Regional Economic Strategy on social inclusion, the Regional Assembly for Yorkshire and the Humber commented that 'many organisations have unrealistic expectations about what the role and remit of Yorkshire Forward is in relation to social inclusion.' They went on to comment that there was more to do to communicate that role and pointed to a need to look at how community and local groups could access single pot funding. This was all fair comment. In direct response Yorkshire Forward established a 'task and finish' group of the Board to examine the issues and to make recommendations. In considering how we should move forward, we consulted all 22 local authorities in the region about what they saw as the key issues facing the local inclusion agenda in their area. In particular we sought their views about the treatment of inclusion within the developing investment planning approach of the use of public and private funds in the region.

The responses, which were all constructive, led us to formulate a simple policy structure for our future investment in the sector. This was set out in simple terms in a letter to all local authorities in the summer of 2004. In it we said that the key areas for our investment would be:

- Support for key bodies or networks which partners regard as important to the delivery of the inclusion agenda in their area, this will form part of the broader investment planning process in bringing partners together and deciding upon priorities for the sub region

- Support for key initiatives which have a track record of success and which partners believe are important in removing barriers to access to the labour market

- Support for initiatives which have a track record of success and which partners believe are important contributors to social cohesion and local economic development

- Support for people who are at a particular disadvantage where intervention can be linked to improved access to mainstream provision leading to greater economic activity.

In promoting this approach we have also been keen to reinforce our role as a development agency. We simply cannot afford to allow our forward balance sheet to become clogged up with revenue funding. We have to set a clear time limit on those initiatives which need revenue funding and try to help them secure a sustainable future. As time goes on, the pressures on us will increase to ease off the revenue funding in favour of capital. This poses particular challenges for us and the sector, and will require further innovation in our approach.

In *Cranes on the Horizon*, Andy Mudd was quoted as saying that regeneration is about people. He is right, and so we are determined that our approach to the renaissance of our towns and cities, including the market towns, should be seen not just as an issue of land and property but also of people. The inclusive community approach to the design and master planning phase of the renaissance projects has been a challenge. But to have excluded the very people who live and work in the areas in which we and partners are investing would have been counter to our approach.

The developments in community capacity and leadership which I have written about earlier showed through in the renaissance programme. In some cases this was a difficult and direct challenge to local democracy. Locally elected representatives suddenly found themselves challenged by an unelected body of opinion, pursuing in some cases narrow partisan issues. Similarly, at the partnership table, at sub regional level, some local authority representatives have commented that the voice of the third sector might be a bit too prominent. I regard all of this as a success. If the voice of inclusion is now perceived as a bit raucous, that is a better position than not being heard at all. As Dorothy Parker said, 'There is only one thing worse than being talked about, not being talked about!'

All things are difficult before they are easy.
Thomas Fuller

So, where do we go from here? The Yorkshire Forward Board has made it clear that over the next five years roughly a third of all our investment should be aimed at connecting people to economic opportunity. Crudely, that is £500 million; a figure remarkably similar to the overall investment in the Single Regeneration Budget inherited by the Board in 1999. When that is added to the inclusiveness of both the business and renaissance approach, Yorkshire Forward's involvement in the overall agenda is alive and well. What has happened is that we have moved the agenda on. Instead of community regeneration being seen as a separate issue, we have connected it to economic opportunity. As Doctor McCoy would have said, 'There is life Jim, but not as we know it!'

OBSERVATIONS

Question: *How many Yorkshire Forward officers does it take to change a neighbourhood's light bulb?*
Answer: *Only one, but the light bulb must really want to change.*

OVERVIEW

- To maximise local regeneration, local authorities may have to reconsider how they award contracts. It makes economic sense to award contracts to local companies even when they charge more, if more of the economic benefit is retained within the local community as a result.

- Different funding streams can distort a project. This happens due to the changes in emphasis made in order to secure funding, but also because it is difficult to achieve continuity and momentum when the next funding deadline is always on the horizon and the conditions of current sources of funding must also be met.

- There needs to be room for creative thinking to overcome artificial constraints set by SRB. The needs of a community are constantly in flux, and meeting them within the short-term, target-led, framework of the SRB is difficult.

- Sometimes the flexibility of SRB funding has led to unexpected successes in the smallest aspects of ambitious projects. It has also been true that some SRB schemes have failed to note the small ways in which they could make a real difference.

- More help is required in guiding projects towards sustainability and self-funding. Local intelligence sparks ideas which local volunteers can translate into a long-term plan, but they need support to help with eventual applications.

- SRB funding often cannot compensate for the lack of a wider and more ambitious regeneration strategy but it can help trigger awareness of the need for such a strategy.

- SRB money can raise expectations and the self-respect of a community.

- A system that gives a portion of an award to the 'accountable body', especially when a pioneering SRB scheme is struggling, is bureaucratic and wasteful.

- Celebrate success stories.

OFFICER SUPPORT

- Joined-up thinking needs more encouragement. Funding pots with tightly defined parameters can deny valid schemes much needed support, and local authorities are under-equipped to encourage social entrepreneurship without stifling it or transforming it into dependency.

- Community skills shortfalls to effectively administer a project are a recurring problem and there should be resources to buy in experts in good time - once monitoring of the project has begun it can be too late to easily address such shortfalls.

- Paid officers need to actively encourage demands on them from community associations.

- Many government officers are every bit as visionary as community activists. The best of them will work for the community they serve.

- Active officer support needs to continue after a strong team of activists has developed, especially when the funders' priorities change. This is when a project is most vulnerable.

- Officers with a long history in community development can sometimes see unorthodox ways to find resources.

Scene: A lecture hall in Asia.
Questioner: 'So, how do you feel, so far, about the dickhead?'
Lecturer: I beg your pardon?'
'Yes, yes, this dickhead and the ones that lie ahead.'
'Well, I'm not sure...'
'You know: the 1990s and so forth.'
'Oh that dickhead!
Simon Schama

ENGAGING WITH COMMUNITIES

- If you have a salary, always ask yourself what is in it for the volunteer.

- Regeneration money cannot compensate for the absence of community activism and is of little use without it.

- Similarly, a driving force of some kind - often a core group of activists - is vital to sustain projects when initial enthusiasm has decreased.

- Respond to sensible suggestions from the local community positively; they often rest on a well grounded knowledge of the immediate area.

- Projects that succeed and prosper are often those with strong community ownership. By contrast, overbearing individual leadership can hamper the evolution that is necessary for a project to thrive.

- In culturally diverse areas, inclusiveness is especially important.

- Projects often meet with a lot of success when fostering new community activism.

- Communities will not be impressed by plans and rhetoric alone. Results and improvements will capture their attention and, more importantly, engage them.

- The professional face of SRB can deter community input and involvement. It is important to find a way to reach down and ensure those with no experience in community activism have their voices heard.

ECONOMIC REGENERATION/CAPACITY BUILDING

- The most successful projects not only serve a community but help build it.

- People want more police and health organisations but they also need access to educational organisations which give new skills and build confidence.

- Treating volunteers as professionals, and providing them with the necessary skills and equipment, ensures a response in like kind.
- Local newsletters produced in a professional way challenge the local community to address local problems.
- Encourage frequent, well-run public meetings. Get members of the community to co-operate and take ownership of the documentation and recording of community decisions.
- Encourage young people to see themselves as citizens and to be involved in community projects.
- In areas of long-term unemployment, volunteering sustains self-esteem and encourages personal development but there are no quick fixes. Modest amounts of regeneration money cannot end severe unemployment.
- Most communities have experts who live in the neighbourhood. Community audits are difficult but informal networks can suggest names of specialists who will volunteer if asked.
- Training courses can be as much about building aspiration and confidence as about ticking off skills on a list.

SUSTAINABILITY

- A sustainable plan needs to be in place, and a long-term future planned, well before the pilot scheme money runs out.
- It is important to distinguish between revenue and capital and to plan for access to both. Some funding sources are diminishing as the European pots get smaller.
- Consider carefully if you need your own building as this carries with it responsibilities which involve hassle and a high level of organisation.

We can travel, if there are openings into other worlds, but we can only live in our own… We have to build a republic of heaven where we are, because for us there is nowhere else.
Philip Pullman,
The Amber Spyglass

- Look for new and sustainable funding and for new initiatives without being seduced into being funding-led.

- A project considering an eventual transition to self-funding must take an open ended approach to the planning of new buildings. Wherever possible rooms should be adaptable for multi-purpose use.

SCHEME MANAGEMENT

- Avoid silo thinking but keep your feet on the ground. Theory and qualifications can be important but they have to be filtered through pragmatism.

- Organisations need strong personalities; leadership matters.

- Sometimes, a carefully planned project can become troubled, and a loosely planned one can have great success.

- Smaller schemes demonstrate that manageable community problems can often be successfully tackled at local resident level.

- Employ people with knowledge of the culture of the area.

- Where outsiders rather than locals got the jobs, the introduction of new businesses to an area may be a success, but this success is limited if it does not improve the employment prospects and education capacities of local people in a direct way.

- Presentation is important but too often style - as seen in glossy brochures - not substance, drives regeneration initiatives.

- There is a temptation to spend grant money on making an organisation appear more professional by buying in expensive office furniture and decor. If a space is not public such expenditure must be carefully justified.

- Make your building beautiful and welcoming to your clients.

- Plans and priorities should always include contingency plans, so that time and focus is not lost when existing plans need to be adapted.

- Face to face communication is more important and effective than printed materials.

BUREAUCRACY

- The eighteen months' journey for a new bid to Yorkshire Forward, travelling there and back along bureaucratic tram lines, is too slow.

- Compared with other funding streams, SRB 4 and 5 were over-bureaucratic.

- In the earlier SRB schemes, and particularly in SRB 1, the pioneering spirit was acknowledged but as the years passed the structures approved by 'accountable bodies' and funders have become more rigid.

- If you preach sustainability and outcomes, officers' work practices should be monitored accordingly.

TARGETS AND EVALUATION

- Fear of the consequences of missed targets sometimes creates unnecessary anxiety and deflects energies from a project. Without space for honest dialogue when difficulties occur, ways of addressing them at the earliest stage can be missed.

- Bald statistics alone remain inadequate as a means to assess the success of a project.

- The demand for over-precise 'outcomes' may promote compliance with funders' expectations rather than data that is useful on the ground.

Let's get one thing clear. This is the golden age – so far. There has never been a better time to be alive in Britain than today, no generation more blessed, never such an opportunity for so many. And things are getting better all the time, horizons widening, education spreading, everyone living longer, and healthier, safer lives. Unimaginable luxuries and choices are now standard.
Polly Toynbee

- Avoid over-ambitious targets. SRB officers need to guide applicants toward realism when setting targets - the bidding process can undermine this realism.

- Test the information and consultation processes on smaller schemes before beginning the operational delivery of regeneration/renewal to an area.

- Have at least one board member who has personal experience of auditing and monitoring.

- Data collected by the community will not be as biased as you might expect. Statistics collected by professionals only have the semblance of objectivity. Data which is stitched to an action-research programme has a vigour absent in paper chasing exercises.

OTHER SRB 4 & 5 SCHEMES

The progressive's endeavour is to persuade people to want and believe things can always get better.
Polly Toynbee

SRB ROUND 4

THE CATTERICK GARRISON

1 April 1998 - 31 March 2002 SRB Grant: £1.1m

Main Objectives: The Catterick Garrison scheme was a four year programme established to tackle the unique problems of an expanding garrison town and was focused on three garrison parishes (Colburn, Hipswell and Scotton) which contain a disproportionate number of economically inactive young women and dependent children. The scheme included crime and community safety initiatives and addressed clear social and economic need by providing training, education, childcare, job opportunities, improved recreation facilities and health advice.

NORTH EAST LINCOLNSHIRE: CREATING A LEARNING COMMUNITY

1 April 1998 - 31 March 2005 Total SRB Grant: £1.765m

Components - Creating a Learning Community

LEAP Support
17 January 2000 - 31 March 2002, £34,951
Description: Creation of a senior post to facilitate the implementation of the North East Lincolnshire Lifelong Learning plan until 2002 and co-ordinate project work under SRB to address learning culture issues.

STEPS
24 November 1999 - 31 March 2002, £129,905
Description: A programme of large scale capacity building designed to raise the motivation, self-esteem and confidence of disadvantaged local communities.

Raising Aspirations
26 January 2000 - 31 March 2002, £48,000
Description: To raise the aspirations, confidence, skills and abilities of multi-disadvantaged community members and engage them in learning as a pathway to employment and voluntary activity. The activities are designed to engage non-participants and provide a forward pathway into, and in particular from, the STEPS programme.

IAG in Communities
6 June 2000 - 31 March 2003, £93,701
Description: Aiming to engage disadvantaged groups of adults in learning, the project will concentrate on reaching adults who do not currently access services by delivering information, advice and guidance to them in their own communities. An additional outreach worker will provide assistance for other community workers through the provision of information and support.

Business and Community Interactive TV
25 November 1999 - 31 March 2002, £80,010
Description: Research, develop and evaluate the role of local, interactive television in community regeneration. Produce local interactive business and community television programmes to be broadcast to viewers in NEL on Channel Seven.

INSPIRE
14 March 2001 - 31 March 2003, £39,834
Description: The project will support the production of learning materials and business support interventions through the use of ICT. It aims to attract and deliver 390 new learning outcomes within NEL through a combination of new learners undertaking units on key skills and employees participating in bespoke training and learning workshops.

Local Small Business Support
1 February 2001 - 31 July 2001, £40,000
Description: A feasibility study to identify the on-going need for business start-up and support services and how these can best be developed for our local community. To assist people along the road to successful trading which will create sustainable full time quality jobs.

Valuing the Volunteer
31 July 2001 - 31 March 2004, £53,913
Description: Develop a community based, collaborative volunteer training programme that provides local people with the opportunity to contribute to improving the quality of life in the region whilst also strengthening their own and the sector's position in the labour market.

Community Learning Fund
26 January 2000 - 31 March 2002, £59,125
Description: Raise the aspirations, confidence, skills and abilities of disadvantaged community members and engage them in the process of learning. Provide a block fund for organisations to apply for funding for small projects.

Common Purpose
26 January 2001 - 31 July 2002, £20,400
Description: Aims to improve the way towns and cities work through delivering a unique educational programme for the rising generation of decisionmakers from all sectors of society.

Communities Explored (Pilot)
1 September 2000 - 1 September 2001, £14,661
Description: Consists of a pilot programme of courses which will explore how core elements of the community, including health, government, crime, education, voluntary sector and wealth creation, impact upon individuals and what opportunities exist for participants to engage in related activities.

Artlandish Skillshare Project
15 December 2000 - 31 March 2004, £17,971
Description: The project aims to enable local people to devise and run basic craft/creative workshops within their communities and so address local need through empowerment and skill share. Further the project will create informal networks between various community groups and offer pathways back into learning using creativity.

Skills Resource Centre
13 November 2001 - 31 March 2003, £62,916
Description: Develop a dedicated Basic Skills resource centre to co-ordinate basic skills support activities such as overseeing training programmes, undertake materials development, manage a practitioners network and equip and mobilise other sectors.

UK Online - Infrastructure
4 February 2002 - 31 March 2004, £160,000
Description: Deliver community led first-rung learning opportunities via twenty-two new online ICT venues. These include a disabled loan equipment scheme, an IT Bus, three mobile media centres, a guidance service (via video-conferencing), a new community campus in St Peters Avenue, three cyber cafés and a range of access points, rising to substantive ICT learning centres for local community groups and residents.

UK Online - Revenue
10 February 2002 - 31 March 2004, £120,163
Description: Revenue support to help with staffing and running costs of the new online ICT venues created by the UK Online - Infrastructure project.

Women into Enterprise - Research Project
11 September 2002 - 31 March 2003, £36,267
Description: Undertake robust and in-depth research into barriers that prevent the greater participation of women in the local economy. This research will provide information that can guide future appropriate and effective practical assistance and support to encourage women to explore their ideas for developing careers, and specifically self-employment.

NVQ House
9 October 2002 - 31 March 2004, £115,500
Description: Produce a simplified building method and new training modules that if successful may develop a new skill operative for the industry which may provide further employment opportunities for young builders from socially excluded backgrounds.

Empowering Residents through Design
9 October 2002 - 31 August 2003, £33,764
Description: Encourage and support people to become more conscious of the opportunities presented to them by regeneration and to take action themselves through working with and considering the needs of communities. To help develop a vision and leadership that is sustainable after the completion of the project.

Food Dynamo
9 October 2002 - 31 March 2005, £142,282
Description: Create a Social Enterprise aiming at up-skilling those in the food sector and providing training for those who wish to enter the industry, as well as establishing links with schools. Give participants the opportunity to run a small food factory covering all aspects of trading as a food processing plant.

Valuing the Learner
1 January 2003 --31 March 2004, £7,191
Description: Employment of community learning outreach worker supported by an experienced and skilled community learning team to further increase the numbers of new learners through partnership with all other active community partners.

Alternative Pathways
1 January 2003 - 31 March 2003, £4,152
Description: A research project to focus on the 'alternative curriculum' opportunities available for the disaffected/disengaged cohort of students who stray from the 14-19 qualification pathways.

BBC Bus Tutor
1 January 2003 - 31 December 2003, £7,500
Description: Provide tutorial support for the BBC Bus when it visits North East Lincolnshire one day each week. The bus is a mobile engagement and teaching unit and an outside broadcast unit, equipped with six computers, all with internet access. The tutor will facilitate the engagement of individuals into first rung ICT based learning opportunities.

Mentor/Network Development
1 April 2003 - 31 March 2004, £20,950
Description: Encourage the sharing of information, removing barriers between local partners in community issues through either direct workshops to enhance skills, by mentor support, or by large networking events.

Community Bowling and Learning Centre
1 March 2003 - 31 March 2005, £58,371
Description: The building of a multi-purpose community centre on the Tollbar Business and Enterprise College site to provide indoor bowling facilities and opportunities to learn and use ICT facilities for senior citizens.

Foodworkers Project
1 March 2003 - 31 March 2005, £65,176
Description: To employ one foodworker to work with the mental health care officer to deliver OCNW basic cookery courses to clients with mental health problems, and to employ a further two foodworkers to deliver the same courses to the 16-24 age group.

Grimsby Learning Shop
1 March 2003 - 31 March 2005, £164,500
Description: The refurbishment of a disused shop into a learning shop to house guidance and training services. This will open up new adult participation with a particular focus on the service sectors.

Learning Partnership Development Manager
1 July 2003 - 31 March 2005, £80,000
Description: Recruitment of a development manager who will: drive and facilitate partnership working in line with the government directives for collaboration and regeneration; develop systems for collection, analysis and sharing of data; monitor and evaluate learning partnership against activities in order to improve performance against targets and quality of provision; direct partnership activity to improve access and choice for local learners.

Evaluation
1 April 2002 - 31 March 2003, £9,539
Description: Mid-term evaluation of the SRB 4 scheme

ROUTES TO EMPLOYMENT IN NORTH HALIFAX

1 April 1998 - 31 March 2005

Main Objectives: To tackle two inter-linked issues facing the Mixenden, Ovenden and Illingworth areas of North Halifax: the lower than (Calderdale and national) average educational attainment of pupils in North Halifax primary schools and low take up of post-16 opportunities, and the higher than (Calderdale and national) average rates of unemployment, including significantly higher than average rates of long-term unemployment.

REACH OUT - WEST YORKSHIRE POLICE

1 April 2000 - 31 March 2004

Main Objectives: The Reach Out project aims to reduce offending behaviour among young adults across West Yorkshire. Working with schools, a series of measures are used to identify susceptible adolescents and then engage with them during their final year at school. This is achieved through provision of appropriate training and counselling services to support their personal development, increase their skills, improve their self-worth and aid their transition into the world beyond school. The developing skills are put into practical use through work placement with appropriately trained participating employers with a view to many securing permanent employment opportunities. A residential course, which combines learning with leisure activity, is also offered to each student.

MANNINGHAM AND GIRLINGTON

1 April 1998 - 31 March 2005

Main Objectives: To raise the level of educational attainment among young people which in some cases is less than half the national average, and to reduce the level of unemployment amongst young people, which is at 30%, by half at the end of the programme.

SRB ROUND 5

SOUTH YORKSHIRE COALFIELDS

1 April 1998 - 31 March 2003 SRB Grant: £16.5m

Main Objectives: This five year scheme aimed at establishing vigorous community and voluntary sectors across the South Yorkshire Coalfield areas of Barnsley, Doncaster and Rotherham to give communities ownership of programmes and resources, to reduce social exclusion and to lay the foundations for stronger, more inclusive and self-reliant communities.

SHEFFIELD: CREATING AN INCLUSIVE AND PROSPEROUS CITY

SRB Grant: £25m

Main Objectives: The scheme, led by Sheffield City Council, delivers a comprehensive regeneration programme combining economic and community regeneration focused on the large housing estates in the Owlerton and Southey Green areas (including Parsons Cross) of North Sheffield. A range of measures aim to tackle multiple deprivation issues in housing, health, education, transport, employment, crime, social, environmental, communication and capacity building issues. The scheme will also develop projects to attract new jobs and industry and encourage business creation and an enterprise culture.

SHEFFIELD: STOCKSBRIDGE'S FUTURE

1 April 1998 - 31 March 2004 SRB Grant: £2m

Main Objectives: A six year scheme targeting Stocksbridge, a single industry, steel dependent town, and the surrounding area. Priorities have been identified through extensive consultation focusing on measures to improve skills, literacy and numeracy, childcare provision and a job search programme. Job creation and the development of local business culture will be encouraged through business start-up, managed workspace and a project to reclaim contaminated sites. The scheme also addresses capacity building through community development workers and the provision of a resource centre. Transport links are to be improved alongside projects to regenerate the town centre.

ENTERPRISE AND EMPLOYMENT: A NEW DEAL FOR BARNSLEY

1 April 1998 - 31 March 2003

Main Objectives: A five year scheme with the purpose of establishing new ways of stimulating wealth, enterprise and jobs in both the mainstream and social economies as part of a co-ordinated programme to create a more inclusive society. The main themes are to develop new and existing small enterprises, implement an investor development programme providing specialist support for established companies wanting to expand, and strengthen community economies through a job creation and community enterprise programme.

DEARNE VALLEY: OPPORTUNITIES FOR ALL

1 April 1998 - 31 March 2003 SRB Grant: £1.6m

Main Objectives: A five year scheme which aims to build on the SRB 3 scheme with a range of initiatives to carry through a strategy for increased local competitiveness, employment growth and improved employability of local people. The emphasis is on returning the long-term unemployed to full-time employment, especially in the Enterprise Zone, through an Intermediate Labour Market project, improving literacy and numeracy, and providing a programme of employee training to improve levels of customer service provided by the supply chain in the Dearne

Valley. The scheme has strong local support and will help local people to take advantage of Enterprise Zone opportunities.

SHEFFIELD GROWING TOGETHER

1 April 1998 - 31 March 2005 SRB Grant: £7.3m

Main Objectives: A seven year scheme to tackle unemployment, educational attainment and poor community infrastructures in the most deprived areas of Sheffield. To achieve these targets the scheme split itself into three main strands of activity; employment, education and community. These sub groups are to provide the strategic direction of the programme. The scheme demonstrates good community involvement, addresses real needs and relates closely to Government priorities.

LEEDS: BETTER NEIGHBOURHOODS AND CONFIDENT COMMUNITIES

1 April 1999 - 31 March 2006

Main Objectives: Targeting the eighteen most socially excluded neighbourhoods in Leeds the scheme, consisting of sixty-four projects, cuts across the range of SRB objectives and seeks to address issues of neighbourhood decline in four areas of concern: community involvement, neighbourhood management, community safety and the improvement of opportunities.

CALDERDALE: COMMUNITIES OF THE FUTURE

1 April 1999 - 31 March 2003 SRB Grant: £1.5m

Main Objectives: Spread across five areas; Mixenden, Todmorden, Brighouse, Elland and Field Lane; this pilot capacity building scheme aims to encourage local groups to participate in the longer term regeneration of their communities. The main objectives are to improve the living standards in the five target communities.

HEMSWORTH

1 April 1999 - 31 March 2005

Main Objectives: A Wakefield MDC led initiative which aims to regenerate the Hemsworth Coalfield area to the South East of Wakefield. It seeks to address problems of low levels of educational achievement, a weak skills base, slow rates of business start-ups, social exclusion, crime and low levels of community activity. Projects have been developed under four main themes: Education and Lifelong Learning (establishing a network of open learning centres), Building Bridges Back to Work (assistance to take advantage of job opportunities and business start up), Healthy Living & Community Safety (health improvement and community safety projects), Community Capacity Building (enablement of local communities including support through community development workers, training support and funding for small projects). The scheme builds upon the experience and partnerships established within the Wakefield District under SRB Rounds 1, 3 and 4, and also complements Working On Cold Coal, an SRB 6 scheme. In particular, it aims to dramatically improve the development and application of education, learning and skills and to implement targeted community based regeneration programmes to improve the living standards of deprived and excluded communities in former coalfields.

KIRKLEES: A PLATFORM FOR CHANGE

1 April 1999 - 31 March 2006 SRB Grant: £15.124

Main Objectives: The scheme will concentrate on the most deprived wards in Huddersfield and will engage, support and achieve by enhancing employment and educational prospects, improving housing and the environment, supporting the growth of the local economy and encouraging new business to the targeted areas, reducing crime, tackling drug abuse and improving community safety.

HIGHFIELD

1 April 1999 - 31 March 2005 SRB Grant £4m

Main Objectives: A five year pilot scheme to address the issue of poor private sector housing conditions coupled with a programme of community capacity building projects. The plan looks to the whole of the Highfield area but SRB investment will be focused on a smaller area comprising of 3,300 people in 1,100 homes.

THE FALSGRAVE COMMUNITY INVESTMENT INITIATIVE

1 April 1999 - 31 March 2003 SRB Grant: £2.9m

Main Objectives: The scheme, led by Scarborough Borough Council, supported activity in the Falsgrave Ward, one of the most deprived wards in Scarborough, and was established to address problems such as difficult to let housing; crime and the fear of crime; health problems; unemployment and a poor social and physical environment. The scheme represented a comprehensive multi-agency plan to tackle current problems in the Ward, which were particularly concentrated on the transport 'corridor', including the Edgehill Estate (the core target area of the scheme).

NORTH CLIFTON REGENERATION INITIATIVE

1 April 1999 - 31 March 2003 SRB Grant: £1.6m

Main Objectives: The North Clifton Communities in Partnership scheme, led by the City Council of York, was established to tackle the underlying problems of one of the most deprived areas in York. The area is blighted by high unemployment and poor health amongst local residents, high crime rates and below average school attainment. There is also a growing problem with drug and alcohol misuse and incidents of anti-social behaviour. The scheme aimed to arrest the decline of the North Clifton area by putting in place a sustainable regeneration scheme that had the active involvement of the community at all levels. This work translated into sustainable economic and social benefits to the area, and improved the ability of local residents to gain access to training and employment opportunities.

SOCIAL AND ECONOMIC REGENERATION OF RYEDALE

31 April 1999 - 1 March 2004 SRB Grant: £2.3m

Main Objectives: The scheme was established to improve the confidence, employability and opportunities of Ryedale's young people in order to enable them to continue to both live and work in their home communities. There are currently more social and economic opportunities for young people outside the Ryedale district than within and the overall aim was to help stem the current trend for outward migration of young people from Ryedale. Most projects are based in and around centres of population, such as the key market towns of Malton, Norton, Kirkbymoorside, Helmsley and Pickering.

COASTAL TOURISM INITIATIVE

1 April 1999 - 31 March 2004 SRB Grant: £0.5m

Main Objectives: The scheme, managed by the Yorkshire Tourist Board and coastal local authorities in the region, encompassed all wards in a coastal strip covering Scarborough, East Yorkshire and North East Lincolnshire, with the bulk of resources targeted in the Scarborough District. The overall objective of the scheme was to improve the economic performance of tourism businesses and to maximise the contribution coastal tourism makes to the economic well being of the coastal communities in the region. This was achieved primarily by the provision of grants to tourism businesses aimed at improving the facilities offered to tourists visiting the area, with the primary focus on accommodation based businesses.

TEAM

Pontefract Press and Yorkshire Forward

Thank you for not smoking while communing with this book. Thank you as well for not burping, drooling, picking your nose, getting drunk, spilling food on yourself, thinking nasty thoughts about anyone, and letting your mind leap from undisciplined ideas to out-of-control feelings like a mean monkey on amphetamines.

Man Sambra of Kirklees

Brian Lewis has been the writer or editor/joint editor of about 70 books or pamphlets on community development and regeneration. Recent relevant books include: *Arts and Regeneration,* Housing Percent for Arts, Bolton (2001); *Renaissance Barnsley,* Yorkshire Forward (2002); *Renaissance Towns,* Yorkshire Forward (2002); *Theories at the Bottom of Our Jargon - SRB 1,* Yorkshire Forward (2003); *Up Sticks and a Job for Life - A History of the Selby Coalfield,* Coalfield Regeneration Trust (2003); *Ten Years of Being Awkward,* Goodwin Centre, Hull (2004); *Pride of Place - The Neighbourhood Agenda, ODPM* (2005) and *A People's History of Pontefract People,* Pontefract Press (2004). He is currently working on the *Creative RES* project in Normanton. He has an honorary doctorate for services to the arts and community and was Deputy Chair of Yorkshire Arts in 1998. He was Birmingham's first Poet Laureate and continues to have his verse published and his paintings exhibited.

Don Stewart is Executive Director, Strategy, Yorkshire Forward. He is one of the founder directors of the regional development agency and his remit covers the Regional Economic Strategy (RES), Investment Planning, Northern Way, Yorkshire Forward Development Fund (YFDF), Culture, Sport, Tourism, Olympics, Major Events and key account management of sub-regional/city-regional partnerships and Treasury.

Don has worked in the public sector for 36 years and has a background that is probably unique in its diversity. His career started in Transport, at a time when night flights out of British airports were rationed, where he had responsibility for aircraft noise control at both major London airports. This gave him a taste for travel so he moved onto the British Overseas Trade Board, started taking flights rather than monitoring them, and spent time in North Africa, China and Eastern Europe organising exhibitions and trade fairs that brought British industry to the attention of the rest of the world.

From there Don moved through most of the major economic Departments of State, including Prices and Consumer Protection, Environment, Housing, Education, Training and Employment, as well as the Office of the Health Service Commissioner, Manpower Services Commission and Government Offices in Manchester and Leeds. His roles as Team Leader, Lecturer, Investigator, Deputy Director, and Regional Director have all been leading him to his current position that of Executive Director here at Yorkshire Forward.

In July 2004 Don assumed responsibility for establishing a Regional Olympic Steering Group for Yorkshire and The Humber. This Steering Group was formed by 4 organisations: Yorkshire Forward; Yorkshire Tourist Board; Sport England; and Yorkshire Culture, and worked very closely with London 2012 and the other Regional Development Agencies in England to help London win the 2012 Olympic Games in July of this year. As part of its remit, the Steering group undertook the first major sports audit for the Region and also developed a Major Events Strategy for Yorkshire and the Humber, both of which are the foundations that the Region is going to build on to maximize the opportunities to the Region from London 2012.

On a personal note, Don is married to Ruth, and they have 5 children ranging in age from 7 to 22. His is a keen club-standard tennis player and an avid Formula 1 Racing fan.

Reini Schühle taught in a local comprehensive after a degree in Russian and German. When she joined Yorkshire Art Circus, she co-ordinated the production of the world's largest peg rug with well over 100 community participants, later she ran their education and publishing arm. She is currently working as a constituency manager. She has co-written a number of books on community development and co-edited an Open College of the Arts course and a book on community publishing. She is a core Pontefract Press team member responsible for strategy.

Ray Hearne has worked across communities of South Yorkshire since early 1980s for the Workers' Educational Association particularly focusing on arts' issues , community writing and community development. He has organised and run writers' workshops across the region and beyond, in communities, schools, and neighbourhood centres. In 2004 he produced and edited a CD for the ODPM's *Pride of Place* project and wrote the section on community governance. Over the last twenty years he has been a key figure in the development of the neighbourhood agendas in SouthYorkshire.

He is a practising writer and performer of poems and songs, on radio, for voluntary and community organisations, and performs at arts and music festivals in this country and abroad, performing his own work and songs by Roy Bailey, Coope, Boyes and Simpson, and Kate Rusby. Ray is chair of the No Masters Music Co-operative. Last album 'Broad Street Ballads' available on the 'No Masters' label He is currently working on BBC Radio 2's Radio Ballads series. He is the presenter of BBC

Ray has a First Class Honours degree in Literature and a Masters' degree in Telematics Learning Learning.

Dee Grijak From 1992 - 2004 she was writer of features and news on arts subjects for the Yorkshire Region. She has worked with Pontefract Press on *Cranes are Flying* and *Pride of Place* contributing articles on SRB/tourism and capacity building in relationship to the built environment, and the faiths agenda.

Vic Allen, writer and art critic, came north twelve years ago to edit the Yorkshire Arts Magazine *Artscene* and in that time his radical voice was much appreciated by the region's artists though not by art administrators. He has been a features writer in national newspapers and the editor of an environmental magazine.

Karen Maitland is a writer and editor with a doctorate in Psycholinguistics. She has travelled extensively from the Arctic Circle to Albania, and has worked in Nigeria, Northern Ireland and Israel. Before becoming a writer, she was employed a variety of posts including hospital administration, college teaching, and in various local government posts. Her first novel was short-listed for *The Authors' Club Best First Novel Award.* She has edited a number of cross-cultural books and been a consultant for a variety of communities and has written a series of innovative 'readable' reports both in her own right and in association with Pontefract Press. She lives in Lincolnshire and has led over 200 Creative Writing Workshops for adults around the country for the Adult Education Service, WEA, Local Councils and a variety of charities. Recently she was Writer in Residence on a council estate working with disadvantaged adults and children and is currently Writer in Residence working with people from rural communities.

Alison Seabrooke is a professional project director, regeneration consultant and writer. She organised the building of the Regen Centre in Riccall and until recently was the Chairman of this innovative community/training centre and responsible for strategy, recruitment and management. In 2002 she was seconded to the Coalfields Regeneration Trust, in order to co-ordinate their response to the Selby Coalfield closure. She was responsible for: co-ordination of multi-agency services including flexible training delivery to 1500 mineworkers. Under her leadership the Regen Centre won two British Urban Regeneration Association awards. Currently she is the interim Chief Executive of the Community Development Foundation.

She has a First Class Honours Degree in Textiles and has run FE college departments. She is both one of Pontefract Press's writers and a key strategist.

Karen Maitland is a writer and editor with a doctorate in Psycholinguistics. She has travelled extensively from the Arctic Circle to Albania, and has worked in Nigeria, Northern Ireland and Israel. Her first novel was short-listed for the Authors' Club Best First Novel Award. She has edited a number of cross-cultural books and has been a consultant for a variety of communities, writing a series of innovative 'readable reports' both in her own right and in association with Pontefract Press. She lives in Lincolnshire and has led over 200 creative writing workshops for adults around the country for the Adult Education Service, WEA, local councils and a variety of charities. Recently she was writer in residence on a council estate working with disadvantaged adults and children. Currently she is writer in residence working with people from rural communities.

Adèle Jagger is a writer and community activist who has lived in Sheffield all of her life. She lives in the Stocksbridge area and is standing for the council.

Porl Medlock is a commercial and arts photographer with a newspaper background. He has worked for most of the Yorkshire papers and also for West Yorkshire MCC recording their regeneration and construction projects. He photographs bands, theatre companies and artists. He was the principal photographer for *Artscene*, the region's arts magazine, until it closed in 2004. His enthusiasm recently took him to Argentina and Chile. He has had several major exhibitions, the last one, *Patagonia,* was at Dean Clough, Halifax (2004). He is the main photographer for Pontefract Press.

Jacob Schühle-Lewis is a website, book and book cover designer with experience of working for Yorkshire Forward, Liverpool HAT, Housing Percent for Arts (Bolton), Interculture and Leeds City Council. Together with Ray Hearne he has developed the interactive *Pride of Place* CD. He has a BSc in Interactive Entertainment Technology.